MAKING
PEACE WITH
THE THINGS IN
YOUR LIFE

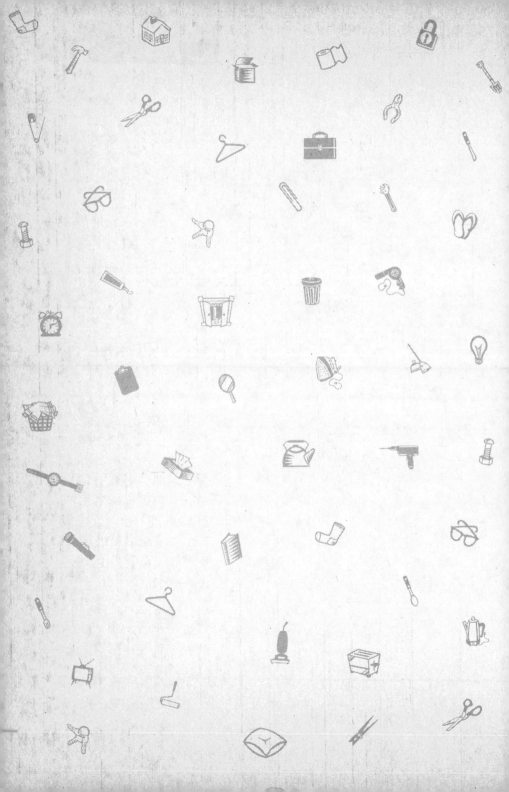

MAKING PEACE WITH THE THINGS IN YOUR LIFE

WHY YOUR PAPERS, BOOKS, CLOTHES,
AND OTHER POSSESSIONS KEEP OVERWHELMING YOU
AND WHAT TO DO ABOUT IT

CINDY GLOVINSKY, M.S.W., A.C.S.W.

ST. MARTIN'S GRIFFIN NEW YORK

www.stmartins.com

Book design by Gretchen Achilles

Library of Congress Cataloging-in-Publication Data

Glovinsky, Cindy
    Making peace with the things in your life : why your papers, books, clothes, and other possessions keep overwhelming you and what to do about it / Cindy Glovinsky.
        p. cm.
    Includes bibliographical references and index.
    ISBN 0-312-28488-8
    1. Conduct of life. I. Title.

BF637.C5 G57 2002
158.1—dc21

                                                                 2001059870

10   9   8

TO EVERYONE WHO HAS EVER LIVED WITH ME

AND SURVIVED BOTH MY OWN BATTLES WITH THINGS

AND MY JOURNEY TO PEACE

CONTENTS

ACKNOWLEDGMENTS

This book was, in many ways, a collaborative effort, and I want to thank all those who helped make it happen. Three wise, generous women deserve special recognition. Judith Kolberg founded the National Study Group on Chronic Disorganization, a group that has influenced my thinking in countless ways, while Judith herself read the manuscript through twice and provided insightful comments both times. Sari Solden, my therapy supervisor and mentor, stimulated ideas through supportive discussion and gave helpful feedback on several drafts of the manuscript. Parang Geri Larkin fostered both my organizing and my spiritual careers personally as well as through her "Building a Business" workshops and, in addition, connected me with her superb agent, who is now also mine.

Two other people played key roles early on. Jim Reisinger, president of the ADDult Information Exchange Network, offered me the opportunity to give workshops at several of their conferences, in preparation for which I developed many of the ideas presented here. Pam Letterman invited me to cofacilitate a support group for ADD adults, and other ideas originated within the context of this wonderful group, which met during the time I was writing the first draft.

Numerous others read the manuscript, gave suggestions, and helped with the editing, including Phyllis Perry, Ruth Greenwood, Mary McKinney, Roger Lauer, Denslow Brown, Seth Warschausky,

Terry Matlen, Sallie Foley, Emily Jernberg, Karen Mikus, Irene Tobis, Marilyn Churchill, Ann Saunders, Sara Bassett, Matthew Ferguson, Betty Housh, and Ira Glovinsky. These individuals' comments were absolutely vital to the quality of the final draft.

I am grateful to Andrea Pedolsky of Altair Literary Agency for believing in this project, for helping me to improve the proposal, for finding me a first-rate editor and publisher, and for her constant availability and support. Andrea's unswerving good sense has helped me to stay focused through good times and bad.

Thanks also to my two editors at St. Martin's Press—to Dorsey Mills for her enthusiastic acceptance of the manuscript and to Marian Lizzi for her thoughtful and thorough editing—as well as to other St. Martin's staff involved in producing and marketing this book.

Most of all, I appreciate the loving support of my husband, Ira Glovinsky, whose patience during this all-consuming undertaking has never flagged; my son, Matthew Ferguson, whose insightful suggestions provided input from generation X; and my mother, Betty Housh, who taught me most of what I know about organizing.

Finally, thanks to the countless clients who taught me everything I know about the issue of Things and none of whom bears the least resemblance to the characters that appear in this book, being infinitely more complex, multitalented, and the nicest people you would ever want to know.

The world is so full of a number of things,
I'm sure we should all be as happy as kings.

ROBERT LOUIS STEVENSON

INTRODUCTION

Living in perpetual conflict gets old. The conflict between people and Things is nonviolent but relentless. You spend an afternoon sorting through mountains of papers and file them all in special color-coded folders, but within a week, your desk has disappeared again. You devote an entire Saturday to decluttering the family room, haul six loads of Things to the Salvation Army, and in a few months you have to do it over. Meanwhile, you do not write your report, work out, or go to the beach with your family. Or you do, but all the time you are engaged in the activity your thoughts are somewhere else, preoccupied by the armies of Things hovering just beyond the horizon.

You know in your mind that Things are not alive, yet you could swear that they gang up on you. Things seem to crawl through the cracks and breed during the night, stacking themselves up in all the most inconvenient places. Although you may bankrupt yourself buying organizing equipment, hire a professional organizer, read every how-to book on the subject, and spend months scaling your Things down to little or nothing, you can be sure that in the end, like the Blob in the '50s movie, THEY WILL BE BACK.

This is not an illusion, as long as you continue to regard your Things as The Enemy. Perhaps you believe that all you have to do to break the cycle is to "conquer" your Things, to impose your will on them by putting every last Thing in perfect order. This will not work. What does work is getting honest with yourself. Change begins with the recognition that YOUR THINGS DO NOT DO ANYTHING TO YOU. You or someone else puts the Things where they are.

If you repeatedly put your Things in places that don't work for you, this is mostly because of what's happening on the inside, not the outside. The problem could be denial about the realities of your present situation, neurological glitches, or a full-blown emotional conflict. All three of these obstacles may be combined with the biggest obstacle of all: the shame you may feel about the state of your Things. Shame gums up your thinking processes and makes it impossible to think clearly about what needs to be done. If you want to make peace with the Things in your life, you must first understand and make peace with yourself. There is no other way.

The focus of this book, therefore, is not external but internal. This is not a book about how to sort papers or set up a closet but about what keeps you from sorting or setting up and how to overcome obstacles to success. It is not meant to replace the externally focused organizing books that you may already have but to enable you to make better use of them after rethinking every aspect of you and Things.

My training as a psychotherapist—I'm both a therapist and an organizing consultant—has taught me that different people may have the same problem for many different reasons. You may have Thing-management problems because you're short on time or space, because of transitions or other people in your life, because you have memory problems, visual processing problems, attention problems, or task completion problems, because you're depressed, ill, grieving, obsessive-compulsive, addicted, or for a host of other reasons. Permanent success in making peace with your Things depends on figuring out EXACTLY what is going on: then you can begin to do something about it.

Figuring out what is going on is hard work. You must first re-examine all of your assumptions about Things, beliefs that you have taken as givens since day one. Then you need to conduct a rigorous inventory of your present habits with Things as well as your feelings about Things. Finally, you must look systematically at the most common causes of Thing problems in order to figure out WHY you're doing what you're doing. Once you've figured out why, then you can figure out what to do. All this self-analysis may seem like a lot of trouble, but once you've gone through it, you'll be able to stop going around in circles with your Things. Only action informed by insight can lead you out of the circles.

Each part of this book is devoted to one of the major tasks you need to accomplish to make permanent peace with your Things. Part I helps you to rethink your assumptions about Things. Part II guides you through a systematic inventory of your Thing habits and Thing feelings. Part III describes possible causes of Thing problems together with suggestions for dealing with them. Part IV is about putting what you have learned into action. Along the way, you'll meet a host of characters with peculiar names, aliens from a planet with an even more peculiar name, and terms that will be both familiar and new to you, such as the word *Things* with a capital *T*. Such non-standard usages throughout this book are intended to help you look at familiar possessions with new eyes, to create new "Thing meanings" in place of old ones, and to detach yourself from automatic emotional responses that perpetuate cycles of clutter.

You may notice that I have frequently chosen to emphasize words and phrases by putting them in all caps rather than in italics. This is because many chronically disorganized people also have attention problems and need more intense, visible stimuli to catch their attention. Through a variety of such stylistic devices, I have tried to make this book as accessible as possible to these readers.

As you begin to make even small changes with Things, you may be amazed at the ripple effects such changes may have on the rest of your life. Because we live in a universe in which everything is connected to everything else, you cannot change one aspect of your life without changing all the others. And because Things are physical and thus easier to get your hands on than relationships, careers, or spirituality, they make a great place to start.

PART I

RETHINKING
THINGS

CHAPTER I

PEOPLE AND THINGS

Silver tea sets. Rock collections. Electric sanders. Stock certificates, marriage licenses, college diplomas, hundred-dollar bills. Blankies, hunting rifles, VCRs, computers, grandfather clocks. Boats. BMWs, Lamborginis, SUVs. The complete works of William Shakespeare. Stradivarius violins. The *Mona Lisa*. The Pyramids. Toothpicks, hooks and eyes, bottle caps, twist ties, cotton balls, brass fasteners, paper clips, dominos, buttons, knives, forks, and spoons.

None of us owns a single, solitary Thing permanently. Each of our Things flows through our fingers temporarily, on its way to somewhere else. Some Things are passed down from generation to generation; others are used for an instant and thrown away, recycled to form new Things, or allowed to dissolve into earth or ocean or air. Some Things become symbols of Things unseen, worshipped in temples constructed solely for their preservation or burned to ashes with incantations against them, others live humbler, more mundane lives: a pot, a stove, a coat, a hat, solid and comfortable, always there for us when we need them, beloved old friends.

Each of us has our own unique style of approaching the Things in our lives. Ruthie Bagger loves to shop for bargains, stockpiling shoes and Tupperware, candles and boxes of greeting cards. Jason Stickshift goes into a rage if anyone touches his car. Griselda Backglance still keeps all of Herbie's Things exactly as he left them even though her husband has been dead for nearly twenty years. Harry Openhand never lets a guest leave his house without a gift. Millie Squalor tosses her clothes carelessly into a heap; Nancy Neatfreak hangs up each garment carefully as she takes it off. Little Marty Gemini screams, "Don't touch MY blocks!" when anyone approaches his tower; Little Mickey Gemini carries his blocks one by one to give to each person around the room.

A lot goes into determining how you and your Things get along. As with most areas of human experience, this is a combination of nature and nurture. Nature consists of genetically programmed "brain wiring," i.e., how much of different types of chemicals you have in your brain and how they're distributed and used. Certain types of brain wiring may predispose you to dysfunctional Thing habits: from hoarding unnecessary Things, to heedless tossing rather than careful placing, to random piling rather than logical systematizing, to fearfully holding on to your Things instead of joyfully sharing them.

Nurture includes the influences not only of childhood caregivers but of family, friends, co-workers, culture, community, nation, and world throughout your life. Little Marty's parents may teach him to share or not to share. Millie's husband may accept her messiness or take issue with it. Ruthie's buying behavior may or may not be encouraged by aggressive, manipulative advertising.

As with people, a dysfunctional relationship with Things is a preoccupied relationship. We are preoccupied with the need to acquire, the need to organize, and the need to hang on to Things, putting off living until we have perfected our control over the material world, which always seems to elude us. Some folks are frustrated by never acquiring the one Thing that will satisfy them, others by their inability to get rid of Things they no longer use. Many feel overwhelmed by piles of Things that seem to breed like rabbits. Others spend hours perfecting already adequate systems, arranging and rearranging, filing and refiling, never feeling organized enough.

The good news is that no matter what your brain is like and no matter what has happened to you, you do not have to remain at war with your Things. Every one of us has the ability to develop healthy Thing-management skills. This means learning to say no to yourself about excess Things, to let go of those Things you can no longer use or enjoy, and to effectively organize and maintain the Things you keep, so that instead of taxing your energy they serve your needs and beautify your life.

To achieve this, all you need is the willingness to take an honest look at yourself.

THINGS AS AN ISSUE

For some of us, Things have become an Issue. An issue is a conflict that is always with you, a little black cloud that hangs over you day and night, no matter where you go, blocking out the sun. You can never quite enjoy yourself as long as an issue continues to hover. An issue prevents you from becoming who you truly are. An issue fills you with shame, often coupled with secrecy. An issue about Things means that you feel that some aspect of your behavior in relation to Things is OUT OF CONTROL.

There are many ways that your behavior may be out of control with Things. Psychotherapists' favorite diagnosis and treatment manual, currently known as the *DSM-IV-TR,* contains a number of psychiatric disorders with symptoms relating to Things, including, among others:

- Developmental Coordination Disorder (Dropping Things)

- Attention Deficit/Hyperactivity Disorder (Losing Things)

- Kleptomania (Stealing Things)

- Intermittent Explosive Disorder (Smashing Things)

- Schizophrenia (Seeing Things that aren't there)

- Phobias (Avoiding Things)

- Obsessive-Compulsive Disorder (Overorganizing Things)

- Obsessive-Compulsive Personality Disorder[1] (Hoarding Things)

- Pica (Eating nonedible Things)

- Anorexia (Not eating edible Things)

- Pathological Gambling (Risking Things)

- Fetishism (Having sex with Things)

- Pyromania (Setting Things on fire)

- Autism (Staring at Things for a very long time)

Of course, you don't have to qualify for any of these diagnoses to have a Thing issue. The most common issue with Things isn't listed in the *DSM-IV* at all. This is the issue of *clutter.* When clutter is perpetual, long-lasting, and resistant to change, organizers call this "chronic disorganization," a term first used by Judith Kolberg, founder of the National Study Group on Chronic Disorganization. When you're chronically disorganized, you feel that you are in constant danger of being buried alive by your Things.

Although millions of people struggle with clutter and chronic disorganization, many have never quite realized that Things are an issue for them, something that they could work on in therapy, in self-help groups, or on their own, using the same techniques that have helped them resolve all sorts of more "legitimate" issues. Their response to the problem has been to read books on how to organize closets or set up filing systems, which is about as effective as trying to lose weight by simply reading books on nutrition. Such information may be helpful, but any progress you make in managing your Things this way will be short-lived unless you're also willing to look inside. *This means giving up the habit of avoiding the issue.*

There once was a princess named Esmeralda who was pursued by a dragon. The faster Esmeralda ran from the dragon, the bigger it grew. After chasing her all over the county, the dragon, gargantuan by this time, chased Esmeralda into a cave. Standing with her lovely face pressed against the dank wall of the cave, Esmeralda screamed for a knight to come rescue her, to no avail. Finally, Esmeralda had an idea. She turned and faced the dragon and looked straight into its eyes. The dragon began to shrink. She leaned forward, and it grew smaller still. She stuck her head right into its mouth, and the dragon disappeared! Many of us have long been pursued by a Thing-dragon composed of papers, books, clothes, and all of the other paraphernalia that human beings can collect. The more we've tried to avoid the piles, the bigger they've grown.

Thus, the first step in resolving the Thing issue is to recognize that, for you, it IS an issue. For someone else—even someone much messier than you are—it may not be, but it's an issue for you because it BOTHERS you. Something about your Things bothers you, and you need to stop avoiding the issue, look right into the dragon's eyes, and begin to make the issue disappear.

CHAPTER 2

HOW YOU LOOK AT THINGS

Recognizing that a particular aspect of your life is an issue constitutes an "aha!"—a revolution in the way you look at it. If change is to come out of this "aha," you must rethink your assumptions about the issue.

Many of the difficulties that we have with Things arise from a perspective that demonizes chaos and idealizes order. This sets us up for failure and, worse yet, shame about failure. It also keeps us living in an impossible future, while the present passes us by unlived. Once you've recognized that organizing possessions is an issue for you, your next job is to reexamine your assumptions about the meaning of chaos and order and their consequences for your life.

THINGS AND CHAOS

Do you think of chaos as evil? Does your clutter remind you of the giant squid in *Twenty-thousand Leagues Under the Sea,* with enormous suckered arms reaching to drag you down to the ocean floor? Titles of organizing books such as *How to Conquer Clutter, Clutter's Last Stand,* and *Taming the Paper Tiger* reflect the view that clutter is something big and scary that can only be subdued by violent action. Yet chaos theorists tell us that chaos, of which clutter is one form, is a legitimate part of our universe. Chaos is everywhere, and so is order, and the two interweave in a perpetual, ever-changing dance.

Stand at a window watching snowflakes on a blustery day. Whirling and swirling, blowing and drifting, skeetering off edges of balconies like white ghosts, all seemingly at random. As you begin to look more closely, however, you begin to discern elements of order within the chaos. One of these is self-similarity: all of the snowflakes are white, crystal shaped, cold. Another is the pattern of descent. Order is always there, somewhere within the chaos, if we look for it.

While order and chaos may exist simultaneously, there is also an ebb and flow between them. In *The Structure of Scientific Revolutions,* science historian Thomas Kuhn maintains that periods of intellectual chaos, when existing theories don't seem to fit together, generally precede a paradigm shift, the birth of a new organizing principle, as in the Copernican revolution. The same idea applies on a personal level. You may, like most people, have periods in your life when nothing seems to make sense. During such phases clutter seems to want to accumulate and may even feel good to you. Then all at once, there it is—the "aha!" the lightbulb that sends you off in an entirely different direction, and you begin to reorganize your Things.

At other times you may feel like a robot, locked into dead habits while somewhere within you a tide of rebellion begins to swell. Then one morning instead of making your bed the minute your feet hit the floor as you have for the past 275 days, you don't. Instead, you leave the covers strewn gloriously every which way and it feels FANTAS-TIC. A whole era of spontaneous, creative living follows. You dig out the novel that you started writing in college or take up karate or join a community group and forget about everything else.

Meanwhile, rather than filing papers, you throw them joyfully over your shoulder. Instead of buying a plain gray suit, you buy a multicolored outfit and toss it over your favorite armchair. Instead of eating your meals at six, twelve, and six, you dine on snacks every hour. Eventually, as the cockroaches begin to creep out from beneath the piles and your friends start to look at you strangely, this wonderful new way of life begins to break down. You feel more and more overwhelmed by the stresses of chaos until suddenly a new "aha!" comes forth and you're ready to reorganize your life around a different center. Out of chaos comes order, out of order, chaos. And the dance goes on.

Human emotional and spiritual growth is largely about learning to tolerate and even celebrate chaos. Chaos means growth, change, freedom, color, creativity, play, joy. This is no less true of clutter than any other kind of chaos. There are times when it may, in fact, be healthy for people to clutter. Writers and artists often feel that they need a nest of clutter around them to do their most creative work. Adolescents make outrageous messes out of their belongings and their bodies so as to reorganize themselves into adults. A life devoid of chaos is a life devoid of growth and fun. Children who grow up in rigidly structured environments may become adults with little or no imagination.

Paradoxically, before you can begin to organize a messy space, you need to take a step back and appreciate the chaos you've created. What does your chaos show about you that's positive? Flexibility? Spontaneity? Imagination? Only when you've looked at your space in this way can you begin to transform beautiful chaos into beautiful order.

THINGS AND ORDER

The human brain is wired to respond positively to order. When an infant first recognizes the ordered pattern of a human face, he or she lights up with a smile of recognition. In *Open Your Eyes,* interior designer Alexandra Stoddard defines order as "a condition of lyrical, comprehensible arrangements among the separate elements of a group." Order feels good to us partly because it's easier for our brains to deal with than chaos. Order is perceptually more efficient than chaos. It allows us to take in a whole group of similar things together instead of one by one by one. Consequently, our brains don't have to work so hard, and we feel both energized and soothed.

Neuropsychologists have found that certain parts of the brain "light up" when confronted with certain "archetypal" patterns, especially the circle, the triangle, and the cross. These patterns, which serve as central symbols in the world's religions, may underlie standard organizing processes such as sorting apples into barrels, lining up corners of papers to form one leg of a cross, or arranging bottles in a triangular hierarchy from smallest to largest.

Infant psychiatrist Daniel Stern, in *Diary of a Baby,* observes how even a six-week-old infant staring at a patch of sunshine on a wall responds to contours: "At this age, Joey is also drawn to areas enclosed in a clearly marked frame. The edges of the square sunpatch catch his eyes at the line where lighter and darker wall meet." In organizing, we create edges between Things that were previously mushed together. Such boundaries keep us safe, containing floods and fires and preventing Cheerios from spilling out all over the table.

When we transform chaos into order, we feel a sense of relief. This makes organizing a wonderful anti-depressant. Have you ever been a patient in an understaffed hospital? As the hours drag by, covers become rumpled, flowers droop every which way, straws drip from plastic cups onto the table, and chaos prevails. In such surroundings, you could care less if someone drags you away with the rest of the trash. Eventually a Candystriper comes in, smoothes your covers, plumps up your pillows, rearranges flowers, throws the cups in the wastebasket, and suddenly you sit up in bed and ask for a glass of orange juice. There can be something almost magical about the process of organizing.

Organizing is about birth: when you organize, you bring something new into being that was not there before. You may begin, for example, with a bunch of books and a bookshelf. If you just put the books on the shelves, that is all you still have. But if you arrange them in a way that makes them easy to find, you give birth to something new: a library.

While order can sometimes feel wonderful, it may not always. Stoddard notes that too much symmetry in a room "when things are too matchy-matchy" may seem cold and uninviting. At times, order even feels tyrannical. On a societal level, obsessive compulsive tyrants such as Hitler and Mussolini have given order a bad name. You may have lived with your own petty Hitler and thus learned to equate order with oppression. But even if this isn't the case, it's natural to feel constrained by order when you're at a certain point in the ebb and flow of your life, when too much order has gone on for too long and you're ready to move in the direction of revitalizing chaos. For most people, the key word is *balance*.

THINGS AND CHAOS/ORDER

Let's take a stroll through three different gardens. The first is a Louis XIV–type garden, like the one at the palace of Versailles. Tree branches have been clipped with manicure scissors to form perfect spheres. Plants are arranged in clever, ornate designs, not a single leaf out of place. Such a garden may be impressive, but standing in it, you're afraid to move.

This is a garden created by the kind of person who would always have to let you know about the spot on your pants.

The second garden is nondescript, overgrown with weeds and brambles. In this garden, you're also afraid to move, not for fear of messing something up but for fear of becoming entangled in a briar patch and never getting free.

The third garden is an eighteenth-century English country garden. Here, nature is allowed to roam fancy-free, but within reason. Flowers are mostly wildflowers, and between naturally curving walkways, wild roses, sweet William, and daffodils mingle in a lovely mixture of chaos and order. In such a garden, you feel as lighthearted as a pink-cheeked cherub dancing around a maypole, sensing the presence of a creator who nurtures but never forces.

In managing your Things, it's helpful to keep the English garden in mind. Perfect order is both less feasible and less satisfying than sensibly and creatively contained chaos. Organization is one aspect of effective Thing management, but so is spontaneity.

Consider a hall closet shelf that contains hats, scarves, and gloves. One way of dealing with the contents is to leave them ajumble. But this would mean constantly sorting through them all to find the garment you need, which could become irritating and time-consuming. Another approach is to separate hats, scarves, and gloves into three clear, plastic boxes, and within the boxes, arrange them by color, size, owner, or some other system. This might seem perfectly natural to some people. But you might feel constricted by having to always put each garment away in exactly the right spot. Your system of choice is to put the hats, scarves, and gloves into the three different boxes and let it go at that. Sorting through the many colored berets and beanies in your hat box might even give you a feeling of abundance that you crave. Should you label the boxes? Maybe and maybe not. If labels on boxes make you feel as if Big Brother is watching you, why not honor your feelings and leave them off?

The whole point of organizing is to increase pleasure and reduce pain, and if your current system is not having that effect, you need to shift gears. Rather than thinking about what you need to organize, you might want to think about where to give yourself permission to leave randomness. You may already have created a junk drawer somewhere or a container for odds and ends. A drawerful of swirling scarves might give you more pleasure than scarves folded into neat squares, one on top of the other. Might you simply let the attic evolve into a magical place where your grandchildren can dig for treasure? Remember that life everywhere is an oscillating dance of chaos and order, and that you and your Things are a part of that dance.

Although disorganized Things may not be the enemy, there *IS* an enemy that keeps us from managing possessions effectively, and it's a big, ugly one: the archfiend of psychotherapy, toxic shame.[2] Striving for perfect order instead of balance with your Things sets you up for failure and shame, which can paralyze your efforts. In the movie *The Edge*, Anthony Hopkins plays Charles Morse, a billionaire who is stranded and stalked by a grizzly bear in the Alaska wilderness with two other men after a plane crash. At one point, Charles tells the other men, "Most people lost in the wilds die of shame." When they ask what he means, Charles explains that most such Hansels and Gretels are so busy blaming themselves for getting lost in the first place that they don't do the one thing needed to survive: think about what to do next.

Are you stranded in a wilderness of papers, old clothes, or gardening tools? How are you responding to the problem? Do you pick up the first object you see and find a home for it? Or do you spend hours staring at your Things and muttering to yourself? "I don't know what's wrong with me." "I can't believe I let it get this bad." "I'm NEVER going to be able to deal with this." "I SHOULD have cleaned this up a long time ago." "I'm such a complete slob." "This is horrible." "I feel like I'm in a nightmare."

Or do you turn your shame inside out and change it into blame? "Arthur never stays home long enough to help me get those files out of the basement." "As long as we have kids, we'll always be living in a disaster area. They're just IMPOSSIBLE!" "I've talked myself hoarse trying to get Jackie to clear out her craft stuff and it's no use. I've given up."

Your first order of business, to begin to manage your Things, is to STOP THIS. To change your negative thoughts about Things, you first have to become more aware of them. For a few days, keep a running list of negative thoughts about your clutter as they occur to you. Then analyze their contents and identify your favorite distortions.

Certain ones—most of which are listed in David Burns's *The Feeling Good Handbook*—happen a lot:

- Should statements: You waste your life trying to meet someone else's ideal standards. Should statements come from old tapes, not from God.

- All-or-nothing thinking: Because your house isn't perfectly organized, it's about to be condemned. Because you can't scrub the entire floor, you don't wipe up the spilled milk. Learn to appreciate shades of gray and to do what you can.

- Mind-reading: If anyone comes to your house, you imagine all the critical thoughts he or she is thinking. Or you don't let anyone come over for fear your friend will have such thoughts. If you're wondering, ask, don't assume.

- Discounting the positive: Six out of seven rooms are neat and one is messy. You focus on the messy room and ignore the others. They count too!

- Personalization: Your spouse, children, or roommate make messes and you blame yourself for them. Be fair to yourself.

- Blame: You make a mess, and you blame your spouse, children, roommate, parents, or society for it. Be fair to others.

- Labeling: Some common labels relating to behavior with Things are "slob," "slovenly," "mess-maker," and "pig." Nobody deserves such words.

- Horriblizing: Favorites are "horrible," "awful," "disgusting," "gross," "terrible," "hideous," "a nightmare," "a disaster area," "a hurricane hit," "a tornado hit," "an earthquake hit," and "I'll NEVER be able to clean this up." When it comes to horribilizing, some people are capable of going on for hours before they put away a single Thing. Stop horriblizing and get moving!

Once you've zeroed in on these distortions and begun to correct them, you can stop filling up your precious mental airtime with negatives and use it instead to think about who could wear the sweatshirt that's too small for you, where to store your income tax papers or whether to use a tower or a shelf for CDs. You may even be able to pick up the next Thing and put it away.

Toxic shame may be a formidable enemy, but four words can serve as a magic formula to vaporize instantly any cloud of shame and get you where you want to go. These four magic words are "DO WHAT YOU CAN."

WHEN I'M FINALLY ORGANIZED, I'M GOING TO . . .

When people don't do what they can, what they often do instead is fantasize. Idealizing order can keep you locked in fantasy, while reality passes you by. Instead of living NOW, you imagine all the wonderful things you'll do once you're living orderly ever after. While it can be motivating to consider what you're making room for by decluttering your home and changing your habits with Things, putting off living until you've reached organizational Nirvana may set you up for backsliding if your fantasies aren't realized.

If organizing has been difficult for you all your life, this makes it the greener grass on the other side of the fence. As a child, you may have been criticized and punished for your messiness. And when, in order to escape from this, you turned on the TV, what did you see? Flawlessly organized homes, complete with smiling mother, in which kitchen appliances eternally sparkled, dogs never wet the carpet, and children's rooms always had neat twin beds and college pennants on the walls. Internalized, such visions of order gleam before your mind's eye like celestial cities that you spend the rest of your life trying to enter. You believe that if you can only realize this vision, you'll finally become what you've always longed to be: a member of the prestigious club of "NORMAL" human beings. The problem is, even once you're perfectly organized, you may have other characteristics that would cause anyone intolerant of deviance to reject you. Such individuals are always ready to dismiss you for your race, religion, politics, class, gender, sexual preference, body size, disability, thinking style, or wearing the wrong shade of pantyhose.

Meanwhile, you make plans about what you will do once your Things are under control. You will get a new job. You will start a business. You will move to another town. You will go on a trip. You will write a book. You will get married. You will get a divorce. You will begin dating again. Looking at the project you are planning from behind a nice, safe barricade of Things, you have no doubt at all that it is what you *would* do, if only those nasty Things weren't in the way. The only problem is, if you get your Things in order, then you will actually have to DO what you planned. So you don't get your Things in order. And you don't move on with your life. You are stuck.

The only way to get unstuck is to begin moving on with life NOW, messy or not. Making a decision to relocate now may spur you on to decluttering, and if it doesn't, you can hire an organizer who specializes in helping people move. To start a business now, all you really need is an empty corner of one room in which to set up a desk, not an ergonomically designed office with state-of-the-art electronics and color-coded file folders. And believe it or not, people have managed to date and get married without ever installing a new closet system.

If you find you're unable to make yourself begin a project before decluttering, then you need to ask yourself if this is really what you want to do or only what you think you SHOULD do. After you've either begun the project or made a definite decision not to do it, you may find that putting your Things in order no longer feels like you're trying to climb Mount Everest. All you're doing is putting your Things in order, which is much easier. Once a shirt is just a shirt— and not a marriage, a job, or a business—you can hang it up—and all its brothers and sisters as well—in nothing flat.

PART II

YOU AND YOUR THINGS: TAKING INVENTORY

Most chronically disorganized people share a common belief in what might be called the Magic System. This system, from their perspective, is a well-kept secret that, despite reading book after book, they have not yet managed to discover. But they have faith: they believe that sooner or later the right book or the right organizer will reveal the Magic System to them, and they will be organized forever after.

This is NOT how it works. While a new system may make it easier to solve problems with clutter and disorganization, no system alone will resolve the issue: in most cases disorganization and clutter result not from lack of a system but from counterproductive habits. Making peace with Things is mostly a matter of replacing counterproductive habits with constructive ones.

Before you can do this, you need to be clear about what your current Thing habits are. A habit is a behavior that is automatically triggered by particular circumstances. You don't have to make yourself do something that is a habit: you can't keep from doing it. Your habits relate to three phases in the flow of Things: how Things enter or don't enter your space; what you do with them while they're in your space; and how Things leave or don't leave your space. Sound familiar? This is the good old input-operations-output model that computer whizzes love.

In assessing your Thing habits, try to ignore your fear of being buried alive under a Thing Mountain as well as your theory about your father-transference and Things and focus objectively on your behavior. Imagine you're being watched day and night by a creature from another galaxy called Gryzypia who understands nothing at all about human psyches and is minutely observing how you interact with the objects around you. A Gryzypian might notice, for example, that a humanoid dressed in blue brings you a stack of white rectangular Things each day, which you add to a pile on a flat surface. It might report that each time you take off an outside layer of skin, you throw it on the floor, or that from time to time you take Things outside and put them into silvery cylindrical Things with lids. You get the idea.

As a preliminary exercise, write out a list of simple propositions describing your current Thing habits, for example:

- I buy a great many books.

- When someone gives me a gift, I always keep it for at least a year.

- I leave my clothes hanging over a chair at night and hang them up in the morning.

- I open my mail as soon as I receive it and throw all junk mail in the recycle bin.

- I keep magazines stacked in the basement and never throw any of them away.

- I take bags of clothes once a year to St. Vincent de Paul's.

Now look at each sentence that you wrote and ask yourself which phase of the flow of Things it relates to: Things coming into your space, Things while you have them, or Things going out. You've made a start, but this approach is hit or miss: many of your actual Thing habits may not have occurred to you. Nothing is more difficult than becoming aware of your own behavior. What helps is to consider systematically all of the possibilities, and that is what we will do in the next three chapters.

Habits, however, are not the only thing you need to consider if you're going to make peace with your Things. Peace, after all, must happen not only on the outside but also on the inside. Many a professional organizer has had the experience of receiving a frantic call from a person who claimed to be "living in chaos" only to discover, upon arrival, that his or her home was as neat and organized as a Shaker village. Such people, however meticulous their Thing habits, are not at peace with their Things. To truly make peace, you must review not only your Thing habits but also your Thing *feelings,* which may have a big effect on those habits. Therefore, the last chapter of this section enables you to assess your Thing feelings.

You will notice that at the end of each chapter is a list of questions under the title "You and Your Things Inventory." These questions are to help you think about your own behavior with and feelings about Things in a systematic way. The ideal way to consider them is with a friend who is also working on Things. Or you might want to use the questions as a basis for journal writing. If the questions remind you of your eighth-grade geography book, you may feel tempted to skip them and go on reading, which is more fun. This is better than closing the book, but if you really want to make peace with your Things, it's important at least to read the questions and get them rumbling around in your brain. Don't worry—you're not being graded.

If taking stock of your Thing habits brings up feelings of shame for you, take care of yourself. Review the section on detoxifying

Things in Chapter 2 and pay attention to your automatic thoughts. Remind yourself that life is supposed to be a mixture of chaos and order. Bear in mind that in Parts III and IV you'll learn new ways to develop more positive Thing habits. And remember: to a Gryzypian, Thing habits and Thing feelings are just stuff for statistics, nothing more.

CHAPTER 3

WHERE YOUR THINGS
COME FROM

Things, as a rule, do not give birth to baby Things. Things in your space multiply only by immigration, not by reproduction. Of course, parts of Things may be broken off and transformed and combined to form new Things, but the amount of stuff in them stays the same— Things do not normally grow new cells (though certain edible Things left in the fridge too long may attract colonies of exotic organisms).

While those of us who have accumulated an excess of possessions may envision a ceaseless parade of Things marching in on little legs through the cracks beneath doors, this is NOT what happens. Instead, Things are BROUGHT in, either by you or by someone else. If you're an adult, you have a legal right to choose what Things you bring or allow into your space. Not all of us, however, choose to exercise this right.

The key word here is BOUNDARIES. If you had carpenter ants in your house, you would need to inspect the walls for cracks and holes through which the ants were coming in so you could stop them up. Where Things are concerned—and sometimes people as well!— you need to conduct an imaginary inspection for "holes in your walls" and figure out what you need to do to fill those "holes" in.

One way to do this is to go from room to room and look at each object in turn, notebook in hand. Spend at least an hour writing down as many of the Things you encounter as you can and note where each Thing came from. List some Things from each room so you'll get a good cross-section. As you list each item, try to remember how you made the decision to bring or allow it in. What thoughts went through your mind? How do you feel about the object now? For example:

- Blue glass mug that says "Class of '66" on it—bought it at my thirtieth reunion to have something to remember the occasion by—LOVE this cup, it makes me feel good every time I look at it.

- Book on fly-fishing—borrowed it from Buddy when he offered to lend it to me rather than hurt his feelings eight years ago. Makes me feel flaky as I still haven't read it. Get real and give it back—if I can find Buddy and he's still alive!

- Green nightgown—bought this on sale with three other nightgowns, knew I wouldn't ever wear it but I couldn't stop myself. I hate it!

- Article on breast-feeding—cut it out of a magazine when Jimmy was a baby, eager to learn. Feel ridiculous for keeping it but I can't get rid of it—I might need it to give to my future daughter-in-law.

- Credit card flyer—threw it on the table, feeling overwhelmed. I hate junk mail—throw it in the trash!

As you begin to look in detail at how you've acquired more and more of your possessions, you will begin to see patterns. Some important ones to look for are:

- Impulsive buying—I saw it and all of a sudden I wanted it and before I knew it I'd bought it; when I got home, I was mad at myself for buying it.

- Compulsive buying—I felt depressed, so I went on a shopping spree; I had to have this to feel good about myself; the Joneses had one of these so I had to get one too; without one of these my life would have no meaning; I went to buy just one and kept on buying—I couldn't stop, I was out of control.

- People pleasing—I didn't want to hurt her feelings, so I accepted it and am still keeping it in case she comes to visit; it's his space too—I don't have a right to tell him what he can keep; they're my children! They'd be furious if I got rid of their Things without asking them.

- Memory aids/connecting with the past—I wanted something to remember our trip by, so I bought it; my grandmother left it to me to remember her by.

- Hoarding—it was on sale; I don't want to run out of these; I might need this sometime; I'm afraid if I get rid of it I'll regret it; I've heard these become valuable really fast. You can never have too many of these.

- Procrastination—I didn't have the time/energy to go through my mail, so I kept everything.

Any of these behavior patterns constitutes a "hole in the wall" through which an excess of Things may be flowing into your space. But all of your Things don't come through the hole from the same place. Things flow in from stores and mail-order houses, from friends and relations, and countless pieces of paper arrive from who knows where through the mail. You may feel horribly victimized by any or all of these Thing sources, believing they're collectively engaged in a plot to keep you buried under Thing mountains. This may, in fact, be the case with some sources, especially mercantile ones. However, the key to change is realizing that none of these people and organizations can legally force you to accept Things that you don't want. YOU AND YOU ALONE DECIDE WHAT YOU WILL ALLOW INTO YOUR SPACE.

In order to make better decisions about what to allow in, consider one source at a time. Just thinking, "I collect too much stuff" feels like a formidable obstacle. "My catalogue buying is out of control" or "We get a lot of Christmas gifts we never use" or "My son's stuff is all still in the basement" are problems that can each be creatively solved, one part at a time.

THE THINGS THEY SELL YOU

Every time you turn around, someone is trying to sell you another Thing. Rarely, however, is this person a gunman with a bandanna over his face who yells "Stick 'em up!" and then hands the goods over when you pull out your wallet. You pay for what you buy of your own volition, which can be burdensome.

To buy means to give someone money in exchange for goods or services. There are many ways to do this, ranging from counting out pennies at a child's lemonade stand to typing numbers into the Internet. Different Things tend to get purchased different ways: you would probably not charge gumballs from a gumball machine on your credit card or pay for a new car in cash.

For some people, buying certain Things has become a little too easy, resulting in debts and/or clutter. This is not just a problem of the affluent, as even the impoverished may go overboard at yard sales and thrift shops. Overbuying happens when we define the word "need" too broadly. When you come down to it, all we really NEED to sustain life is food, water, clothing, shelter, and medical care. Everything else is a luxury. Luxuries, however, can have a strong appeal, especially those that your neighbors already have.

If Roger Suburb has a new power mower, his neighbor, Eliot Status, feels that he must have an even fancier one and make sure that

Roger sees him with it. Why is this? One possible motive is the biologically programmed instinct to dominate. On some deep, totally irrational level, Eliot may hope that when Roger's crummy old lawn mower breaks, Roger will come over to Eliot's house, fall groveling to his knees in the driveway, kiss Eliot's shoes, and beg him to let him use his infinitely superior lawn mower. Things are about power.

Another reason Eliot might want a lawn mower like Roger's is the chemically programmed instinct to belong. Human beings are herd animals, though some seem to follow the herd more than others. If everybody in the neighborhood but Eliot has a fancy power lawn mower, he may feel like an outcast. If Eliot wants to belong, he must own the Things that everyone else owns. Things are about belonging.

Not everyone, however, is strongly motivated to belong. Some are more interested in being different. Eliot Status may want a lawn mower just like Roger's, but Andrew Oddfellow, who lives next door to Roger on the other side, does not. Andrew, in fact, doesn't even HAVE a lawn mower, which he regards as much too boring. He doesn't have a lawn either, opting instead for the only rock garden on the block, complete with driftwood sculpture, terra cotta figurines, and bonsai. Owning these Things instead of grass and a lawn mower gives Andrew a feeling of identity. The Things that we own tell us—and others—who we are. Things are about identity.

The identity aspect of Things presents a problem to those who aren't sure who they are. All of us know people who adopt a new hobby—and buy all the paraphernalia attached to it—every month. Their basements are filled with rusting golf clubs, warped tennis rackets, cobweb-covered easels, boxes of piano music, unfinished manuscripts, half-knitted sweaters, and unfilled stamp albums.

If part of how you think of yourself is avant garde, a person at the head of the fashion parade, this can also be problematic. Such image consciousness can lead to buying a new wardrobe and redecorating your house every six months while the passé possessions accumulate into Thing mountains. Fashionable Things are about trying to achieve a perfect image. Things are about perfection.

Some advertisers dedicate themselves to keeping our lust for power, belonging, identity, and perfection alive and associated with possessions while anesthetizing our intelligence about what these Things will actually DO—or NOT DO—for us.[3] A great deal of advertising is done not merely through ads but through implicit media messages about how the rich and famous live. Hence, the Roger Suburb that Eliot imitates may not be his actual next-door neighbor, who has an income comparable to his own, but his TV "neighbor" with an income twenty times greater. The result is that huge numbers of people currently live beyond their means.

Those whose brains are wired to function mainly on a concrete level are particularly susceptible to this kind of influence, but the truth is that we are all brainwashed about Things. We don't like to admit this to ourselves, preferring to believe that we buy what we do only because WE want it, not because we've been convinced of a need we don't truly have. Once we've recognized this, however, we can begin to fight back by tracing Thing messages to their original sources and taking a more critical look at them.

Not everyone has the same degree of control over his or her buying behavior. There are two ways that your buying behavior may be seriously out of control: impulsive buying and compulsive buying.[4] When you go into a store with the intention of buying nothing and come out with a new waterbed frame and realize when you get home that you don't have a waterbed, that is impulsive buying. When you buy impulsively, you buy without thinking.

When you buy compulsively, on the other hand, you think a lot. Compulsive buying—also known as oniomania—pits you in constant battles against yourself. You know you shouldn't buy but you can't stop—YOU CAN'T STAND IT IF YOU CAN'T HAVE THE THING RIGHT NOW. If it's the middle of the night and you have to drive all over the county in a snowstorm to find a store that's open and sells what you want, you will do so. But nothing that you buy satisfies your craving for long, and once you have begun a spree, you are powerless to stop until you've maxed out all of your credit cards. In the end, you're consumed with guilt, which only makes you buy all the more. Oniomania of this magnitude is rare, but many individuals experience a milder form of compulsive buying that causes debts and clutter to pile up over time, if not instantaneously.

In *Women Who Shop Too Much*, Carolyn Wesson maintains that women are particularly susceptible to compulsive buying, especially for clothes. According to her, the women most at risk for this problem are those who feel powerless in relationships that do not meet their needs and are unable to express anger directly. Another theory is that compulsive buying may be caused by faulty brain chemistry: your brain needs more exciting sensations than other people's brains need or your "satisfaction system" simply doesn't work right. Compulsive buying is often found in conjunction with depression, bipolar disorder, or obsessive-compulsive disorder, and many compulsive buyers have been treated successfully with antidepressants or other medications. Psychotherapy and twelve-step programs such as those offered by Spenders Anonymous and Debtors Anonymous are also helpful.[5] This disorder can have serious consequences financially, emotionally, socially, and environmentally. If you are a compulsive buyer, do not try to handle your problem alone: GET HELP BY CONTACTING AN APPROPRIATE MENTAL HEALTH PROFESSIONAL.

THE THINGS THEY GIVE YOU

Getting a gift from someone can feel great, but not always. Sometimes it makes you want to dance and sing. At other times it makes you want to groan and sigh, especially if you believe that once you've received a gift, you have no choice but to keep it for the rest of your life. If you believe this, you may become a gift slave whose life is devoted to organizing these unwanted objects. As more and more hand-crocheted tissue-box covers, dollar-bill toilet paper rolls, and chrome-sailed ship clocks flow into your space and none flow out, it becomes increasingly impossible to find places to store them, and clutter is the result.

In our culture, a large proportion of gift giving and gift receiving is done within the family. The idea is that when you give someone a gift, this strengthens a tie between you and the receiver. Families have different traditions when it comes to gift giving. The Bountifuls exchange gifts on Christmas, Hanukkah, New Year's, birthdays, Mother's Day, Father's Day, Valentine's Day, St. Patrick's Day, Passover, Easter, "Sweetest" Day, Halloween, Thanksgiving, Memorial Day, Labor Day, and the Fourth of July. The Skinflints never exchange gifts at all, grumbling about the "commercialism" of all holidays. Not everyone within the same family necessarily feels the same about gifts as everyone else, however. This can cause a lot of confusion and strife. Bobby Bountiful, who married Susie Skinflint, has come to resent his family's constant gift expectations. Susie, on the other hand, feels that her family has cheated her out of the gift fun that other families have.

Whether given within the family or outside of it, gifts, like water, have varying degrees of purity. Impure gifts have hidden obligations or even barbs attached. Hence Virgil's expression "Beware of Greeks bearing gifts." This phrase refers to the legendary big wooden horse that the Greeks gave to their enemies, the Trojans, without telling them however that it was filled with Greek soldiers. The Trojans rolled the horse into the city and during the night, the soldiers came out, let their compatriots in, and burned Troy. The size 2 dress a disapproving mother gives her overweight daughter, the tuition check to be used only for the college of Junior's grandfather's choice, the football helmet a father presents to his ballet-dancing son—these gifts are contaminated by selfish intentions. A genuine gift is given freely, respecting the well-being and autonomy of the receiver and accompanied by the best gift of all: the right to give the gift away and thus experience the joy of giving oneself.

When you give a loved one a leather-bound book of poems for

which you combed every used bookstore in the state and on which you spent your entire paycheck, it doesn't feel good if he or she says, "No, thanks, I've already read it," and gives it back to you. Thus, in most circles, refusing gifts, especially on formal occasions, is taboo. There may also be a rule that you have to pretend you like a gift even when you don't. Taking a bite from a chocolate you received for Valentine's day and going "Blech!" in the name of honesty is considered bad form. While refusing the gifts of those who are inappropriately generous or who use material objects to manipulate others may be necessary at times, in most cases it's sensible to do what is both culturally appropriate and kind, and accept what's offered.

If you habitually accept good and bad gifts alike, however, you may begin to feel that gift giving is something that is done to you, especially if some gifts are impure. This is not the case. Your choice to accept is still your choice to accept. And although you may reasonably deny yourself the choice of refusing a gift, you can still choose what you do with it once you have it. Some people get rid of all the gifts they don't like the moment their benefactors have driven away; others hang on to them and even go through the motions of using them for a brief period and then get rid of them; still others hold on to them for life. Which of these people you happen to be may have something to do with how overwhelming your Thing mountains become.

THE THINGS THEY SEND YOU

Human beings everywhere in the world receive mail. Most people receive it every day. For some, it's delivered by mail truck, for others by dogsled, helicopter, bicycle, elephant, or llama. Some simply have to step outside their door, while others must ski down a mountainside to a post office or stand at attention while their commanding officer passes out letters that have flown thousands of miles and exchanged hands dozens of times and yet somehow miraculously managed to get to them. To further complicate things, many people receive electronic Mail over the Internet, sometimes in enormous quantities, in addition to paper and package mail.

Not everyone responds the same way to the daily miracle of mail. To children homesick at camp or soldiers at the front, mail call may constitute the high point of the day, a reason for continuing to live. Others have come to take their mail for granted or even to feel oppressed by it. In general, the principle that governs sentiments toward mail is the law of diminishing returns: the more mail you receive, the less you appreciate it. Because most of the mail we receive is printed paper, this is the kind of mail we tend to appreciate least, especially papers that demand money or try to sell us something.

Behaviors in dealing with paper mail are as varied as attitudes. Some people process their mail as soon as it's in their hands; others allow it to pile up for weeks before they open a single envelope, regardless of consequences. As piles of unread mail begin to accumulate like mountains of dirty snow, you feel more and more like avoiding them. The more you avoid the piles, the bigger they grow. And still the mail keeps coming.

Dealing with mail takes time, energy, the cognitive ability to distinguish subtle differences and make decisions, and the emotional ability to get rid of the extraneous. If you're short on any of these, papers tend to accumulate. Studying your own behavior with mail enables you to identify points where the flow of mail gets stuck, and to develop some kind of mechanism to keep mail moving. If you're a visual thinker, making a flowchart may help you see where your mail goes. The more conscious you become of the flow of your mail, the easier it will be for you to develop a better system as well as the habits to make it work. If mail systems are totally alien to you, don't worry: in Part IV you'll learn how to set up a simple system that you can then adapt to your own personal style.

Sheldon and Biffy Splitup have been divorced for fourteen years, but Sheldon's old golf clubs are still in Biffy's garage. Madge Youngblood graduated from college ten years ago and got married several years later, but all of her stuffed animals are still on the closet shelf of her childhood room. Roberta Keepit recently moved into a retirement home, and now all of her old living room furniture is in her daughter and son-in-law's basement "to keep it in the family."

Sometimes we hold on to significant amounts of Things from people who've moved out of our homes. This is not unhealthy if it's only temporary. When someone leaves, it's normal for us to try to cushion ourselves from overly abrupt change by allowing some of their possessions to stay around for a while. Doing so may enable them—and you—to feel that the bridge behind them is not yet completely engulfed in flames even though the match has obviously been lit. As you wander through empty rooms with tears rolling down your cheeks, you may welcome an old teddy bear or even a pair of shoes to serve as surrogates for the loved one you miss. Somehow, it feels better than nothing. As time goes on, however, many of the Things that at first were comforting may become an annoyance. If you DON'T begin to feel this way, then you may need extra help in grieving and letting go. Once you have done so, you will want to reorganize your Things so that your space serves the needs of its current occupants.

However, sometimes the transition isn't so smooth. Something may hold you back when you consider making an ultimatum to the owner of the old autograph books or Depression china. You know you should set a deadline and perhaps offer help in moving the Things, but you don't.

You may be afraid that you'll lose the person completely if you set limits about his or her Things, but such fears are based on mind reading and fortune-telling. The reality is that in the vast majority of cases, setting firm boundaries with others improves relationships with them rather than causing them to deteriorate. And it's much better for THEM if you do so. One of the worst things you can do to another person is to encourage his or her thoughtlessness by rewarding it. While Junior may fuss when you tell him you'll be giving away his football gear if he hasn't claimed it by June 1, he will almost certainly come and get it—AND be less likely to impose on others in the future.

THE THINGS THEY LEAVE TO YOU

Griselda Backglance is touring her house with her organizer. "These conch shells belonged to my grandmother, God rest her soul," she says. "And over here on the shelves are Uncle Albert's stamp albums, all fifty of them. I wish they didn't take up so much space. And my kitchen cupboards are filled with odd china pieces from different people in the family. I hardly ever use them, but I know it's my duty to pass them on to my daughter. Heaven knows what she'll do with them—she doesn't like old things. The basement and attic are filled with boxes and boxes of Herbie's model trains. I don't know one from the other, but I can't bring myself to get rid of them. And of course I've kept his study exactly as it was when he died."

Do you have a great many Things that were left to you by people who've passed on to the place where Things can't go? When a loved one departs, his or her Things may become your Things, whether you want them or not. Everyone reacts to this situation differently. Some people keep countless Things for years knowing they'll never use them, simply because they belonged to a loved one. Others keep next to nothing, caring little about the past, perhaps even finding it therapeutic to get rid of an intimate's belongings, especially if the relationship was a difficult one.

When you really begin to think about your inherited Things, you may realize that you've been hanging on to some of them for years out of sheer habit, keeping objects that mean little or nothing to you along with those that mean a great deal. As with Things left in your space by the living, what may hold you in bondage to the Things of the dead is an irrational fear of being a Terrible Person. This may prevent you from setting boundaries with your departed loved ones, which are just as important as the boundaries you set with the living. The dead have no more right to impose on you than the living. If you cannot use the Things they left to you yourself, then not only are you not a Terrible person for giving them to someone who can enjoy them, you're a wonderful person for being willing to share what is now yours.

YOU AND YOUR THINGS INVENTORY:
PART A: THING ACQUISITION HABITS

BUYING THINGS

1. What kinds of Things do you typically buy in stores? From catalogues? Over the Internet? In other ways?

2. When do you typically shop for groceries? For clothes? For books? For household items? For other Things? Do you shop for particular Things at regularly scheduled times, when you run out of them, or whenever the mood strikes you?

3. Do you make lists when you shop? Do you often come home with Things that were not on your list?

4. Do you usually shop alone or with someone else? How is your shopping behavior affected by your companion(s)?

5. What are your favorite stores? What do you like about them? What "snares" do they contain that invite you to buy more than you intended to buy? How frequently do you give in to them?

6. Do you ever window shop? Do you enjoy looking through catalogues? What thoughts go through your mind when you're doing so?

7. Impulsive buying: Do you often buy Things you had no intention of buying when you entered a store? Do you sometimes not realize you're buying something until after you bought it? Do you often regret purchases after you've made them? Do you take the Thing back when this happens? How would it feel to do this?

8. Compulsive buying: Do you often go shopping to forget your troubles? Do you ever feel as if you can't wait to go buy something? Do you often feel guilty after shopping? Are you unable to keep from making purchases even when you know this will result in negative consequences such as debt, lack of time, inconvenience, or displeasing someone else? Once you start buying, do you sometimes feel that you've lost control and can't stop? Do you ever hide the Things you buy or quarrel with others about them? Are you deeply in debt?

9. To what kinds of advertising are you most frequently exposed: TV, radio, newspapers, magazines, junk mail, telephone solicitations? How often do you buy the products these ads are selling? When a new product comes on the market, do you immediately rush out and buy it, or do you wait and consider the purchase first?

10. How much do the people around you talk about Things they've bought? Which objects do they talk about the most? When you hear people talking about a new type of product, do you immediately buy one too? Do you deliberately NOT buy it? Do you always have to have the best on the block?

11. Make a list of ten Things that you own and consider how you decided that you needed each of them. What role did friends, relatives, or advertisers play? Were you imitating someone when you bought it? What did you hope it would do for you? Did you see it as helping you to create a new identity? as empowering you in some way? as enabling you

to belong? as making you or your life perfect? How did owning the object affect you once you made the purchase? Pay special attention to fashionable Things that have only recently come on the market.

GIFT THINGS

1. On what occasions do you typically receive gifts? With whom do you exchange them? Do you like and/or use most of the gifts you receive?

2. When someone offers you a gift, do you automatically accept it even if you don't like it and can't use it? If you don't like it, do you pretend that you do?

3. Does anyone in your life offer you Trojan horses, gifts that feel disempowering or even harmful to you? Does anyone use you as a dumping ground for his or her useless Things? Do you accept these gifts? What would happen if you didn't? How would you deal with this?

4. How much control do those who give you gifts exert over what you do with them? In what ways do they exert their control? How do you respond?

5. Does anyone in your life offer gifts that you feel wrong accepting—gifts that he or she can't afford or are inappropriate for the type of relationship you have? Do you accept these gifts? What would happen if you didn't? How would you deal with this?

6. Do you often feel and/or express resentment at others for failing to give you the gifts you'd hoped for? Where did these expectations come from?

7. Once you've accepted a gift, do you feel obligated to keep it forever? What would happen if you gave it away yourself? How would you deal with this?

MAIL THINGS

1. When do you usually receive mail in your hands? Do you put it down to sort later, or do you open it right away?

2. Do you throw some envelopes away without opening them, or do you open everything? Do you separate mail addressed to different people in your household immediately or later? What proportion of commercial mail do you open and keep and what proportion do you discard?

3. If you allow mail to accumulate, where do you keep it in the meantime?

4. To how many magazines, newspapers, and journals do you subscribe? What proportion of articles do you read? Do you ever clip out articles and throw the rest away? If so, where do you keep the articles until you read them?

5. When and how often do you pay your bills? Do you ever pay them late?

6. When and how often do you look at your E-mail? Do you feel a compulsion to check for new messages frequently? Do you deal with E-mail when you receive it or do you put it off? Do you print out all E-messages, or only some of them? What do you do with the ones you print out?

LEGACY THINGS

1. What Things in your home were left by someone who's moved away? How much of your space do these objects take up?

2. How did the person who left these Things with you justify doing so? Did you agree to this at the time? Has this person's situation changed? Have you talked with him or her about it?

3. What do you think would happen if you asked the person to

remove his or her possessions from your home? How would you deal with this?

4. Do you have lots of Things that were left to you by people who've died? Do you like or use them? Do they have good, bad, or neutral memories attached to them?

5. Are you keeping a lot of family heirlooms in order to pass them on to your descendents? How do you and your potential heirs feel about these Things?

6. Are you keeping an entire room exactly as a loved one left it? How long has it been kept intact? Have you created any special memorials for the person?

7. At times of loss, how did you decide what to keep and what to give away? If you were making such decisions now, would you do it the same way?

8. Would you feel guilty if you got rid of something left to you by a deceased person? How could you manage your guilt feelings? What are you afraid might happen if you gave the item(s) away? How would you deal with it?

CHAPTER 4

WHAT YOU DO WITH THINGS
WHILE YOU HAVE THEM

Nancy Neatfreak gets up and puts her dishes in the sink the minute she's taken her last bite. Millie Squalor lets dishes pile up for days at a time. Alan Orderly files papers in file cabinets, Wilbur Seebottom in milk crates, and George Shovit in paper bags. Marcy New Age scrutinizes feng shui diagrams to ensure that her furniture won't block off the energy flowing from the trees outside her windows. Joshua Random throws whatever is in his hands down when he comes in the door and there it stays.

Many people believe that getting organized is simply a matter of reducing the number of Things they acquire and keep. This is not the case. It's perfectly possible to have even a small number of possessions and still have clutter problems. Each of us is engaged in a dance with our Things that has different steps. Our habits vary not only in how we acquire Things but also in how we manage them while we have them.

How organized you feel depends largely upon whether or not all of your Things have homes—places where they belong—and how successful you are at keeping most Things in their homes most of the time. Putting Things away, however, is only one way that we deal with Things while we have them. We also use, mix, throw, hug, clean, fix, lose, find, wear, talk to, and do a great many other things with our possessions. To make peace with your Things you need to consider organizing within the context of all of these activities.

THING HOMES

Some people live by the rule of "a place for everything and everything in its place." These people have a home for every single object that they own. If a new type of Thing arrives on the scene, they immediately assign it a home. People who know where all their Things belong are usually much more at peace with their Things than those who don't, even if they don't always keep them there. Having a mental map of all your Thing homes gives you a sense of security that enables you to relax.

Some Things, like some people, are natural vagabonds. These objects seem to resist settling down into definite homes. Large, oddly shaped Things such as skis, baskets, salad swirlers, and baseball bats may fall into this category. So may smaller Things that you constantly use and throw down, use and throw down. These are Very Important Things (VITs) such as keys, watches, eyeglasses, wallets, purses, briefcases, shoes, gloves, notebooks, planners, and Palm Pilots, which you may waste precious minutes—or even hours!—looking for every day of the week. Since you use these Things so frequently, you may never have bothered to create homes for them. Leaving your VITs homeless saves you a few seconds here and there, as it means you don't have to get up out of your chair every time you finish using a VIT to go put it away. The only drawback is the hours and energy you may squander on VIT searches.

Just as different kinds of people have different kinds of homes, so is it with Things. Some people are highly conventional in the homes they choose for their Things: they keep their books on bookshelves and their underwear in dresser drawers. Others are more unconventional: they keep their underwear on bookshelves and their books in dresser drawers. There's nothing wrong with this if it works. What's important is not where a Thing's home is but that you KNOW where it is and that you keep putting it there every time you put it away. As long as every time you put a Thing away you put it in a different place, it's still a homeless Thing.

If you feel overwhelmed thinking about Thing homes, don't worry. All you need to do at this point is consider which of your Things already have homes and which don't: you won't have to actually create homes for Things until Part IV, when you'll get lots of help.

PUTTING THINGS IN THEIR HOMES

Even the youngest camper at Camp Hammerhead knows that the daily agenda, following flag raising, breakfast, and singing the camp song, includes a period known as chore time, a frantic scramble of bed making and bathroom scrubbing in preparation for the collective ordeal of inspection. Chore time at camp is the ultimate Thing routine, a structured time period for putting belongings in their homes, when blankets are spread wrinkle free over beds, shoes are lined up beneath bunks, and flashlights and canteens arranged beyond reproach.

Some of us have carried the ritual of chore time from camp, school, or home over into our adult lives and others have not. Some may never have been exposed to its delights in the first place. Devoting a daily, weekly, monthly, or yearly block of time to putting Things away can be an effective method of keeping most of your Things in their homes most of the time, but it's only one of many means of accomplishing this purpose. Not everyone lives strictly by the clock. If you don't, this does not necessarily mean you don't put your Things away. Clocks, after all, are simply triggers to which you may or may not respond. But other triggers may likewise inspire you to hang up your clothes and put away your crayons.

The most common trigger for putting Things away, to which

some people are trained to respond as consistently as Pavlov's dog responded to the bell, is the trigger of having just used a Thing. While you may prefer not to engage in such meticulous robotics, you may still automatically put away certain objects some of the time, under some circumstances—or you may not. As organizer Julie Morgenstern points out, you're more likely to put Things away after using them if their homes are near the "point of use."

Another common putting-away trigger is simply the act of finishing a job or other activity. "Part of any job is putting your tools away." "Winner cleans up the game!" "After lunch, we have to do the dishes and put them in the cupboards." If this type of training stuck, you may find it impossible to finish anything without immediately dealing with the Things involved. In this case, congratulations. For you, the battle with Things, if there is one at all, is caused only by how they come in and out of your life, not the middle piece, and you can skip ahead to the next chapter.

A third, powerful trigger to sending Things scurrying into their holes is the expectation that someone is going to see your space. "We have company coming over—I've got to clean up!" "I'm getting the house in order for my daughter's wedding dinner." "Uh-oh, here comes the boss—gotta get these papers in order." Panic at the prospect of being seen, however, tends to result only in the APPEARANCE of all of your Things being put away, not the reality. Your space may look tidy on the surface, but if the guest is your nosy Uncle Phineas, he may be shocked to find beer cans and paintbrushes in your medicine cabinet, and clarinet reeds, water pistols, and brassieres in your kitchen cupboards.

Not everyone, of course, is triggered into action by clock, completion, or guests. Some habitually drop an object wherever they happen to be as soon as they've used it, then wonder where their Thing mountains came from. Such people may be at peace with their Things only if they have servants, spouses, or others who are willing to pick up after them. As a rule, peace with Things requires that you not only have homes for your Things, you also need to have at least some habits, rules, or routines that result in regularly marshaling Things into homes. There are many ways to make this happen. There are also many ways not to make it happen. What you need to get clear on right now is which of these, if any, you're already using.

PAPER THINGS

Paper Things are unique. Pieces of paper large and small are mixed up in every aspect of your life, from whether you're seen as promising or hopeless to what vegetables you put in your soup to whether or not the plugs will be pulled that attach you to life. Because paper can exercise so much control over your future, it becomes extra important for you to know exactly where each piece of paper is when you need it. Alas, this can be challenging.

Each person has a particular style of dealing with paper. When handed a piece of paper, some folks add it to the piles without even looking at it. Others glance at it cursorily, make a decision, and do something with it. Still others spend hours scrutinizing it without doing anything, paralyzed by its power to affect their lives. While the information age demands ever more efficient visual processing in dealing with paper, not all brains have such capabilities wired into the system. Many brains do not allow their owners to read quickly, concentrate on what they read, make sense out of it, or categorize it. This can be a source of intense frustration.

Viewing pieces of paper en masse also produces different reactions in different individuals. Some tend to view their papers much more collectively than others do, as if all the papers in a pile are glued together and can only be dealt with as one. These people are most likely to have paper-management problems. While they may occasionally extract an individual page from the heap, they will look at it for only a second, fail to make a decision about it, and quickly allow it to go back into the All. They may repeat this process for hours without permanently separating a single piece of paper from the rest. Eventually, when they're cleaning out their office for the last time and none of their papers are now of use to them, they dump the whole pile into the wastebasket, TOGETHER TO THE LAST. Not everyone responds this way to a pile of papers, however. Believe it or not, to some individuals, a pile of papers is a pile of individual items, each of which can be completely dealt with before going on to the next.

Those who mismanage paper may choose from several mismanagement options. Sammy Spreader spreads his papers out on all available surfaces, so that he can read them all without ever having to move any of the others. He claims that he can only find those papers he can see. Sammy's "system" worked well for his first few days on the job, but as layer upon layer of papers have begun to accumulate, the system has broken down, and Sammy feels overwhelmed. Henrietta Stasher stuffs her papers randomly into closed boxes and filing cabinets with drawers that slam shut, protecting her from the critical scrutiny of others. Henrietta leads a double life: to the world she looks great, but her stashes of paper constitute a guilty secret. Harold Stacker is somewhere between Sammy and Henrietta. Harold, like Sammy, keeps all of his papers in plain sight, but instead of spreading them out he stacks them in neat piles.

Dealing with paper is not an easy matter for anyone, and it gets harder all the time. Enormous amounts of paper flow through all of our lives, notwithstanding the predictions of computer lovers. Compared with dealing with most other kinds of Things, organizing papers is slow and tedious, and not all brains have the requisite patience wired into them. For this reason, you need to pay particular attention not only to what kinds of paper you allow into your space but also to the intricacies of how you sort, spread, stash, or stack them. If you're drowning in paper, just try to keep swimming for now: in Part IV you'll learn what to do with the piles.

Each time you finish using an object, you have a choice. You can put it away now or you can leave it for later. Many people assume that the ideal is to always put each Thing away the minute they're done using it. If your only goal in life is to keep your Things perfectly organized at all times, then this probably is the ideal. Most of us, however, place a higher priority on nonorganizing activities than on organizing, and nonorganizing activities may be either enhanced or constrained by such behavior. Psychologist Mihaly Csikszentmihalyi writes about "Flow," an ecstatic feeling of being totally engaged with an activity we enjoy. Good organizational habits minimize interruptions of this Flow.

One kind of interruption occurs when you can't find something you need in order to continue with the activity. Such interruptions can be reduced by getting out all the things you need for an activity before you begin. If you're making a dress, for example, get out your fabric, thread, patterns, pins, buttons, scissors, tape measure, and sewing machine. When you've finished laying out the fabric, you won't have to go look for the pattern, and when you have to cut the pattern pieces out, you won't have to go look for your scissors. You can flow through the sewing process uninterrupted.

As an experiment, try performing one of your favorite activities two different ways. First, do the activity for an hour without getting out anything ahead of time—go get each object as you need it. Second, spend another hour on the same activity after gathering all the Things you need ahead of time and organizing them so they're readily accessible. How did the first experience compare with the second?

Interrupting an activity to go find something you need is only one type of Thing related interruption to Flow. You also intrude upon Flow when you stop to put something away, especially if it belongs FAR AWAY. How often you do this, or whether you do it at all, is a matter of choice. In general, the more deeply engaged you are with an activity, the less willing you may be to stop and put Things away.

If you're on a creative roll while writing an opera libretto, chances are you're not going to want to put books back on shelves or file manuscript pages away until the roll is over. As the roll begins to die down, however, taking a break to put these objects away may let you gather strength for another wave. Allowing Things to remain out temporarily does not mean ever-increasing clutter *if* you intersperse periods of Flow with cleanup times.

In identifying your Thing habits, consider how often you stop what you're doing to deal with a Thing—whether to go find it or to put it away—and how these interruptions impact Flow. Once this has become clear to you, adapt accordingly. Either getting a few more things out ahead of time or leaving a few more around until you've finished the job may have a big effect on how well you bake a strudel, write a poem, plan an experiment, or build a gazebo—and on how much joy you get out of the experience.

THING MARRIAGES

Sometimes Things get "married." Usually this is more than just a monogamous marriage. In general, this kind of marriage can only take place at the hands of a human being. Food Things get married a lot: eggs, milk, flour, sugar, vanilla, baking powder, salt, and oil are mixed together to form a new food, a cake, for example. Setting aside food Things, all sorts of other objects may be mixed, glued, cemented, nailed, screwed, or otherwise joined. Some of us do more of this than others. In the past, of course, when people made bread from scratch, sewed their own clothes, and built their own furniture, a lot more Thing marriages took place in most households than in our current age of ready-made products. Even now, however, many people enjoy arts and crafts of all sorts that involve putting Things together, and working with machines such as vacuum cleaners, cars, electric mixers, or computers often involves performing temporary or permanent marriages between parts and wholes.

As with people waiting to be married, Thing engagements may vary in length. Some folks buy fabric, thread, and buttons or wood, nails, and varnish, and immediately put them together. Others put them away and meanwhile buy more Things to be married. Their shelves are filled with objects caught in the limbo of long engagements.

While Thing marriages may sometimes reduce the quantity of objects overall, they may also present a challenge to the chronically disorganized: leftover Things. Sewing a dress leaves scraps and loose threads, building a bookshelf leaves small blocks of wood and bent nails, making a salad produces unused vegetables rotting in the refrigerator. If you're a person who uses ready-made everything, leftover Things will not be a problem for you. If you're a do-it yourselfer, however, you need to consider just exactly how the Thing marriages at which you officiate impact your organizing habits.

BROKEN THINGS

Broken Things are prime candidates for Thing limbo. As a rule, household objects do not sprout little hands and fix themselves when they break. Consequently, a broken Thing, especially a broken machine, places you in a dilemma: should you try to get the broken Thing fixed, try to repair it yourself, or simply chuck it and buy another one if you need it? The result is a basement filled with broken coffeemakers and automatic card shufflers awaiting your verdict.

You may feel paralyzed at the thought of taking something to a fix-it shop, or, indeed, of figuring out WHERE to take it—no easy job in today's world. Gone are the days of the kindly old fix-it man on the corner who could resurrect everything from alarm clocks to electric sanders and charge you $1.50 for the job. Finding the right place to take a broken Thing can consume a whole afternoon of being put on hold, going up blind alleys on the Internet, or crisscrossing the county. And if you do manage to locate the proper service depart-ment, swallow your chagrin at having lost the warranty, and actually TAKE your broken Thing there, more often than not you'll be told in a voice reserved for technological kindergartners that it would cost far more to repair your pathetic old gizmo than to buy a brand-new model. Many of us have been trained by a few such experiences to immediately respond to a machine breaking by going out and buying another without even trying to get machine A repaired. Meanwhile, machine A is assigned a permanent place in Thing limbo.

Some Things you may be able to repair yourself. If you're mechanically inclined, you may even be able to repair most of your broken Things. This can save you a great deal of money. The prob-lem, however, is that you have to DO IT. Fixing Things takes time, and consequently do-it-yourself repair people often spend much of their lives making toast in the oven, hanging clothes out on the line, and taking the bus to work, all "just until I have time to fix the _____ machine." Also, if you try to fix something and fail, you may feel like a failure, especially if you've been taught that you're not a "real" man or "liberated" woman if you can't fix Things yourself.

Take a walk around your space and ask yourself how many bro-ken Things are taking up space while waiting for you to put them out of their misery, one way or another. Once you've figured out what broken Things require action and screwed up your courage, you may find that you can cut your clutter in half by making just a few deci-sions, taking a few items to the right people, and fixing a few others yourself. And, best of all, you won't have to make your toast in the oven anymore.

LOST THINGS

How much of your life do you spend looking for Lost Things? Many people devote enormous amounts of time and energy to frantic

Thing searches, quadrupling their stress level without being aware of it. Others vaguely realize that this is going on but may never have broken down the problem enough to break the pattern.

In looking for lost Things day after day, you may become aware that you're somehow repeating yourself. As you think back through multiple incidents when you turned your entire house upside down, patterns begin to emerge. These patterns can tell you a lot about how your mind works. Some possibilities are the following:

- It's in a perfectly logical place, you just forgot where you put it. Your memory may not be so good as you think—it's time to start writing notes to yourself. Think of them as your external memory, which is every bit as good as the other kind.

- It's someplace extremely strange. You find the teakettle on the back of the toilet or a box of birdseed in your dresser drawer. You're probably a dreamer who engages in a lot of activities while mentally writing poetry, winning the state lottery, or improving on the theory of relativity and rarely notice where you put your keys down. Best not to put things away until you're sure you're focused.

- It's the same place it was yesterday and the day before. You may live in the present, which makes it hard to learn from past experience. Develop a habit of asking yourself, whenever you can't find something, where you found it the last time you had to look for it. When you do find it, write down where.

- It's in plain sight. Your brain may be slow to make sense out of what your eyes take in. When searching, scan systematically, as if you're reading a page, or use someone else's eyes.

- It's exactly where it's supposed to be. You're probably moving too quickly, perhaps out of anxiety. Slow down and look at each page in the folder where the paper belongs, especially if your boss is looking over your shoulder.

- It's at the bottom of a pile. You move your Things around quickly and rarely put anything away. Slow down and place, don't throw.

- It's mixed in with someone else's Things. Either somebody else has been messing with your Things without your permission or you've been messing with his or hers. Set boundaries if you need to, and observe those of others.

- It's under a piece of furniture. Unless you have small children, you may be on the lethargic side and fail to put Things away due to lack of energy. When your energy is up again, use some of it to clean under couches and beds.

- It's up on a high shelf. You're unusually tall, you have small children, you're short on space, or you have issues around trust. This may include not trusting yourself to use pretty dishes and vases without breaking them. (So what if you do? They're just Things.)

- It's down in the basement back behind the furnace covered with cobwebs. You may have trouble prioritizing where storage is concerned. Make a list of the objects you use on a typical day and be sure they're easily accessible.

- It has totally disappeared and is never found again. Either you throw Things out while sleepwalking or you have a raccoon in your backyard. Pay closer attention when you dispose of Things or consider building a fence.

Not everyone reacts the same way to not being able to find something. It happens to all of us, no matter how meticulous we happen to be. No amount of organizing and reorganizing can prevent losses from ever occurring, and when they do, this does not mean that you or someone else is a Terrible Person. Believe it or not, it is quite possible to spend hours looking for something without crying, yelling, swearing, accusing, or turning all the drawers upside down on the floor. It helps to remind yourself that the more you allow your emotions to run away with you, the less likely you are to find the Thing for which you're looking.

ESCAPES FROM THINGS

The dishes are waiting, overflowing out of the sink and onto the counters, coated with grease and green slime. Baskets of laundry have yet to be folded and put away. The desk and the floor around it are a sea of papers. The storeroom is so full that the door can no longer be opened and there is a suspicious scurrying sound in one corner. Piles of books, tapes, and CDs are everywhere. In the midst of this chaos, where is Olivia Ostrich, the proud owner? In front of the TV set. On the Internet. At the bar. On the telephone. In bed. On the golf course. At the casino. At the gym. At the movies. On a cruise. In the garden. At the library. In the car. At the office. In her own head. Anywhere Olivia can find to be except in the middle of the mess she has made, putting away one vagrant Thing after another.

Knowing what you do when you're NOT dealing with your Things is as important as understanding how you deal with them. Avoidance of clutter and addictions feed into each other. It's hard to take care of your Things when your brain is stupified by too much food, alcohol, drugs, TV, Internet, reading, sex, or work. At the same time, the desire to avoid messes that fill you with shame may drive you right into the jaws of your favorite fix.

Along with the usual addictions, a host of more subtle evasive tactics may infiltrate your organizing efforts even when you do not actually flee the scene. Between brief spells of actual work, you stop to get a drink of water, go to the bathroom, get a snack, answer the phone, answer the door, walk the dog, and leaf through the first four volumes of the *Encyclopedia Britannica.* Then you tell yourself that decluttering takes too much time for you ever to be able to finish, throw up your hands, and turn on the TV.

Or you may favor escapes that are inside your own head. Fantasies and obsessions may paralyze you for hours. Strangely enough, one of the most common escapes from dealing with clutter is obsessive analysis of the problem itself. While you must figure out what's going on to make progress with Things, when you make analysis an end in itself, substituting thought for action, it becomes self-defeating.

Giving up these escapes requires rigorous honesty. This is not easy. Where serious addictions are concerned, it's virtually impossible without outside support. The brain can play all sorts of twisty-turny games when it craves, which may, in fact, be what's going on RIGHT NOW. Is your brain suddenly telling you that this is a stupid book that you didn't really want to read anyway, that the author does not know what she is talking about, that this is all a bunch of hooey and that all you really need to get organized anyway is a new filing cabinet? If that's what's happening, instead of throwing the book in the garbage, ask yourself what you don't want to stop doing in order to face up to your piles of Things. Then, if you can't get yourself to stop it, GET HELP. (If that doesn't work, then you can throw the book away.)

YOU AND YOUR THINGS INVENTORY: PART B. MAINTENANCE HABITS

THING HOMES

1. What proportion of your Things have homes? Do you know where all of these homes are? Do you use any tools such as labels, indexes, or color coding to remind yourself where each object goes?

2. How appropriate is each home for each Thing that you have? Is the home big enough to hold all the Things of that type? Are some Things spilling out of their homes due to lack of space?

3. How close is each Thing's home to the place where you usually use it? How easy is it to reach? Are the Things you use most frequently in the most accessible places?

4. When your Things are not in their homes, where are their favorite hangouts? In other words, are there certain places where possessions tend to accumulate?

5. What patterns can you identify in how you arrange Things? Do you leave your clutter out for all the world to see or hide it away in closets and drawers? Do you favor vertical or horizontal arrangements? Do you have a habit of stacking things vertically and then pulling out the bottom one, so the rest of the stack topples?

6. What Things do you tend to keep with what other Things? Which of your Things are totally disorganized, loosely organized, or fastidiously organized?

7. What types of containers do you use the most and why? Do you favor containers that keep Things out of sight or those that leave them visible? Are your Things organized within the containers or not?

PUTTING THINGS AWAY

1. Do you usually put Things away as soon as you've used them? In what situations do you do this and in what situations do you not?

2. Do you have certain times, either daily, weekly, monthly, or annually, when you routinely clean and/or put Things away?

3. When an unusual mess occurs, as, for example, when a string of beads is broken, do you deal with this immediately, considering it an emergency, or do you let it wait?

4. Do you often put Things someplace "temporary" that turns out to be permanent?

5. Do you ever schedule decluttering times in your planner or on your calendar?

6. How do you distribute the time you spend arranging and decluttering? Do you spend time organizing some of your possessions much more minutely than others?

PAPER THINGS

1. Do you keep your papers in closed containers such as filing cabinets, in open containers such as milk crates, or outside of containers altogether? Do you fear that if you put them in closed containers you'll forget where they are?

2. Do you spread your papers on horizontal surfaces such as desktops? Do you believe this is the only way you'll be able to find them?

3. Do you stash your papers in drawers without sorting them so that others will not see how disorganized they are? How does this make you feel?

4. Do you stack your papers without organizing them? Are you able to find papers that you need?

5. How much time do you spend looking for lost papers?

THINGS AND FLOW

1. Do you take Things out before you start a project so that you won't have to stop and look for them?

2. When you're engaged in a project, do you stop and put Things away after you use them?

3. If you don't, do you put them away during breaks? after you're finished for the day? after you're finished with the whole project? What proportion of Things do you put away as you work, and what proportion do you put away later?

THING MARRIAGES

1. When and how frequently do you combine Things to form other Things? What sort of leftovers do these projects leave?

2. Do you keep many Things on hand for long periods of time before putting them together? Where do you keep them? What is keeping you from following through with your projects?

3. Do you keep a lot of leftover objects to use later on? Where do you keep them? How often do you actually use them?

BROKEN THINGS

1. What broken Things do you have in your space? Where are they stored? What do they have in common? What was your original plan for getting them fixed? At what point did they become stalled? What happened?

2. How familiar are you with service centers in your area? How would you go about finding a place to get something fixed? What anxieties does this present?

3. Do you know where the warranties for your belongings are? Do you know where the instruction manuals and other maintenance paperwork are?

4. Do you REALLY have the time and skills to fix all your broken Things yourself? What keeps you from getting the job done?

Do you need to get parts and supplies? Do you need someone to help you? Are you afraid you'll fail?

LOST THINGS

1. Think of the last time you lost and found a particular Thing. What was it? Was it a VIT? Do you remember where you found it? Look at the patterns described on pages 50–51. Which, if any, describes your experience?

2. When you lose something, how do you react? Are you able to search calmly and do what you can to replace it, or do you have problems dealing with your frustration? Are you constantly trying to get someone else to "rescue" you by finding things you have lost?

THING ESCAPES

1. Each time you think about decluttering and don't, what do you do instead? How free do you feel to NOT do the escape activity?

2. Once you've shifted from cleaning up to an avoidance behavior, how long does it take you to get back to the task at hand?

3. Once you're back on track, how much time goes by before you start thinking about doing something else? What automatic thoughts go through your head? What, if anything, do you tell yourself in response to them? How long does it take for you to stop your work and do something more fun?

4. While you're engaged in your escape activity, are you fully able to enjoy it, or are thoughts of your neglected clean-up responsibilities lurking somewhere in the background? How does this experience compare with using the same activity not as an escape but as a reward for a job well done?

5. Once you've started a decluttering task, what percentage of your time goes to actual work and what percentage to escapes? How much time do you spend thinking as opposed to acting? How does this affect your sense of how long decluttering actually takes? What can you do about this?

CHAPTER 5

HOW YOUR THINGS LEAVE
YOU—OR DON'T LEAVE YOU

At some point, all beautiful friendships must come to an end, including those between you and your belongings. Some people find it easy to say good-bye to Things; others find it next to impossible.

A lot has been written about the "excuses" people make for hanging on to excess Things. But why might a sane person get rid of a Thing? Here are some possibilities.

I haven't used this Thing in a long time.

I have too many of these Things.

I just got a new one Thing to replace this Thing.

This Thing doesn't work anymore.

I don't have room for this Thing.

This Thing is too hard to move.

This Thing is too hard to take care of.

This Thing is *ugly.*

This Thing smells bad.

This Thing is sinful.

This Thing is dangerous.

This Thing is hazardous to my health.

This Thing has bugs in it.

This Thing makes too much noise.

This Thing scratches.

This Thing is full of holes.

This Thing has a spot that won't come out.

This Thing gets on my nerves.

This Thing keeps breaking.

I don't like this Thing.

I don't need this Thing.

I don't like the person who gave me this Thing.

This Thing doesn't belong to me.

This Thing brings back bad memories

My spouse/parent/child/roommate can't stand this Thing.

So-and-so would really like this Thing.

This Thing could be recycled.

I could get money for this Thing.

I could put this Thing in the rummage sale.

I could use this Thing for firewood.

One would think that with so many excellent reasons for getting rid of unwanted items, it would be easy to do so, but for many it is not. The problem is, such criteria are often superceded by other, more seductive "reasons" for hanging on to Things:

This Thing was a great bargain.

I paid good money for this Thing.

This Thing is a family heirloom.

This Thing is practically brand-new.

This Thing will be valuable someday.

My spouse/parent/child/roomate will have a fit if I get rid of this Thing.

This Thing belonged to Great-aunt Zelda.

This Thing has sentimental value.

This Thing is a great conversation piece.

This Thing is from France/China/Africa/Atlantic City.

This Thing was a gift.

This Thing just needs fixing.

They don't make Things like this one anymore.

This Thing could come back in style someday.

This Thing is handmade.

This Thing is still perfectly good.

I wouldn't be me without this Thing.

I wouldn't want this Thing to go to waste.

This Thing can't be recycled.

I don't know who I would give this Thing to.

Somebody put a lot of work into this Thing.

I have to use all of these Things up.

This Thing is made of solid walnut/granite/rubber/plastic.

This Thing is part of a whole set.

I save these Things for parts.

I still haven't finished this Thing.

I'm going to make this Thing into a lamp.

This Thing brings back memories.

I'm not ready to let go of this Thing.

I'll figure out what to do with this Thing later.

I'd be lost without this Thing.

I MIGHT NEED THIS THING SOMEDAY.[6]

When we do manage to get rid of Things, there are various ways of doing this:

- destroying them.
- trashing them.
- abandoning them.
- recycling them.
- giving them away.
- selling them.
- trading them.

Part of successful Thing management is being responsible about how you get rid of unwanted Things. Getting rid of Things may be easier if you feel good about where they will be going next. Giving Things to those who can enjoy them and recycling objects to make new ones may diminish guilt and even give you pleasure. Selling and trading might enable you to get Things that you like better, including money. You always pay a price when you choose to keep a Thing: the time, space, money, or energy needed to house and maintain it. Thus, getting rid of something doesn't just mean getting rid of the Thing itself; it also means gaining other, intangible rewards such as space, light, a boost to your self-esteem, and, best of all, FREEDOM.

THING ADDICTION

Elsie Clutcher is cleaning out her bedroom closet with her organizer, Judy Stackwright. The closet is packed to overflowing, and the garments are badly rumpled. "Why don't you start by separating the clothes by type," Judy suggests, "then you can choose your favorites from each pile and give the rest away."

"BUT I CAN'T DO THAT!" Elsie wails, "I MIGHT NEED THEM!"

Elsie is addicted to clothes. Addiction has to do with attachment, the glue that holds all human relations together. Good-enough parents are attached to their children. Intimate partners in a healthy relationship are attached to one another. Workers perform better on the job if they're attached to their work. Even nuns and monks are attached to God or to their spiritual practice.

Psychologically, a person with no human attachments is in deep trouble. In solitary circumstances, humans instinctively turn to inanimate objects as people substitutes. In the movie *Cast Away,* Tom Hanks, bereft of human companionship on a desert island, keeps himself sane by painting a face on a volleyball and develops such a strong attachment to "Wilson" that he risks his life trying to catch his friend when it floats away.

While attachment to material objects is often scorned as unspiritual, being able to attach to Things shows that you're also able to attach to human beings. In *The Meaning of Things,* Mihaly Csikszentmihalyi and Eugene Rochberg-Halton describe the results of interviews they conducted with over three hundred members of eighty-two Chicago families about themselves and their possessions. They report that interviewees who appeared unattached to belongings, even those who vehemently asserted that friends were more important to them than material possessions, tended to be lonely and isolated.

Attachment to our own Things makes life more predictable: Without such attachment, we would all be wearing each others' underwear, which could get complicated. To some, having an abundance of Things feels good, and there's nothing terrible about indulging these feelings when you have the space to house a collection or two. But when the glue between you and your belongings becomes super glue, so that you hang on to multiple Things for dear life despite overwhelmed feelings and other negative consequences, then you have to face the fact that your attachment has become an addiction.

Some Thing addicts are addicted only to certain types of objects, others to all types. In extreme cases, people may not be able to throw ANYTHING away, accumulating thousands of margarine containers, plastic bags, balls of string, newspapers, and other disposables. While in cultures of poverty this makes perfect sense, the amount of throwaway items produced in present-day developed countries makes hoarding a serious health and safety hazard, potentially leading to illnesses, cuts, fires, falls, and other causes of death. Extreme hoarding can be a life-threatening problem.

Biochemically, what Thing addicts seem to lack is a mechanism that causes hoarding to shut down when it reaches a certain level. Human beings, like squirrels who bury nuts for winter, are a hoarding species, but most human beings hoard selectively and stop hoarding when they have a reasonable amount of something stored away: these folks don't. Their brains become locked into repetitive patterns that don't allow them to stop hoarding and move on to other activities. Excessive hoarding is symptomatic of obsessive-compulsive disorder and requires psychiatric treatment.

Not everyone who is at war with his or her Things suffers from mild to severe Thing addiction, but for many it's a major source of clutter. Part of the inventory at the end of this chapter is a series of questions relating to Thing addiction. The more of these questions you answer yes to, the more severely addicted you may be to your Things.

Facing the fact that you have any kind of an addiction is difficult, but addictions have a way of not getting better until you do this. It may help to realize that if you do have Thing addiction, it's not your fault. Addictions—even those that don't involve substances—are caused by brain chemistry, family problems, and traumatic experiences. Now, think about it logically. Did you choose your brain? Did you choose your family? Did you choose to be traumatized? Obviously, you did not, which means that HAVING THING ADDICTION DOES NOT MAKE YOU A TERRIBLE PERSON.

As with all addictions, the key word where Thing addiction is concerned is *honesty*. Honesty becomes possible once you recognize that having a brain that responds differently to Things doesn't make you a Terrible Person. Then you can begin to face the fact that you need to let go of some Things, get the support you need, and begin to do so, one Thing at a time.

GIVING THINGS AWAY

One of the pleasanter ways of getting rid of unwanted Things is to give them away. Some of us do more of this than others; Those who do it less are not necessarily monsters of greed. These people may have fewer Things to get rid of, or they may never have thought about giving Things to others as an option.

Finding the right person to whom to give the right Thing is an art. Some people put more effort into this than others, whether they're dealing with family and friends or with strangers. A few thoughtful souls carry this to the point of actually doing research to determine others' tastes and needs. Such people may notice, for example, that their next-door neighbor repairs old radios as a hobby and ask him if he would be interested in the box of old vacuum tubes that their grandfather, also a radio buff, left behind.

Where giving to groups of strangers is concerned, some folks have only a vague idea of which charities accept which kinds of Things, while others have it down pat. It's easy to miss the boat in contributing Things to drives put on by religious organizations and schools, for example. You may take your old clothes across town to St. Vincent de Paul's and then have nothing to contribute for the school bundle drive the next week. Even if you mark such events on your calendar and save Things up for them, you may somehow still miss the day when it arrives, so that the Things go on piling up for next years' drive.

Figuring out exactly the right way to give away your Things takes time and energy that you may not have, especially if you're in a clutter crisis. Putting off getting rid of Things because you haven't found the right person or organization to which to give them can hold you in bondage for years. Are some of the Things moldering away in your basement or attic ungiven gifts? If so, you need to haul them out and find appropriate recipients or begin to consider other options for disposing of them.

SELLING AND TRADING THINGS

Two methods of Thing disposal that most of us seriously underuse are selling and trading. These methods can enrich you, but they require work. When you offer to give people Things, most of the time they accept them. This is a lot less likely to happen if they have to give you something in return. To sell or trade something, you have to find just the right person with whom to transact business, which takes time and energy. The danger is that you'll become stuck between the idea of selling or trading a Thing and actually DOING so.

Large objects, like cars, refrigerators, or pianos may merit putting an ad in the paper. This requires that you compose the ad, pick up the phone, read the ad to someone, and give the person a credit card number or mail in a check. None of these tasks are likely to take more than a few minutes, yet some people put them off for years, meanwhile enduring the annoyance of having two washers and dryers taking up most of their basement.

A multitude of options allow you to sell smaller items, ranging from informal sales to friends, to yard sales, to flea markets, to consignment shops. Of these options, yard sales are the riskiest—not the sales themselves but the PLANS for "The Yard Sale": as soon as you make such plans, you begin putting aside Things for The Yard Sale instead of getting rid of them then and there. This may go on for years without The Yard Sale ever taking place, due to scheduling problems, weather concerns, and plain old procrastination.

An alternative to The Yard Sale is the consignment shop, to which you can take Things any time you like. Most shops, however, are selective about what items they accept, and many require a membership fee. Consignment selling necessitates gathering information about which shops buy what. The risk is that you'll haul a lot of Things across town and watch some shop owner manhandle the lovely but wrong-sized tablecloth your mother gave you only to be told that it's worth next to nothing or even that he or she doesn't want it at all. This is not a pleasant prospect and keeps many an unusable Thing sitting securely in the closet where no one can possibly disappoint its owner.

You may sometimes be able to sell Things to friends and neighbors, but too much of this may have the potential to damage friendships. Likewise with trading, though this can be fun. A social gathering where everybody brings old books, clothes, or whatever to trade can leave everyone richer, yet organizing such an affair is no easy job.

All of these difficulties with selling and trading may contribute to stalled Things in your nooks and crannies. Is your space filled with

Things that you keep promising yourself you're going to sell or trade ONE OF THESE DAYS? If so, you need to figure out what the hang-ups are and either get the Things out to where they can help pay off your credit card balance or find another means of getting rid of them.

WHERE YOUR THINGS GO WHEN THEY DIE

There comes a time when we all have to deal with those Things that, during their brief sojourn with us, have passed into the Great Beyond. While many of your possessions will still be hale and hearty when you say good-bye to them, some (sob, sniff) will spend their final days with you, and you're responsible for disposing of their remains.

A dead Thing is an object that's unlikely ever to be of use to anyone in its present form: a dress that's hopelessly stained or torn, a book that has lost half its pages, a couch with stuffing bursting out of the seat, a rusty set of bedsprings. It can be hard to face the fact that a Thing has died, and to go about disposing of it. It can also be hard to do away with certain Things yourself, eternally usable but fast-breeding Things such as bottles, cans, margarine tubs, and plastic bags. Disposing of such Things can make you feel like a Terrible Person, especially if you live in an area where recycling is minimal, and some folks would rather perish under a mountain of old tin cans than bring such guilt down upon themselves.

If you're fortunate, you may live where most disposables are recycled. In *Waste Not, Want Not: A Social History of Trash,* Susan Strasser explains how in America before the twentieth century most goods were recycled in one way or another: food scraps were fed to animals, peddlars exchanged tea kettles for rags, children's toys were made from adults' cast-offs. Alas, this is no longer the case, but most communities have at least some recycling facilities.

Recycling is a form of giving, but doing so knowing that old

Things you give will be transformed into new Things. This feels great: a triumph of rebirth over death. But keep in mind that there are different ways of recycling, and some require more effort than others. Some people dutifully squash all cans, tie up newspapers into bundles, and remove the little rings from bottles. Others are less conscientious. Some communities make it easier for you to recycle than others do. If recycling in your community takes significant time and energy, this can lead to recyclables piling up and taking over. Give yourself permission to cut corners if you need to and get the job done! Remember your goal, which is to unload unwanted items. Recycling can help you accomplish this while also doing your bit for the environment.

Some people make use of extra help in getting rid of Things. Many cities provide pick-up services for large items for an extra fee and individual haulers do this as well. Other folks, however, put off arranging for such help, ashamed of the fact that they don't have the muscles or the friends with muscles to do the job themselves. Meanwhile, the Things just sit.

Dead Things can make us feel guilty. For this reason, facing up to them and deciding on a course of action can be one of the most liberating steps you can take in making peace with your Things.

A FINAL NOTE ABOUT
GETTING RID OF THINGS

If the task of getting rid of Things seems daunting, relax. Do not try to get rid of anything at this point: all you need to do now is consider your Thing Habits. In Chapters 12 and 13, you'll find lots of help in actually disposing of excess Things. By then, what you've learned about yourself and Things will make the job a lot easier.

THING ADDICTION

1. Do you own dramatically more of certain Things than most people seem to own?

2. Are you unable to get rid of anything at all?

3. Do you feel obligated to protect "the environment" by keeping more Things than other people do even though the environment in your home is overflowing?

4. Do you personify your Things, thinking and talking about them as if they're alive and have feelings?

5. Are you unable to use areas of your home for activities for which they were designed because of excess Things?

6. Do you feel overwhelmed by the sheer numbers of some or all of your Things?

7. Has anyone else in your household complained about how many Things you own?

8. Have Things caused conflict between you and others?

9. Have you ever lost a relationship over your Things?

10. Have you been called names like "greedy," "stingy," "miser," or "pig" in reference to your keeping Things?

11. Do you feel guilty when you get rid of Things?

12. Do you feel guilty when you *don't* get rid of Things?

13. Have you ever been evicted for having too many Things?

14. Is your home unsafe or unhealthy due to excess Things?

15. Do you feel ashamed about how many Things you have?

16. Do you try to keep the sheer quantity of your Things a secret?

17. Have you suffered other negative consequences due to excess Things?

18. Have you made numerous unsuccessful efforts to get rid of Things?

19. Do you spend a lot of time thinking and talking about your Things?

20. When you try to get rid of Things, do you always come up with reasons why you can't?

21. Do you feel physically anxious when you think about getting rid of Things?

22. When you do get rid of a Thing, does this leave you feeling depressed?

23. Do you react angrily when others suggest you get rid of Things?

24. Have you ever hurt a person or animal in defense of your Things?

The more of these questions you answered yes to, the more likely you are to be suffering from Thing addiction.

If your problem is severe, consider contacting a therapist specializing in hoarding obsessive-compulsive disorder—see the Appendix for help with finding such a person. Suggestions for dealing with Thing addiction are provided in Parts III and IV.

GIVING THINGS AWAY

1. How frequently do you give Things to others? To whom do you most often give Things—family, friends, or strangers?

2. Do you give specific Things to people you think can use that item, invite others to choose from a variety of Things, or give Things away indiscriminately without considering whether the recipients can use them or not?

3. Once you've decided to give someone something, do you keep it moving until it has reached its destination, or does it sit on your back porch for three years first?

4. Once you've given a Thing to someone, do you continue to monitor what he or she is doing with it, or do you let it go?

5. Are there any charitable organizations to which you regularly donate Things? Do you know which charities in your area accept which kinds of Things, who picks them up, and where the organizations are located?

6. Do you regularly take advantage of public events such as school bundle drives, church bazaars, or white elephant sales to get rid of excess Things? Do you often discover that such events have taken place and you've missed them?

SELLING AND TRADING THINGS

1. Do you have Things you don't want that you might be able to sell? When was the last time you made use of this alternative?

2. Do you have any excess Things for which it would make sense to place an ad in the newspaper or on the Internet? What has kept you from doing so?

3. Have you ever given a yard sale? What was this experience

like? Do you have Things accumulating in your space in preparation for a yard sale? How long has this been going on? Have you ever participated in a collective yard sale?

4. Do you ever sell Things at a consignment shop? Do you know what shops are in you area, what they accept, and what their terms are?

5. Did you ever trade any of your Things for services or Things? Did whatever new items you received take up more or less space than the original did? Was trading a positive experience?

DISPOSING OF DEAD THINGS

1. What dead Things do you have? How long have they been deceased? Can any of these objects be used to make other Things? Do you save large numbers of dead Things with the intention of making new Things out of them? When did you last actually make something?

2. Do you habitually hang on to disposable Things even when you don't know what you can do with them? Would you feel like a terrible person if you got rid of them?

3. How familiar are you with your community's recycling criteria? Do you use recycle bins regularly?

4. Do you prepare Things for recycling or just throw them in as is? Does the tediousness of preparation discourage you from recycling?

5. Do you have to drive loads of Things somewhere to recycle? How often do you do this? In the meantime, where do the recyclable Things accumulate?

6. Do you put Things in the trash that could be recycled? How does this feel?

7. Do you know where your community's landfill is? Do you know of at least one person or organization you can call to haul large objects away that can't be recycled? When was the last time you hauled Things to the landfill or called a hauling service?

8. Do you keep dead Things moving until they're where they're going to end up, or do they sit for months on your closet shelves, back porch, front porch, or front lawn or in your basement, attic, garage, barn, car, or truck?

9. Do you ever burn, bury, or dump dead Things illegally? How does this make you feel?

CHAPTER 6

THINGS AND FEELINGS

Every time Griselda Backglance looks at Herbie's pipe, she bursts into tears. Jason Stickshift swells with pride as he polishes his car. The sight of Roger Suburb's power mower fills Eliot Status with envy.

Things can trigger every conceivable kind of feeling in human beings, both pleasant and unpleasant. Individual Things may evoke strong reactions, often because of people or events with which you associate them. When feelings run high, you may confuse a particular Thing with something it represents, especially if your brain is wired in a way that does not easily distinguish symbols from what they symbolize. Some people, for example, experience a flag as a country. To others, a flag is just a flag.

Collective Things may also trigger emotions. You may feel pride or pleasure at the quality or abundance of what you've accumulated. Or you may feel fear, helplessness, rage, shame, anxiety, grief or despair at the sight of your out-of-control, overaccumulating Things.

Or you may feel nothing. Most of us have neutral feelings about at least some of our Things. You may feel nothing at all about your stapler or your garden hose, for example. Some people feel little or nothing about any of their Things, viewing those which are out of place as simply a problem to be solved.

Whatever you feel or don't feel, remember this: THERE IS NO RIGHT OR WRONG WAY TO FEEL ABOUT THINGS. All feelings about Things are okay, though all behaviors are not. Wishing you had your neighbor's bicycle is all right; stealing it is not. Hating a particular painting is harmless; slashing it up is not. But even when you don't let them control your behavior, unpleasant feelings about Things can be inconvenient. You don't WANT to feel so attached to all your old magazines that you can hardly let them go, but you do. You don't WANT to feel terrified of your cluttered basement, but that's what you feel. Because you don't want to feel these feelings, you may keep yourself convinced that you DON'T feel them, and that's where the trouble starts. As long as you deny to yourself that you feel something, the feeling will control your behavior.

Feelings are mostly physical. When you feel, some kind of chemical substance or electrical charge is moving around inside of you. This doesn't mean you have to *stop* the feeling, any more than you have to stop food from moving through your digestive tract. Trying to stop a feeling is just about this effective.

Just as you examined your behavior with Things as if you were a creature from Gryzypia, you can study your feelings about Things with the same detachment. Imagine that a really advanced Gryzypian is able to shrink itself down to the size of a pea, float through your skull, and sit up in the front of your brain observing your feelings as they pass through your body down below. Each time the Gryzypian observes a new feeling coming through it goes BEEP! Angry BEEP! Scared BEEP! Happy BEEP! Sad. That's the attitude that you need to take in observing your feelings about Things.

Sit quietly, close your eyes, and focus on your breathing. Then open your eyes and look around the room. What's the first Thing that your eyes encounter? What feelings hit you when you look at it? Put names on them, the way a Gryzypian might. Move your eyes from Thing to Thing around the room, naming feelings.

Feelings about Things have a lot to do with how successful you'll be at changing Thing habits. Feelings can tie you up in knots if you're unaware of them, but even the most negative feelings lose some of their power once you can name them to yourself. Then you may begin to act constructively with your Things.

THINGS AND LOVE

Love is a many-splendored word, with as many meanings as there are popular songs to celebrate it. How this queen of feelings relates to material objects may depend partly on how we choose to define the word.

To some, love is simply attachment—the feeling that you CAN'T STAND to be without that which you love. You feel that the love object (the person or Thing you love) is attached to you by invisible rubber bands that will always snap you back to it any time you venture out too far. Attachment is most visible with toddlers as they run along the sidewalk ahead of their caregiver until they get just so far away, stop, turn around and look, and come running back to Mom or Dad. As children, some of us never quite mastered the running ahead part, never feeling safe enough to venture out. Perhaps they were naturally fearful, or perhaps their caregivers were never able to attach to them, preoccupied with their own fears or problems.

Adults who were never securely attached to a caregiver in childhood are often unable or unwilling to tolerate separation from love objects in adulthood. The love object has to be right there next to them at all times, preferably in a wire cage with a padlock on it. The insecurely attached may also tend to become Thing addicts, especially if no one's available who's willing to spend his or her life in a cage.

Anyone who has ever raised a child knows about what D. W. Winnicott called transitional objects—blankies, Teddy bears, and other warm, fuzzy Things to which children may become attached as substitutes for caregivers. Children are tactilely oriented, but adults may replace warm fuzzies with less cuddly Things. A photograph, an art object, a piece of jewelry, a book of poems, a musical instrument, a car, a house, a piece of land may all become the objects of intense attachment, conflict, and/or grief. You may even feel that a Thing is alive and experience pain if you get rid of it. While these feelings are not abnormal, allowing them to control your behavior with Things can lead to clutter, Thing conflicts, and other negative consequences.

Not everyone equates love with attachment, however. If you were lucky enough to have formed secure attachments in childhood, love may mean something different to you: fostering the wellbeing of the love object, even at the sacrifice of your own interests. Is it possible to love a Thing this way? Perhaps. The artist who risks his life to paint frescoes on a cathedral ceiling, the scientist who devotes her whole career to studying the geology of another planet, the preservationist who collects thousands of dollars to save a historic building, the pilgrim who travels thousands of miles to enter a holy city: none of these people seeks to possess the beloved Thing but rather to create, to understand, to worship, or to preserve it. Yet behind such Love always lies a willingness to share what is loved with others. For the sad fact is, although you may love a Thing to distraction, no mere Thing will ever love you back.

THINGS AND HAPPINESS

It's hard to be honest with yourself about happiness. Your mind may be filled with "shoulds" that prevent you from recognizing what *really* makes you happy and what *really* doesn't. You may think you SHOULD like Waterford crystal better than tumblers from your local hardware store, so you assume that you DO but just haven't felt it yet. But you don't, not if you're honest with yourself.

Such counterproductive "shoulds" can cause you to obtain and hold on to many Things that leave you cold. Distinguishing Happiness Things from meaningless or even negative ones can be difficult, especially if you grew up in a home where either you were given no

Things of your own at all or you were treated like a little monarch and given every Thing you looked at. In neither situation did you learn how to CHOOSE, which involves noticing what feels good to you and what doesn't. The result is that you try to take it all.

Of course not every Thing you own has to give you pleasure. Few people experience joy at the sight of a toilet plunger—unless they're about to experience a flood—but a good plunger can come in handy at the right moment. A certain percentage of your Things are simply there to be used. But other Things are luxury items. If these Things don't make you or someone else in your home feel good, their presence is meaningless. When we walk into a home, most of us can sense immediately whether it contains Things that their owners cherish and enjoy or Things that are there simply for show. Such homes do nothing to nurture their occupants.

You may have Things that once gave you pleasure that no longer have this effect. If you have a lot of Things that you've lost interest in, you may be tempted to respond by buying a lot of new Things. STOP. BEFORE BUYING, ASK YOURSELF WHAT'S GOING ON. The answer will most likely be one of three possibilities:1) You have a certain type of neurochemistry that's attracted by novelty, and chances are you'll soon be as tired of the new Things as you were of the old. 2) You've become depressed and need to seek professional help. Once your depression has lifted, you may enjoy your Things as much as ever. 3) Your taste has changed due to emotional growth and/or passing into a new stage of life. In this case, it makes sense to get new Things, but be sure to also dispose of the old ones.

The best way to deal with Things you no longer like is to find someone who likes them better. Slow down and give yourself time and space to contemplate and enjoy the Things—and the people— you love without the distraction of too many other Things. For one thing is certain: the people who get the most fun out of their belongings are not necessarily the people with the most Things. On the contrary, when it comes to Things, the law of diminishing returns seems to apply. A child living in a grass shack in a poor country may feel ecstatic over a box of crayons that a child in a wealthier country would have merely tossed aside. When you cut down the number of treasures you try to hang on to, you may find that each treasure you keep grows brighter and more beautiful every day.

THINGS AND FEAR

Fear is a double-edged sword: you can't live with it and you can't live without it. Fear keeps you from getting sick, burned, smashed, or stabbed in the back by some stranger lurking in the shadows. Fear screams STOP, DON'T GO THERE and saves your life again and again. The problem is, in a world now mainly devoid of saber-toothed tigers, fear can be overzealous in doing its job, and sometimes it causes harm to your body and soul by working overtime.

Are you afraid of any of your Things? This fear is rational only if the Thing actually has the power to hurt you, as is the case with certain machines. You NEED to be afraid of your electric saw. It can cut off your hand if you let it. If you're afraid of your saw, you'll either learn how to use it safely and thus reduce your fear, or you'll leave it alone.

Are you afraid of any Things that have no power to harm you at all? This may be because you associate these Things with times you've been hurt, physically or emotionally. If you were hurt by a bicycle when you were six, you may be frightened even by a picture of one. People who have been severely traumatized or who have a certain type of anxious neurochemistry may be afraid of the whole universe and everything in it, including their Things. These folks handle Things differently than others do, picking them up gingerly with the tips of their fingers instead of with their whole hands. To them, every Thing—as well as every person—is a bomb that might go off at any moment.

Perhaps your fear is not that Things will harm you but that you will harm them. Behind this fear is the belief that harming a Thing makes you a Terrible Person, which is not the case. For some of us, however, fear of harming Things is at least partly reality based. Certain people may, in fact, be unusually likely to drop or break Things because of neurological glitches that affect their motor skills. Not everyone is equally adept at grasping Things and moving them around. If you know that your coordination is weak, it's rational to approach your Things more cautiously than others do, use extra tools and strategies in dealing with them, or even allow others to handle certain objects for you. Disabilities are all a matter of degree, and you do not have to have a serious coordination disability to have trouble handling Things.

Fear of harming Things, however, does not always mean you really have coordination problems. You may just have grown up with someone with unrealistic expectations of children's motor skills, someone who screamed, yelled, or hit when you spilled the milk or failed to tie your shoes. Such caregivers train children to be afraid of Things.

Not all coordination problems are physical: some are mental. Hence technophobia, the fear of electronic devices such as computers, VCRs, and fax machines. Only some brains are wired to perform the intricate gymnastics involved in operating such gadgets easily. And as with physical coordination, internalizing comments from the peanut gallery can cause you to see yourself as more technologically challenged than you really are. Has fearing that you'll break electronic Things or simply feel stupid using them resulted in large numbers of them gathering dust in your basement? If so, you need to either take the time and get the help you need to use these machines or get rid of them. Whatever you decide, remember this: NOT BEING ABLE TO USE A MACHINE DOES NOT MAKE ANYONE LESS THAN A FULL-FLEDGED ADULT.

When dealing with their Things en masse, some people seem to react phobically to their sheer numbers. Multiple Things can feel scary, just like hordes of ants become frightening—and dangerous, after all—when a single ant, or even an anthill full of them, is not. Horror movies such as Alfred Hitchcock's *The Birds* have frequently capitalized on human beings' fear of being overrun and attacked by large numbers of something small. When it comes to hordes of insects or animals, the flight, fight, freeze, or faint response may be adaptive, but it's counterproductive in dealing with Things.

Fear of objects themselves, however, is not the only kind of fear to cause problems between people and Things. Fears relating to yourself and/or other people may be triggered by your dealing with Things and may cause even more trouble. You may be afraid of not having enough, of feeling empty, of not being perfect, of making a mistake, of forgetting something, of going to extremes, of having to face reality, of being bored, of changing relationships, of feeling helpless, or of having your weaknesses exposed.

Throughout most of history, fear has been given a bad name. Many people see it as a bad feeling that must be kept hidden at all costs, but it's silly to be ashamed of a feeling that's so necessary for survival. As long as you deny your existing fears, you will not be able to manage your Things effectively. Progress begins with naming your fears, giving yourself permission to feel scared, and going ahead anyway.

THINGS AND ANGER

Professor Tightstring is approaching his breaking point. The professor has had an unusually trying day. First, he gave back an exam on which all of his students did miserably and had to listen to them whine about their grades. Then he learned that his chief competitor, Professor Goodie, was appointed chairman of the Review Committee. After that the department chairman's secretary scolded him for failing to turn in his expense report on time, and he received a letter rejecting his grant proposal. And now, just when he's about to escape to a nice, peaceful dinner with Mrs. Tightstring, another graduate student shows up and asks for the recommendation letter he forgot to write.

After apologizing to her *again* and seeing her out the door, Professor Tightstring buttons his coat and reaches up to a top shelf to grab a journal issue he intends to take home with him. Yanking it down, he's assaulted by the entire contents of the top shelf, which rain down on his head, knocking his glasses to the floor. From the hallway outside Professor Tightstring's closed door, students and faculty are surprised by a wild, subhuman yowl followed by a stream of curses accompanied by smashing, pounding, and ripping noises. The sounds go on for a long time. After they stop, Professor Goodie knocks timidly on Tightstring's door and enters. Books, torn papers, and overturned furniture are strewn everywhere, and in their midst stands his colleague, beet red, shame-faced, and panting.

Human beings' dealings with Things are not always peaceful. When Things fail to cooperate with us, especially if people have also been giving us trouble, they can sometimes set off a volcano. Some people find it difficult to express anger at other people, fearing that they'll lose them or hurt them if they do. Things, especially your own Things, are much safer targets: they make great people surrogates. They can't talk back to you, and they can hurt you only if you cause them to. The only problem is, when you're through venting your rage at a Thing, you may feel *very* silly. Suddenly you remember that the Thing you just destroyed couldn't possibly have behaved maliciously to you, because IT DOESN'T HAVE A BRAIN. If you're lucky, no one saw what you just did. If you're not, whoever did see it will probably never let you hear the last of it.

Machines can be particularly anger inducing Things. Some folks seem to believe that they can use or fix any machine ONLY if they fumigate the air around it with a thick cloud of swear words, meanwhile threatening to decapitate anyone who comes within ten feet. Wise intimates of such individuals stay clear until the worst is over and assume that the person is temporarily insane, discounting anything that's said during machine encounters.

When you feel angry at a Thing, ask yourself three questions:

1. Who does this Thing represent?

2. What feelings lie beneath the anger?

3. What is the problem to which the anger is linked?

Often when you think you're angry at an object, you're actually angry at a person it represents to you. The child who left her roller skates on the stairs for you to trip over, the spouse who bought a computer without consulting you, the intellectual foe who wrote a book that attacked your beliefs. The old saying in French murder mysteries, *cherchez la femme* ("look for the woman") could be degendered and applied here. Whenever you believe you're truly angry at an inanimate object, try looking for the person at whom you're really angry. When you do this, you may discover that the original source of your anger is nobody else but yourself.

Anger, unlike fear, is often a surface-level feeling, beneath which lies an underlying feeling such as fear, shame, or frustration. Some people change all these feelings instantly into anger because they've been taught that if they have any other feelings they're not macho, and if they're not macho, life is not worth living. This is not true. Anger is an unpleasant feeling to feel, so why should anyone want to feel only anger? A little anger is necessary to let you know what problems you need to solve, but too much of it eats holes in your stomach and makes your heart clog up. You deserve better! Anytime you find yourself shaking your fist at a Thing, ask yourself what feelings lie beneath the anger.

While some people change all their feelings into anger, others don't let themselves feel it at all. Anger is about action, and denying anger has a way of keeping you paralyzed. People who allow enormous Thing mountains to build up without even trying to pick up anything usually look depressed on the outside, but beneath their depression they're ANGRY. Boy, are they angry! THEY'RE SO ANGRY THEY COULD SMASH UP EVERYTHING IN THEIR HOUSE IF THEY JUST KNEW THEY WERE ANGRY. So they don't let themselves know.

If you're depressed about the state of your Things, it's important to ask yourself if you're angry and, if so, what the problem is. Then you can figure out how to solve the problem, which makes the anger go away. Anger is a great teacher. Your imaginary Gryzypian, whom you met in the prologue to Part II, can be of help here, sitting up in your cortex going BEEP! Anger BEEP! Anger BEEP! Along with identifying feelings, Gryzypians are also good at identifying problems. BEEP! Daughter forgets to put skates away. BEEP! Spouse ignores wishes when buying. BEEP! Belief attack. Some problems are solvable and some are not. You don't necessarily need to solve a problem to resolve anger if it's truly unsolvable. You need to realize that it *is* unsolvable and GET USED TO IT.

The trick is not only to resolve anger but also to harness it and make it work for you. If you can do this, it may enable you to establish good Thing habits and declutter your whole house in nothing flat. For anger is not only a great teacher, it also makes great rocket fuel. Once you're in touch with its energy, there's nothing like it.

THINGS AND SADNESS

Sadness is an absence of energy accompanied by longing. Sadness is wanting things to be different from the way they are, often wanting them to go back to the way they were before. The way they are feels flat, as if an EEG of your feelings would be a straight line. Sadness stretches across your psyche in a perfectly still blue-gray lake. Nothing will ever change. You just know. When you're feeling sad, you may sometimes cry, but not so hard as when you're frustrated, angry, or in pain. Sadness is not altogether unpleasant: it incorporates both unhappiness and calm, which can feel good. Singing the blues to yourself captures the calm "blue" side of sadness.

Sadness has less stigma attached to it than anger or fear, but because of its negative aspect, you may still try to avoid naming it to yourself. Often sadness causes people to have ambivalent feelings about certain Things. A picture of a person you've lost, for example, may be both soothing and upsetting at the same time.

Of all emotions, sadness has been the most romanticized—in other words, the most loaded with "shoulds." You're supposed to feel sad and cry when your grandmother dies, but you're not supposed to feel sad when your sister gets married. The trouble is, you may feel the exact opposite, though you may not want to admit it to yourself. If what you feel doesn't match what you're supposed to feel, you may hang on to all sorts of Things you don't really want in order to prove that you're sadly correct.

Throughout life, all of us experience true losses and failures from time to time, leaving objects that remind us of them tinged with sadness. When you let go of or lose Things you may feel not only sadness but grief. The grief may be about an object itself or about the person with whom you associated it. Grief is a hodgepodge that may involve many other emotions besides sadness—denial, anger, and guilt, to name a few—as well as periods of apathy and indifference. Gryzypians can come in handy in observing your personal parade of grief feelings.

Grieving any major loss in your life can radically, though usually only temporarily, affect your behavior with Things. At such times it's normal to want to hang on to Things that you associate with your past so as to cushion yourself from the emptiness left by your loss. Also, grief ties up a lot of time and energy, which leaves you less of both for dealing with Things at all. When you're bereaved, it's normal, perhaps even healthy, to let your Things pile up for a while, forming a nest in which you may begin to heal yourself. If this goes on too long, however, and you continue to put decluttering off, this is a sign that you need to get some extra help.

Insufficiently resolved grief is one of the primary reasons people hang on to excess Things. Recognizing what objects are related to grief is the hardest part of taking inventory, and acting on your discoveries is even harder. Just because you've identified the Things that have sadness or grief attached to them does not mean that you'll instantly be able to get rid of all these Things, nor should you. You may choose never to get rid of all of them, but in time you may let go of some. The key to success is to give yourself time.

THINGS AND FATIGUE

Sometimes you're just plain tired. Sometimes you're just plain tired surrounded by Things. Sometimes you're just plain tired surrounded by Thing mountains. Sometimes you're just plain tired surrounded by bigger Thing mountains. The Things look at you. You look at them. You don't move. They don't move. Dust accumulates on them. Ants crawl out from between them. You think if you wait long enough they'll give up and put themselves away without you. But they don't. You think about putting them away. You talk about putting them away. You tell yourself you SHOULD put them away. You call yourself lazy, lousy, and worthless for not putting them away. You call someone else selfish, uncaring, and unsupportive for not putting them away. You analyze why you can't put them away and they don't put them away. But you don't and they don't. Sometimes you're just plain tired.

There are a lot of reasons why you may feel too tired to put your Things away. You may have just been through a big ordeal—an exam, a daughter's wedding, a gallery show, a concert debut, a play opening, a book deadline, a presentation, a filming, a harvest, a labor contract, an election, a corporate deal. Night after night you sat up into the wee hours, and now that the strife is over, you need time to recharge. You may also have been through a trauma or a loss that has sapped all your energy and left you running—or not running—on empty. You may be experiencing burnout from too much prolonged stress in your job or at home. Fatigue may be a normal, natural response to what's going on.

Or it may be a symptom of something. Medical conditions such as chronic fatigue syndrome, Lyme disease, mononucleosis, hypothyroidism, diabetes, anemia, cancer, or clinical depression, as well as the treatments for some medical conditions can drastically reduce your energy level, and if you feel immobilized for no apparent reason, you may need medical attention.

One of the most common causes of fatigue is clinical depression, a condition that lies somewhere between the physical and the emotional, causing both kinds of symptoms. When you're depressed, all your Things become five times as heavy as they really are. A piece of paper weighs as much as a book. A book weighs as much as a couch. A couch weighs as much as a car. Even your own body feels like a ball and chain dragging along behind you. You may literally feel unable to move for long periods of time, even while enormous Thing mountains pile up and collect filth. People who are disorganized but not depressed usually keep their environments clean, but people who are depressed may not. They may hate the dirt around them, but they feel unable to do anything about it.

If this is you, get help. Call your therapist or talk to your doctor. Treatment for depression is highly successful, leaving most folks feeling better than they've ever felt in their lives, but psychiatric treatment can only happen if you're willing to pay the price of the treatment, which is not only money but swallowing your pride and getting help.

One sign that you might be depressed is that you hear yourself saying "yes, but" to anything anyone suggests that might make you feel better, especially the suggestion that you get professional help. IF YOU THOUGHT "YES, BUT" WHEN YOU JUST READ THE WORDS "GET HELP" ABOVE, YOU MIGHT NEED TO GET HELP. Anybody who's been successfully treated for depression will tell you that it's worth it.

The challenge when you're fatigued is not to get caught up in horriblizing and self-blaming and instead to keep DOING WHAT YOU CAN. Even if you have only half your former energy, you still have half your energy, usually at certain times of day more than others. You don't have to stop picking up anything ever again just because you can't do as much as usual. It's a matter of studying your fatigue closely, identifying patterns, and figuring out how your tiredness affects what you do with your Things.

THINGS AND EXISTENTIAL DESPAIR

Life presents us with many problems that appear unsolvable. One of these is the problem of sustaining life itself. We are all on the *Titanic* going down, and our only choice is in how we will deal with this. But this is not all. A host of other seemingly immovable obstacles, some of your own making, others totally unsolicited, may appear on your path to invite despair. You may be unemployed, with only bad references, hugely in debt, evicted, or starving. You may be blind, deaf, or weigh three hundred pounds despite trying every diet known to man. You may have a child who's autistic, a spouse who's alcoholic, a best friend who has cancer, or simply love someone you know will never love you back.

We could go on and on listing all of the big-time slings and arrows that life can hurl at us. And along with these go countless more trivial but equally resistant little darts: a car that keeps breaking down, a boss who has it in for you, a printer that won't print, a friend who's a terrible bore. To this catalogue of miseries may be added a home or office that has become so overwhelmingly cluttered that you feel you can never master it within a single lifetime, given all the other problems with which you have to deal.

Existentialism teaches us that not all human beings respond the same to situations that appear to be hopeless. When confronted with such circumstances some folks throw up their hands and walk away, while others continue to face facts and DO WHAT THEY CAN. Existentialism as we know it, the brainchild of Camus, Sartre, Kierkegaard, Frankl, de Beauvoir, and other Europeans, blossomed out of the horror and rubble of two world wars. Anyone who traveled across Europe after Germany surrendered could easily have been filled with despair at the possibility of ever cleaning up the mess, much less healing the scars on people's souls. Yet a trip through the same countries today reveals an existential triumph: despite ongoing pain, traumatic memories, and enormous human loss, Europeans threw themselves into rebuilding and in almost all countries, their surroundings are now as magnificent as ever. If you feel that your messes are too horrific ever to be eliminated, spend a few moments pondering this.

When it comes to clutter, it seems all too easy to conclude that the situation is hopeless, even in response to just a few piles. At the same time, clutter seems too trivial a matter to evoke the kind of existential heroism we may display in other circumstances. People who would be heroes in facing up to cancer or bankruptcy or losing an arm may blanch and flee at the sight of their own cluttered garage. If their Things remain out of control year after year, the primary cause of this is their flight response to a situation that they impulsively judge to be hopeless.

The hopeless-helpless reaction may be related to past circumstances in which you were truly helpless to prevent bad things from happening and were forced simply to endure them. Psychologist Martin Seligman calls this response *learned helplessness,* citing studies in which dogs received shocks no matter what they did to try to avoid them. These dogs soon quit trying to escape being shocked, EVEN WHEN THEIR ENVIRONMENT WAS ALTERED SO THEY COULD EASILY HAVE AVOIDED THE SHOCKS HAD THEY TRIED TO DO SO. If your best efforts have led only to disappointments and disasters in the past, it's easy to begin to believe that nothing you do can have an impact on the world around you, including your Things.

If you're feeling hopeless about your clutter, don't try to talk yourself out of your hopelessness. Instead, think of a situation in which you faced hopeless circumstances like an existential hero and do what you did then: THE NEXT THING. So, maybe you *are* doomed to perish under a heap of old tennis shoes and bicycle tires—they can at least find you sorting away. The funny part is, when you begin dealing with your "hopeless" clutter this way, you soon discover that it isn't. As you begin to move more of your Things to convenient places, you discover that you have the power to transform hopelessness into hope and to triumph over despair. This is great practice for life.

THINGS AND LOVE

1. Which of your Things feel comforting to be near? Do you associate them with anyone or is there something about the objects themselves that comforts you? To which of your senses does each Thing appeal?

2. Would you feel depressed if you lost certain Things? Do you have any possessions you would fight to protect?

3. If there were a fire in your home, are there any Things that you would try to rescue even at the risk of your own safety?

4. Does the thought of certain Things being harmed affect you physically?

5. Have you ever sacrificed yourself or another person for the sake of a Thing?

THINGS AND HAPPINESS

1. Choose a room in your home. List every Thing you can see in it that is not essential for your survival. On a scale from 1 to 10, how much pleasure does each of these Things currently give you? The items with a score of at least 6 are among your "happiness Things." Now focus on the Things that received a score of less than 6. What "shoulds" are motivating you to hang on to these belongings?

2. What do your "happiness Things" have in common? What do they tell you about yourself?

3. Do you have Things that no longer give you the pleasure they used to? How do they fit with your current life and view of yourself?

THINGS AND FEAR

1. Are you afraid of any of your possessions? Are they actually dangerous or harmless? If they're harmless, do they remind you of anything that once happened to you?

2. Are you afraid of your Things collectively? Does the sight of a cluttered room make your heart speed up with fear?

3. Are you afraid that you'll harm some of your possessions? What are they? Do you have coordination problems? Were you ever abused for being clumsy?

4. Are you afraid of using machines? Are you keeping machines that you're afraid to use?

5. In dealing with Things, are you afraid of

   - not being perfect?

   - making a mistake?

   - forgetting something?

   - going to extremes?

   - having to face reality?

   - being bored?

   - ruining a relationship?

   - feeling helpless?

   - having your weaknesses exposed?

- going without?
- feeling empty?

What could you do to diminish these fears?

THINGS AND ANGER

1. Do you ever take your anger at people out on Things?

2. Have you ever broken or destroyed a possession out of anger? Was it something valuable? Did it belong to someone you cared about?

3. When you're angry, do you throw Things? Tear Things up? Smash Things? Burn Things? Yell or swear at Things?

4. When you express anger at inanimate objects, what feelings most often lie beneath the anger? Do you convert other feelings into anger?

5. Have you ever felt foolish after displaying anger at Things in front of other people?

6. Do you routinely swear and throw tantrums when you have difficulty running or fixing a machine?

7. Do you allow Thing mountains to build up out of anger? Do you believe anger is bad?

8. When you feel angry at or about objects, are you able to identify the problem that produced the anger?

THINGS AND SADNESS

1. Walk through your home and ask yourself what you feel as you encounter different Things. Make a list of ten "sadness Things." Then look at each one and consider the following:

- Do you really feel sad when you look at this item, or do you just think you *should* feel sad?

- What is the loss or failure you associate with this object?

- Is your sadness mixed with other feelings? What are they?

- Why have you chosen to keep this Thing even though it makes you feel sad to look at it? Is there a "should" involved, or do you feel it will help you to heal yourself? If there is a "should," what is it?

- How would you feel if you got rid of the object? Would you feel better or worse about yourself?

2. Make a list of the major losses you've suffered in your life. Have a good cry if you need to. Then go through your space and look for objects that you associate with these losses. Are they many or few? Which objects are associated with which loss? Are some Things more closely associated with it than others?

3. What grief emotions have you recently experienced in response to each major loss? How have these feelings affected what you're doing with belongings?

THINGS AND FATIGUE

1. How long have you been feeling fatigued?

2. Did something happen recently that might account for your tiredness?

3. Do you have a medical condition or symptoms of a medical condition commonly associated with fatigue? How long has it been since you saw a physician?

4. Are you always tired, or are there times when you're more tired than others? Are you able to do any decluttering during your less tired times?

5. What do you say to yourself when you neglect your Things because you're tired? Do you make a lot of negative statements to yourself or overanalyze? How does this affect your energy level?

6. When you've been able to put any Things away, how have you motivated yourself to do this? Can you apply what you've learned at other times?

7. What are your beliefs about emotional energy? Do you feel you have to save energy in order to have enough, or do you think in terms of momentum, i.e., the more you do the more you have?

THINGS AND EXISTENTIAL DESPAIR

1. When you encounter a cluttered room in your space, do you immediately declare your situation to be hopeless?

2. Do you spend a lot of time "horriblizing" about your clutter? Do you often tell others how hopeless you are about it? If someone tries to suggest ways to deal with your Things, do you instantly come up with a "yes, but"? Do you ever get angry with others for suggesting that your situation with clutter isn't hopeless?

3. Have you ever gone ahead and started working anyway even when you thought you could never, ever clean up a cluttered area? Did you keep working until you were finished or did you give up before finishing? How did this feel?

PART III

WHY THINGS KEEP OVERWHELMING YOU

Why does Griselda Backglance keep all of her relatives' Things forever? Why does Millie Squalor throw her clothes on the floor? Why does Professor Tightstring take his anger out on Things? Why does Olivia Ostrich try to escape from Things? What's really going on here? What can we suggest to help these people? The main reason people get caught in such maladaptive Thing habits is that they don't have a clear understanding of why they do what they do. They may not even know there is a why.

WHY can be a scary question. You may associate the word with prosecuting attorneys whose "why" always implies that the defendant is guilty. Also, if you ask why, you might find out why, and then you might feel obliged to change what you're doing. Many people go through life assuming that they have no choice but to continue doing what they've always done. They feel that if they did things differently, they would be SOMEONE ELSE. Believing that you would be someone else if you did what would make your life happier comes from defining your identity too broadly. You assume that "I" includes all sorts of habits, positive and negative.

Try this: Take out a piece of paper. Sign your name the way you've always signed it. Now sign it the way a superneat bookkeeper might sign it. Now sign it the way a glamorous movie star might sign it. Now sign it the way a mafia boss might sign it and a corporate executive might sign it. Guess what? You just did something differently than you've been doing it your whole adult life. Now look in the mirror. Are you still you? You bet. SO DON'T SAY YOU CAN'T CHANGE YOUR BEHAVIOR JUST BECAUSE YOU'VE BEEN DOING SOMETHING FOR A LONG TIME. YOU JUST DID!

Although "why" can be a scary question, not asking it sets you up for failure when it comes to solving problems. Suppose you had a stomachache and you went to your doctor. If, instead of asking you questions and doing tests to try to determine what was going on, your physician simply took out your appendix, how effective do you think this would be? Constructive change requires self-assessment: asking why you do what you do and coming up with answers that are not vague generalities but instead zero in on the SPECIFIC problems behind the problem for YOU. To begin to discover the problems behind your problems with Things, you'll need to explore three questions in depth:

1. How does my situation affect what I do with Things?

2. How does my unique brain chemistry affect what I do with Things?

3. How do the people around me, past and present, influence what I do with Things?

Exploring these questions systematically will result, for each person, in a list of factors that FOR YOU add up to conflict with Things. Your list will not be the same as someone else's list. This means that what you need to do to make peace with your Things will be different from what someone else will need to do.

Whether you're looking at your situation, your brain, or the people in your life, the jack-in-the-box that's likely to pop out at you at every twist and turn is the same: it's called DENIAL. It isn't easy to ask yourself what your situation REALLY is, face everything about it, and deal with it. It isn't easy to admit to yourself that certain kinds of tasks are hard for your brain to do, name these problem tasks to yourself, and find ways of working on or around them. Nor is it easy to look at the people you've known, see them exactly as they were and are, and ask yourself how they've influenced your Thing habits.

This job won't be easy. It will take courage. But it will reward you many times over. It will truly change your life.

CHAPTER 7

THINGS AND
YOUR SITUATION

Sandy Chaser is a single mother of three young children, all of whom have been diagnosed with attention deficit/hyperactivity disorder. Sandy works long hours as a waitress to support her family and also does extra sewing to supplement her income. When she comes home, she's exhausted, but her children are not. They always seem to have enough energy to take the air conditioner apart, play Frisbee with Sandy's favorite CDs, and cut up hundreds of pieces of paper to make "collages" while Sandy weakly protests from her chair in front of the TV, too tired to stop them.

When Eric Crampit separated from his wife, he moved into a tiny efficiency apartment, which was all he could afford. By being exceptionally clever, Eric managed to squeeze all of his power tools, his bicycle, his computer, his clothes, and his entire library into this space. In order to put anything away, however, he always has to move at least five other Things. Eric reacts to this by building Thing mountains.

Louisa Braveheart is getting on in years and finds it more difficult than she once did to remember certain things. Also, six months ago she was diagnosed with cancer. Although she's done well in chemotherapy, she does not have the energy she once had, and she finds herself less and less able to keep her belongings organized. Louisa hates watching them pile up under layers of dust, but she just doesn't know what else to do.

Many issues with which people struggle, including clutter issues, can be attributed to a challenging situation. People who might be able to manage their Things just fine in a different situation may not be equal to doing so in the circumstances in which they find themselves. Some depressed folks, whose favorite words are "if only . . ." are forever blaming their situation for their problems. Strangely enough, however, many other people seem to prefer blaming themselves to confronting their situation EXACTLY AS IT IS and asking how it impacts the issue at hand.

In some cases this may be because the situation is just too painful or frightening to take in, so that the brain resorts to "defense mechanisms"—Anna Freud's term for the various mental gymnastics we use to avoid unpleasant realities. If you allowed yourself to recognize your situation for what it is, you might feel obligated to try to change it—if it is changeable—or you might have to do the emotional work, the grieving, involved in accepting it if it's not. Both of these activities take energy, and energy is what human brains are programmed to conserve—even if it means playing tricks on ourselves.

Failure to face facts does not always have an emotional cause, however. Many of our brains are just not wired in such a way as to easily process the details of such circumstances. Such difficulties have nothing to do with intelligence. Absentminded professors, whose high-powered cortexes are busy calculating the effects of the lunar eclipse on the mating habits of kangaroos, may have only a hazy idea of how long it takes to wash a car or how many volumes can go on a shelf. Some brains are naturally repetitive, playing the same tapes over and over while the rest of the world goes by. Others are like butterflies, flitting here and there, taking in a fragment of this, a fragment of that, but never putting the pieces together to make sense out of things. All have something to contribute to the world, but not all are equally able to come to terms with The Facts.

To make peace with your Things, a good, systematic review of all relevant situational factors—time, space, money, health, disabilities, other people, and life changes—is a must. You need to look at these factors one by one and consider what effect each has on your current Thing habits. If Sandy Chaser did this, she would see that other people—namely her children—along with lack of time, energy, and money, have created havoc with her Things. Eric Crampit would realize that lack of space as well as the life transitions of moving and divorce are primary for him. Louisa Braveheart would understand that her Thing troubles relate to health problems and aging, and that she may be in transition to accepting more assistance from others.

When it becomes clear that a situational factor is causing you serious problems with Things, you have two options: to try to change your situation or to devise strategies that take your situation into account. Which option you choose will depend on how easy it is to change the situational factor, if you can change it at all. Just because you can't change it, however, does not mean that you're doomed to live in chaos until your circumstances change. It just means you may have to use some special strategies and/or outside help to deal with your Things.

TIME AND THINGS

Albert Juggler is a fast-track marketing consultant with a zillion new ideas, all of them great. Al flies all over the world helping multinational corporation heads plan their marketing campaigns. Arriving back at his office after his latest trip to Geneva, Al shuffles through mountains of paper and other Things, dumps out a briefcaseful of papers, and sits down to go through the backlog of mail. He's just opening the first envelope when his assistant comes in and asks for his help with a project she's working on. Al immediately sets the mail aside and becomes engrossed in problem solving, pulling out manuals, leafing through folders, and printing out scores of Internet pages.

Suddenly Al remembers that he has an article due tomorrow for a marketing journal. Without putting anything away he launches into writing, printing out multiple drafts and throwing papers all over the floor while consuming a "lunch" of pretzels and black coffee. He puts the finished article in an envelope and takes it out to the mail basket with satisfaction. Finally, a break. Maybe now he can get to the mail. As he returns to his office, Al hears his phone ringing and barely answers it in time. An enthusiastic client, excited about their new project together, wants him to fly to New York right away and work on it with her. No time to deal with the mail now—Al has to go!

He leaves the piles of envelopes, books and papers, and the unrinsed office dishes and races off to the airport, brainstorming with clients on his cell phone as he drives, and just barely makes the next flight. When Al arrives in New York, he realizes he has forgotten half of the materials he promised the client there he would bring. He can't call his secretary for help, as she quit a month ago out of frustration with his habits, and he hasn't had time to hire a new one. Coming back into his office early the next morning, Al looks around in despair. How did his office get like this? But there's still no time to do anything about it—he has an all-day meeting scheduled for which he has to get ready.

Many Thing-management problems relate to time-management problems. Most chronically disorganized people are overcommitted, and those who aren't may still have trouble planning and remembering their sparsely scheduled activities. Nearly all are in denial about one basic situational reality that everyone on planet Earth shares: THERE ARE ONLY TWENTY-FOUR HOURS IN ANY GIVEN DAY.

Being overcommitted has important ramifications for Thing management. When you're overcommitted, you tend to allow insufficient time for each activity, as well as insufficient time between activities. In consequence, you constantly leave Things from unfinished projects uncontained by drawers and closets as you dash off to whatever's next on the agenda.

Overcommitted people like Al are often pleasers who are willing to stop in midair the moment others snap their fingers. They fail to take charge of their own schedules and instead leave them up to the whims of everybody else. Consequently, they spend most of their time in crisis mode, which, along with flooding their bodies with adrenaline, triggers an automatic mechanism to save five seconds here, ten seconds there by not putting things away. Then they use up three hours frantically searching for something they can't find.

Overcommitted people generally wind up in vicious circles with their Things: they see themselves as too busy dealing with the next emergency to take the time or even hire the help they need to make inroads into their clutter.

If you're overcommitted, the solution of choice is to try to scale back your commitments. To do this, you must stop the merry-go-round, let what's going to happen happen, go off to the north woods—or at least to your own attic—and spend at least three days thinking about what matters most to you. Thinking about WHAT you commit to is important; thinking about HOW YOU DECIDE to commit is even more important. To improve gatekeeping, before you leave for your retreat, keep a log for three days of all moments when you committed to do something, then study your entries:

- What happened during the moments when you committed? How did you decide to accept the commitment?

- Did you agree to a time without looking at your calendar or planner?

- Did you consider travel time from one job to another?

- Did you think about what you would NOT do in order to make time for the job?

- How long did you think the job would take and how long did it actually take?

- How firmly did you commit—"I'll do it if it kills me" or "I'll do it if I can"?

- How much will your commitment benefit you? benefit others?

- How does the commitment relate to your long-term goals? What would the consequences have been if you'd chosen not to commit?

- If you made the commitment in order to earn more money, will you be spending the extra cash on necessities or luxuries? on debts accumulated buying luxuries?

Rethinking your obligations this way may enable you to stop overcommitting or it may not. Working parents, low-wage workers holding multiple jobs, professors, physicians, lawyers, congresspeople, corporate executives, and many others in today's world may be in positions in which being overbooked comes with the territory. If you're hopelessly overcommitted, this does not mean that you have to live in perpetual clutter, however. Once you've faced up to your hopeless overcommitment, you can begin to strategize accordingly:

- Make time to learn to use a planner even if it means putting a few less critical activities on hold while you're learning. Take a time-management workshop if you need to, but don't go berserk. (For more on planners, see Chapter 12.) LOOK INSIDE YOUR PLANNER EVERY DAY.

- For one day, write down an estimated time for each task before you do it, then time yourself and compare the actual time with the estimated time. Many people grossly underestimate how long activities will take.

- Pay particular attention to the time you allow *between* activities, and schedule travel time—even to go across the street—unpacking time, and catching-up-with-mail time as religiously as you would appointment time.

- Do not do ANYTHING that you can persuade someone else

to do. Take the time to train others to organize your Things the way you like them, even if it means allowing a few minor slip-ups to happen while they get up to speed. If you can afford it, hire extra help.

- Make homes for all your possessions as near as possible to where you use them.

- Set up way stations, containers where you can temporarily put Things until you can put them completely away: a box next to the stairs, an indoor mailbox for the mail, a "to-file" tray. Keep Things you need to take with you at a moment's notice near entrances and exits. Empty way stations the moment a crisis is past as part of regrouping.

- Train yourself to keep ALL of your VITs (Very Important Things that you constantly use and put down again such as keys, wallet, glasses, watch, shoes, planner, purse) in their homes except when you're using them.

- Keep your possessions as minimal and as low maintenance as possible. Always ask yourself, whenever you buy a new piece of clothing, appliance, or other type of Thing, how much time this purchase will take to maintain.

- Accept the fact that you cannot deal with your Things in the same way as you would if you were not overcommitted. Instead of cleaning the whole house each week, just clean the parts that need it the most. Redefine "finished."

- When you're in crisis mode, don't think you have to follow the triggered instinct that tells you not to put Things away. Remind yourself that the seconds you save now while creating clutter may result in hours later looking for something lost. No matter how serious the crisis, you'll deal with it better—and feel more confident—if you keep your environment organized. People who are trained to deal with crises on a daily basis are always taught this principle. Have you ever seen a cluttered emergency room?

Because overcommitment is such an important cause of clutter, many people assume that it is the ONLY cause. This is rarely the case. If your Things are out of control, don't stop reading here. Instead, continue on at least through Chapter 10 and ask yourself if each possible factor described relates to you. You may be surprised at what you discover.

SPACE AND THINGS

There are two kinds of Things: containers and objects to be contained. Not having enough containers for your possessions usually leads to clutter. Many of us need to be reminded of a simple principle: ANY GIVEN CONTAINER CAN HOLD ONLY A VOLUME OF THINGS EQUAL TO ITS OWN VOLUME—without something spilling over, that is.

Although not all Things are normally kept in containers—a life-sized replica of Michelangelo's David is unlikely to be stored in a closet or filing cabinet—in well-organized households most Things are "containerized," to use Julie Morgenstern's term. Having the right type of container for the right type of Thing can help you to use space more efficiently, but it isn't necessary to spend hundreds of dollars on organizing equipment to do this. Never underestimate the value of the cardboard box.

Unless you're part of a nomadic tribe, you'll probably keep most of your containers in some type of enclosed space. It's perfectly possible to have all of your Things in containers but have your space cluttered by excessive and poorly organized containers. Some people, on the other hand, favor contained chaos, in which all Things are contained, but completely randomly.

Ask yourself two questions: Do I have enough containers for my

Things? and Do I have enough space for my containers and Things? If you don't have enough containers for your Things, you have two and only two choices: Get more containers; or Get rid of some Things. Likewise with space. While it often makes sense to acquire more containers, getting more and more space is usually a bad idea. Wealthy people have been known to die leaving literally dozens of rented storage cages packed with excess Things, none of which had been opened for years.

You may, for whatever reason, be living in a situation that's *space poor.* People living in small apartments, dormitories, overcrowded households, trailers, tents, and submarines may need to face the fact that space poverty is part of their current situation and that, in consequence, they must deal with their belongings differently than they otherwise would. Suggestions for coping with the reality of space poverty:

- Accept the fact that YOU CANNOT HAVE AS MANY THINGS AS PEOPLE HAVE WHO ARE NOT SPACE POOR. This is not the worst problem you could have. Read Thoreau's *Walden,* particularly the part where he talks about how all any of us really needs is a coffin-sized box to sleep in. At least you have more than that. Meditate on people in poor countries, many of whom would be thrilled to have what you have.

- If you want to feel rich, instead of going for quantity, go for quality in your Things: since you can only buy a few Things, you can afford to get thicker towels, softer blankets, prettier dishes than if you could buy these Things in quantity. Notice how much more you enjoy the Things you have, now that you have fewer of them.

- Read books on storage and home decorating magazines to learn about ways to use normally unused space such as areas high on walls, above rafters, behind doors, and under beds. Buy Things that serve dual purposes: a table that is also a chest, a couch that is also a bed, a nightstand that is also a bureau. Build or hire someone to build shelves wherever possible. Don't be afraid to store books in the linen closet or keep your extra cosmetics in your kitchen cupboards. Be creative.

- Try to get extra storage space somewhere. Although this is a bad idea if you're not space poor, it's a good idea if you are. Talk to your landlord, hire a storage cage, or ask a friend or relative to keep your Things for a while. If someone's keeping Things for you, give the person a definite date when you'll come to get them, honor this when the time comes, and do something nice in return.

- Enjoy the FREEDOM that comes with being space poor. Remember that when you've succeeded in increasing your space you'll have to spend a lot more time caring for your Things and your space than you do now. Many people with larger households look back on a time when they were space poor with nostalgia, remembering it as a time when life was simpler and they didn't have to work so hard to hang on to so much stuff.

MONEY AND THINGS

Money is a Thing. As a Thing, it isn't really of much use: it's neither edible nor wearable, and it doesn't even make very good wallpaper. Its only value is the value we assign it, and whatever the exchange rate, not everyone gives it the same value. Some people are money addicts, whose lives revolve around piling up more and more of it; others are money anorexics, who dedicate themselves to remaining uncontaminated by it, forgetting that it is "the love of money" not money itself that the Bible calls "the root of all evil."

In actuality, money, like water, is neither good nor evil, but sim-

ply a type of Thing that flows more continuously and more perva-
sively than all other Things. Making use of money requires trust in
the universe. If you ask someone to give you a bicycle that can carry
you all over town in exchange for some crinkly little bills, your friend
will probably refuse unless he or she totally believes that somebody
else will be willing to trade a Thing as useful or pleasing as a bike for
those crinkly little bills.

Money means different things to different people. To Elsie
Clutcher, it means having dozens of brand-new outfits. To Nicholas
Climber, it means being admitted to the best club in town. To Joe
Parkbench, it means another shot of whiskey. To Charles and Betty
Average, it means going on a vacation each summer, sending their
children to college, and a carefree retirement.

For some people, money is more tightly connected to tangible
Things than for others. This may be partly a matter of upbringing.
Those who grew up deprived of certain Things are likely to value
money primarily for its potential to give them what they didn't get.
But as with everything, brain wiring may also play a role. Some
brains are wired to think mainly on a concrete level. To their owners,
the sooner coins and bills are exchanged for davenports and snow-
mobiles the better. Numbers in a bank book or stock certificates
mean nothing, nor do intangible purchases such as a college education. Such people tend to become spenders.

Spenders are often broke and almost always have too many
Things to fit into their homes, no matter how palatial, including the
latest, fanciest organizing equipment and books. You don't have to be
rich to be a spender, at least not in modern Western culture: it isn't a
matter of your income but of what proportion of it goes into purchasing physical objects. And anyway, spenders buy most of their
Things on credit, which, in their minds, is the same thing as getting
them for free, since credit is intangible, and therefore unreal. Need-
less to say, spenders may experience clutter problems on their way to
bankruptcy.

A second group of folks seem to have little connection at all with concrete Things. Such a connection may have existed at one time, but early in their owners' lives, their thoughts seemed to float free of all concrete moorings, to drift among the clouds from then on. These are the philosophers. You can tell philosophers by their lean physiques and unfashionable clothes. To the philosopher's mind, Things are mere shadows of abstract ideals, and of little or no consequence. They pass through Things the way Casper the Friendly Ghost passes through walls.

Because Things are not real to philosophers, they tend to be clumsy and forgetful in dealing with them. They cannot understand why Things are so important to other people. Money is just as unreal to them as any other Thing, and they put little effort into earning it. This does not mean they're always poor. They may inherit money, or, if they're lucky, they may even get paid for philosophizing. But if this happens, they either give all the money away or leave it sitting in the bank compounding 1% interest: anything but use it to buy Things. The Things philosophers buy are few, though the Things they get rid of are also few, as they fail to notice that the Things are piling up around them, and are constantly forgetting where they left them. Thus, philosophers can have clutter problems just as severe as spenders can, but the difference is that their clutter tends to be dingier and covered with stains.

Somewhere between these two extremes are the balancers, to whose brains a savings account is real enough to prevent them from converting entire paychecks into Things, but who also are able to enjoy trying on a new dress, collecting china angels, or buying a boat. Balancers are able to both control their purchasing habits and get rid of Things when they need to, knowing that "the best Things in life are free." If they have clutter problems, it's not because they have too many Things, though they may still have problems for other reasons.

If you aren't a balancer yourself, this is probably because you have only a vague idea of what you're doing with your money. Because money is composed of so many little Things that flow continuously in and out of your life, clarifying your money habits and figuring out how to improve them can be particularly challenging. Suggestions for would-be balancers:

- Create a balance sheet that includes your liquid assets— various forms of money and investments; your fixed assets— Things translated into monetary terms; and your liabilities— unpaid debts. Then consider which fixed assets (Things) could be liquidated (sold) in order pay off liabilities (debts) and increase your liquid assets (savings).

- Buy a little notebook to keep in your purse or pocket and, for one month, keep track of every penny that flows in or out of your life and where it goes. At the end of the month, set up categories that include intangibles such as tuition fees or health insurance as well as tangible goods such as food, clothes, or books. Calculate the amount you spend on tangibles vs. intangibles. Look at your list of tangibles. Are you spending a disproportionate amount of your income on a particular type of Thing? Put an asterisk next to each of these Things of choice. Now look at your list of intangibles. Are there intangibles you would like to have on this list that aren't there because you spent so much on Things? Would you like to take a class, go on a trip, or give more to a charity? What possessions could you do without in order to acquire the necessary funds?

- Make a bank from a jar or some other type of container. Each time you pass up an opportunity to buy one of your Things of choice, write yourself a check and put it in the container. At the end of the month, deposit these checks in your savings account or add them to what you would normally spend to pay off debts.

- Translate the space your Things take up into monetary terms: divide your monthly mortgage payment or rent by the number of square feet in your dwelling to calculate the cost per square foot; estimate the square footage occupied by a particular type of Thing—newspapers, for example—then multiply the cost per square foot by the square footage occupied to calculate the cost of housing the Things. If your mortgage payment is $1000 per month for a dwelling of 1500 square feet, the cost per square foot is $.67. If your newspapers take up nine square feet, you're paying about $6 per month to house them. If they take up a whole 10 × 14 foot basement, you're paying $93 per month for them. Are they worth it?

- Keep track of the amount of time you spend on Thing maintenance for a week, then translate this into monetary terms by multiplying the number of hours spent by the amount you earn per hour. What are your high-maintenance Things? Do they give you enough pleasure or usefulness to be worth the cost of maintaining them?

- Read *Your Money or Your Life* by Joe Dominguez and Vicki Robin. Dominguez and Robin offer an excellent nine-step program to help you become more conscious of your own choices with money and consider how you can better make use of the "life energy" that money represents. Be sure to take a look at the list of resources they have at the end of the book. They're great!

HEALTH, DISABILITIES, AND THINGS

It's hard to care much about your Things when the Thing known as *your body* is ailing. As a general rule, Things can only be moved by bodies interacting with them, directly or indirectly. Some of us have bodies that, either temporarily or permanently, resist such interactions. When you're sick, the thought of carrying your clothes across the floor to the hamper may feel like moving a mountain. If you're lucky, someone else may be on hand to do this for you; if not, the piles quickly begin to grow, to be removed only when you're feeling better. For some people, this will never happen.

Many people also have physical challenges that make managing Things more difficult. Any disability that lessens your ability to pick up an object and move it somewhere else that makes sense to you will affect your style of Thing management. This includes visual impairments as well as cerebral palsy, multiple sclerosis, arthritis, carpal tunnel syndrome, injuries, and other conditions that affect mobility and may require canes, crutches, walkers, braces, wheelchairs, and other special equipment. Folks living with such special challenges often need to arrange Things differently than the rest of us do and/or require special equipment to make their Things accessible.

Illnesses and disabilities that affect the way you think can be even more problematic for organizing Things than those that target your body. The most common of these among the chronically disorganized is attention deficit disorder (ADD). This disorder is caused by neurological anomalies, especially in the prefrontal area of the brain, and insufficient dopamine, a neurochemical needed for good attentional and executive functioning. When the attention/executive system doesn't work right, a wide variety of problems can result, including distractibility, impulsivity, difficulty staying on task, memory problems, under- or overactivity, social problems, and organizing problems. Each person with ADD has some of these difficulties but most do not have all of them. The majority have problems organizing Things, but not all do, and not all people with Thing problems have ADD.

Psychotherapist Sari Solden, in *Women with Attention Deficit Disorder*, writes that disorganization is a primary symptom of ADD, especially for women:

> *The whole experience of living with ADD is one of disorganization—both internally as well as externally. It includes not only environmental disorganization, such as a messy house, office, or*

*stacks of unpaid bills, but also an inner experience of disorganiz-
ation. The cognitive and emotional experience of not being able to
"hold things together" is disorganization on another level.*

Part of the reason organization is so problematic for ADD
women, Solden says, is the expectations that are put on women to be
superorganizers. She points out that the job of homemaker requires
fantastic organizing skills, and that even when women work mainly
outside the home, people in the working world may expect them to
play organizing roles.

Many individuals with ADD—women *and* men—have exceptionally low self-esteem, often related to a history of verbal or physical abuse in response to their brain-based difficulties. People with
ADD live with failures and accusations every day of their lives,
though they're just as intelligent as anyone else. The problem is,
many people with ADD are too afraid of being belittled—and why
wouldn't they be?—to go find out if they have ADD. Consequently, a
lot of people with ADD don't know they have it. If you're chronically
disorganized, and especially if you identify with many of the difficulties described in Chapter 9 of this book, you may want to consider
getting evaluated by a neuropsychologist or other mental health professional. For referrals, contact ADDA or CHADD, support organizations for people with ADD (see Appendix).

ADD is not the only mental disorder associated with chronic
disorganization. Another common source is learning disorders (LDs),
especially reading disorders, visual processing problems, and visual
motor problems, all of which impair our ability to make sense of
what we see and act in response to it. Sensory integration dysfunc-
tion (SID) affects people's ability to interact with their environment.
People with SID have trouble organizing the information from their
senses and may have problems handling Things due to clumsiness
and/or hypersensitivities.

Probably the most severe cases of chronic clutter are caused by a
type of obsessive-compulsive disorder known as hoarding OCD.[7]

People with this condition habitually hoard enormous quantities of Things. While their clutter may be monumental, they may also suffer from severe perfectionism, which pits them against themselves when they try to do anything about it.

Mood disorders, such as chronic depression and manic depression, also challenge people's ability to deal with Things. When people are depressed, they lack the energy to move even themselves, let alone anything else. They may also find it more difficult to let go of Things, as depression increases dependencies. When individuals are manic, on the other hand, they may create incredible messes while racing around the house repainting all the rooms in a single night.

Conditions that severely affect memory, such as dementia or Alzheimer's disease, can make it impossible to keep track of Things. Head injuries, strokes, and brain tumors may cause symptoms associated with most of the above conditions, depending on what part of the brain has been damaged, with the same consequences for Thing management. The mental health problems listed here are by no means the only ones that can lead to clutter problems. The fact is, almost any psychiatric DISORDER is likely to create disorder with Things.

When it comes to managing Things, some people with illnesses or disabilities are much more successful than others. The folks who do best are not those who try to pretend that they can deal with Things exactly as they would without their condition; they know exactly how their particular challenge affects what they do with their Things, and thus they're able to devise ways to compensate for it. They can also accept the help of others without feeling disempowered.

What keeps many people from doing this is our old friend, toxic shame, grandchild of the belief that we're supposed to be able to do everything OURSELVES. This is especially the case with mental disabilities. The erroneous belief that any reasonably intelligent human brain is supposed to be able to deal with Things easily has wreaked havoc in people's lives throughout history.

When it comes to getting help with Things, the best suggestions for those with special challenges generally come from those who share the same challenge. In today's world, support groups abound for those with most chronic illnesses and disabilities. Members of such groups, their partners and caregivers, and professionals who habitually work with the populations that they represent are the greatest source of help with Things for the physically or mentally challenged. This is not to say, however, that professional organizers and coaches have nothing to offer people with special needs. Some organizers and coaches, in fact, specialize in helping individuals with a specific disability. They can be contacted through the organizations listed in the appendix of this book.

OTHER PEOPLE AND THINGS

One of the most formidable obstacles you may encounter in managing your Things is *other people*. Be careful not to minimize the role of other people in creating clutter in your space. While it's easy to blame others unjustly for your own clutter, it's also easy to do the opposite, especially if you're afraid of being abandoned or abused if you assert yourself. Two kinds of other people can be particularly troublesome: automatic clutter makers (ACMs) and compulsive neatfreaks (CNs).

Automatic clutter makers come in all shapes and sizes. These people literally cannot move without making a mess. Many ACMs are children, especially very young children. These are trainable ACMs. They're trainable both because they're at the stage of life when learning is easiest and because you have authority over them. Most child ACMs do not have to stay ACMs, and in most cases they won't—*if* you train them kindly but firmly and set a good example for them with your own Things. The topic of training child ACMs requires a whole book of its own and hence will not be dealt with here.[8]

Unfortunately, some child ACMs *do* remain ACMs even after they become adults. Adult ACMs are only trainable if they wish to be. Not all do. Some of those who don't may be charming human beings that you want to keep in your life, but THEIR CLUTTER DRIVES YOU CRAZY. When dealing with adult ACMs,

- DON'T TRY TO CHANGE AN ADULT ACM. This is not possible. Don't lecture, scold, analyze, supervise, yell, swear, or otherwise attempt to bully or manipulate the ACM into changing. Remind yourself that other people are OTHER people.

- Tell the ACM what you would like him/her to do with Things. State specific goals clearly and in terms of asking for help, which minimizes defensive reactions. Use "I" statements: "I need you to help me keep the hall table clear from now on." If the ACM agrees to help, ask permission to issue reminders when needed.

- Never organize or get rid of the ACM's Things without his or her permission. If an ACM is uncooperative, put the ACM's Things where they won't bother you and focus only on organizing your own Things.

- Find ways to contain the ACM's Things. Ask if he or she would be willing to divvy up space into mine, yours, and ours. This will allow the ACM to clutter to his/her heart's content in a restricted area and allow you to keep your space as neat as a pin if you like. Watch where the ACM tends to create the most piles and place strategically located containers there into which you or the ACM can simply sweep Things.

- Don't spring decluttering surprises on the ACM. Let him or her know your plans well in advance and make changes gradually, in stages. Sometimes adults need weaning from Things.

- Expect the ACM to be upset about any actions you take with his/her Things. Don't allow yourself to be deterred by accusations and "change-back" strategies on the part of the ACM. If you stand firm, the ACM will get over it.

- Allow the ACM to experience the negative consequences of the clutter and gently point out connections between behavior and consequences.

- Don't deny your own anger at the ACM to yourself. Acknowledge it, take it as a signal that you've lived too long with an unresolved issue, and look for solutions.

- Don't allow yourself to become depressed by the ACM's clutter. Create orderly sanctuaries for yourself, and go places that feel good to you.

- Keep the boundaries between yourself and the ACM clear in your head. Just because he or she clutters does not mean you have to.

- Ask yourself how much the ACM's clutter bothers you. If you can live with it, fine; if it makes you miserable, decide on a bottom line. A bottom line means you'll leave if it gets any worse. Do it if you have to. You don't deserve to be miserable. If the ACM is abusive in response to your efforts, WALK AWAY. If he or she attacks your belongings violently, LEAVE. This is unacceptable, and you may be the person's next target.

- Read Sandra Felton's book *When You Live with a Messie,* from whom some of these suggestions were borrowed, for a more comprehensive treatment of this issue.

The compulsive neatfreak is the second type of other person who can wreak havoc on your dealings with Things. CNs are people who not only drive themselves crazy trying to have everything perfect but who insist that you adhere to their standards as well. They fuss and nag and scream at you for spilling blood on the carpet instead of getting you a Band-Aid if you cut yourself. Nothing you do with Things can please them.

There are two ways that most people instinctively react to CNs. One is to stay up all night scrubbing the floor with a toothbrush to try to please them. The other is to dig in their heels and refuse to pick up a Thing—in other words to become an ACM. Both of these responses are counterproductive. Trying to please a CN only reinforces the person's behavior, making it more likely to persist. Becoming oppositional toward a CN starts a vicious circle in which the more you clutter, the more he or she nags, and vice versa. This is because neither of these responses does anything to counter the extreme anxiety that underlies CN behavior. While most of us can accept the fact that the universe contains a lot of uncontrollable chaos, CNs cannot. Their futile response to the chaos they find so scary is to try to organize the entire universe, starting with YOU.

Suggestions for dealing with CNs:

- Remember that the CN is motivated by fear, and do anything you can to reduce that fear. Reassure the person that you're working on your clutter and continue to do so at your own pace without trying to meet the CN's perfectionist standards.

- Don't get pulled into playing the role of the rebellious child just because the CN is acting like a tyrannical parent. Decide what steps you're going to take to change your own Thing habits, and let the CN know what they are. Take only those steps, but be consistent with them.

- Don't let the CN brainwash you with critical statements about your Thing habits, which may gradually become part of your own thoughts. Acknowledge any truth in what the CN says, empathize, and confront the strategy he or she is using: "It's true I haven't been hanging up my clothes, and I can see this frustrates you, but your labeling me as a slob only makes me want to get away from you."

- Set limits to the CN's badgering, especially if it amounts to abuse. Distance yourself anytime these limits are violated. Be rigid about this even though you wouldn't be rigid about other things. If the CN is abusive to you over Things, WALK AWAY. PEOPLE DO NOT DESERVE TO BE HURT OVER THINGS.

CHANGE AND THINGS

Any time a major change occurs in your life—a birth, a move, a graduation, a marriage, a divorce, a new job, a retirement, a death—everything else in your life shifts, sometimes slightly, sometimes drastically. This includes the Things in your life. Any transition has the potential to alter your habits and feelings about Things.

Change always involves uncertainty. Your mind is filled with questions: will your fiancé still love you once you've said your vows? What will your new boss think of you? How will you keep from getting bored once you're retired? How will you keep from going crazy once your spouse has retired? Will you be able to make friends in your new location? What will you do if your new baby won't stop crying? How will you ever fill the void after a loss?

Because you're uncertain, you may not know what Things you need to have most accessible. You try out different activities and even different personalities, all of which have different paraphernalia attached to them. Meanwhile, objects from prechange times begin to gather dust while connecting you with the stage of life that you left, for better or for worse.

Suppose you've just started your first full-time job after graduating from college. The first day, you're determined to look professional, so you wear your classiest tailored suit. When you get to work, you discover that everyone is in casual clothes. The next day, you arrive in a sweater and slacks. This feels comfortable socially, but you discover that your office has an overactive heating system and spend your whole second day mopping sweat off your brow. The day after that, you wear a lighter outfit and this feels better, but you learn that on Friday an important meeting is scheduled for which you'll need your suit, which now needs cleaning. Meanwhile, at home your closet gets shuffled and reshuffled.

Eventually, you pull together five or six outfits that become your work "uniforms" and keep these in the front of your closet, ready for mornings when the alarm fails to go off. As time goes on, you begin to buy more clothes that suit your present position. Meanwhile, most of the jeans and T-shirts that you lived in during your college years are stuffed into the back of your closet while some college student goes away from a resale shop disappointed. It may feel good to you to hold on to your college clothes to remind you of your past, but eventually you'll feel ready to move forward and pass them on to someone else, keeping only a few to wear on weekends.

Some people find change easier to deal with than others. Some rush headlong into it, never looking back, while others have to be dragged into the present kicking and screaming, hanging on for dear life to the Things of their past. Life transitions, even the good ones, can involve grief. Grief is a kind of emotional time lag in which your attachments fail to keep up with the speed of change. The train your body is on has moved out of the station while your soul is left standing on the platform. When you feel that part of you has been left behind, it's normal to want to hang on to Things that you associate with your past.

A few people seem never to get rid of anything from their past lives at all. Decluttering for these folks is like digging through layers of buried cities. Their problem is not so much grief over a particular loss as it is overattachment to the past in general. In some cases, this behavior may also relate to memory problems. People with poor memories may fear that they will not have a past at all if they don't hang on to every single Thing they can to remind them of it. If you're having trouble letting go, try this:

- Choose certain Things to represent whole categories of memorabilia and get rid of the rest. Then do something special with the memorabilia.

- Buy pretty boxes covered with patterned papers, a carved wooden box, or a trunk for your memorabilia.

- Take photos of Things before getting rid of them. Put the photos in an album, organized in a way that makes sense to you.

- Perform a "funeral ceremony" for dead Things relating to your past. Say a prayer, read a poem, or do whatever else gives you closure. Then let go of them.

- Write a poem or song or paint a picture to commemorate Things that you're relinquishing.

- Declutter with a trusted close friend or professional organizer at your side and recount memories attached to Things as you let them go.

The process of decluttering old Things, once you are ready for it, can be a wonderful aid to the grieving process and to your emotional growth. As you begin to sort through and dispose of books, clothes, papers, and toys from a bygone era, memories will surface, emotions churn up and wash away—sometimes with tears—and in the end you'll feel lighter and more energetic, ready to form new attachments and arrange your remaining Things—and life!—in a new design.

CHAPTER 8

THINGS AND THE BRAIN

The human race is in the midst of a revolution. Throughout most of history, people have explained behavior purely in terms of angels and devils. Originally, these angels and devils were literal, but more recently they were replaced with human angels and devils, better known as moms and dads. For a long time, the predominant psychological view—existing alongside the theological angel/devil view—was that all of the unpleasant things we felt or did were because either mom was a devil or dad was.

In the latter decades of the twentieth century, however, more and more people began to experience a certain big shift, a flash of insight, which upon arrival, made them want to run naked out into the streets like Archimedes, shouting "Eureka!" Neuroscientists who, as a result of World War II, began studying what damaged brains couldn't do, were the first to experience the big shift. This was followed by the development of brain-imaging techniques, the amazing success of psychoactive medications, and dramatic advances in the study of genetics, which collectively forced many an established psychotherapist, experiencing the big shift, to think about changing careers. Meanwhile, all kinds of other people experienced the big shift. Some ran into it when they realized that they were powerless over a brain-based addiction or successfully tried medication for some kind of psychological condition or experienced the effects of brain damage on themselves or someone they knew. Others were enlightened by living or working with, studying, or treating people who had these experiences. While many still cling to the angels-and-devils philosophy—either theological or parental—their numbers are dwindling.

Everyone who experiences the big shift arrives at exactly the same conclusion: SMALL DIFFERENCES IN THE BRAIN CAN MAKE BIG DIFFERENCES IN WHAT WE'RE ABLE TO DO AND WHO WE BECOME. Many ideas and habits we thought we had because we were good or bad, smart or dumb, crazy or sane—or because our parents were—are simply the result of subtle distinctions between brains. If my brain works differently from your brain, then some things that are easy for me may be hard for you and vice versa without either of us being stupid, lazy, or crazy. Everything from our ability to draw or do math to our ability to control our emotions and cravings to our ability to fit into society is wired into the system, though the wires are constantly being eliminated and crisscrossed and disconnected and reconnected by encounters with the brain's environment, including good or bad parenting. Brain wiring is no less important for how we manage Things than for anything else. Many difficulties with Things relate to the particular quirks in our own unique neurochemistry.

Brain-based thinking applied to Thing management can be tremendously empowering, as you begin to ask yourself specifically what's easy, difficult, or impossible for your particular mound of gray and white matter to do, and to take this into account in developing strategies. Thinking this way allows you to break out of circular patterns you may have repeated for years with your Things and begin to make genuine progress.

FIVE KEY BRAIN SYSTEMS FOR THINGS

According to John Ratey, in *A User's Guide to the Brain,* the brain is not just a big organic computer. For one thing, it's infinitely more complex, with billions of neurons and trillions of synapses. For another, it works differently, operating not by "the predictive logic of a microchip" but by "analogy and metaphor." However, in one way, the brain IS like a computer: both brain and computer perform a host of different tasks. Just as the same computer can be used to write and edit a novel, balance a checkbook, send a message around the world, and order flowers for Mother's Day, the same brain tells your heart how fast to beat, forms words into sentences, decides which type of lettuce to buy, generates an idea for an experiment, and tells you to duck when a ball is thrown at your head.

Each task that your brain performs utilizes different "hardware," a different system composed of key parts of the brain, neurotransmitters (brain chemicals), and hormones (the brain's messengers to the body) as well as, in many cases, the rest of the nervous system and other parts of your body besides the brain. Each system is extremely complex. Although certain parts of the brain are primary for certain tasks—as demonstrated by the fact that people whose brains have been damaged in those areas can no longer do them—most systems make use of networks of neurons from many areas. Furthermore, when a brain has been damaged, other areas may compensate by taking over certain functions from the damaged areas.

Some brain systems, such as the auditory system, for example, are not particularly relevant to organizing and managing Things. Others are highly relevant. Suppose Nancy Neatfreak is reorganizing a kitchen cupboard. In the cupboard are mixing bowls, baking pans, utensils, pots, and jars. To organize the Things in the cupboard, Nancy first has to know that they're there. To do this she must somehow perceive them. Messages from Nancy's eyes must enter areas of her brain that make up the VISUAL-SPATIAL SYSTEM. Seeing the pots and pans will not help Nancy if her brain does not remember what the items are and where they belong by means of the MEMORY SYSTEM. Then she must decide whether to keep or get rid of the extra frying pan and which shelf to put the sifter on, plan how she'll do it, and stay on track in implementing her plan. This is high-level thinking in the ATTENTION/EXECUTIVE SYSTEM, the big boss of the brain.[9] Once she's decided what to do with the sifter, Nancy's MOTOR SYSTEM sends out messages down her arm to tell it to pick up the sifter and put it on the desired shelf. Meanwhile, if any of this is to happen at all, Nancy's AFFECTIVE SYSTEM, which involves not only her brain but the rest of her body as well—the brain and body communicating via both nerves and hormones (chemical messengers)—must provide the energy and regulate her emotions, including the attachment feeling.

If any of the Five Key Brain Systems—visual-spatial, memory, attention/executive, motor, or affective—isn't working just right, Nancy will have trouble organizing her cupboard and may also have difficulties relating to both Thing acquisition and Thing disposal. Even minor glitches in the flow of chemicals and electricity in certain parts of the brain can have big effects on whether you're constantly at war or comfortably at peace with the Things in your life.

BRAIN GLITCHES

Every normal brain, regardless of IQ or mental health status, contains both glitches and strengths in at least some systems, as well as individual quirks that neither help nor hamper the systems. When a system doesn't work right for accomplishing a particular task, this is because of GLITCHES—minor differences occurring in some element of that system. HAVING GLITCHES IN YOUR BRAIN DOES NOT MAKE YOU STUPID OR CRAZY. What constitutes a glitch depends on what you're trying to do: what might be a glitch for accomplishing one task might be a strength for accomplishing another. Glitches may be permanent—differences we were born with that can be altered, if at all, only by medical interventions—or they may be temporary, the result of health problems or of the wrong balance of neurotransmitters and hormones.

Troubleshooting for glitches within key brain systems tells you what you have to do to resolve a particular problem with clutter. If you discover, for example, that you have a glitch in your visual/spatial system, you might decide to use color-coded folders to make papers more visible. If you discover a glitch in your affective system that limits your energy, you might plan short but frequent decluttering sessions instead of lengthy, less frequent ones.

But how do you discover a glitch? Are you supposed to run out and have an MRI? No. You don't need to look at your physical brain to troubleshoot for glitches, only at its output: your thoughts and feelings about Things as well as your habits, in other words, what you learned when you took inventory in Part II. This is not the only useful source of information for identifying glitches, however. You can also make use of any information you have about which tasks in general—with or without Things—are particularly troublesome for you. All your life, people have been evaluating you according to various criteria, and you've also been evaluating yourself. What subjects caused you the most trouble in school? What tasks have been most difficult for you at work? Were you ever given intelligence or achievement tests? What were the results? When others have picked on you, what have they criticized? If the task of identifying glitches seems puzzling, don't worry: Chapter 9, "The Four Brain-Based Troubles with Things," will describe many of the most common "subtroubles"—i.e., glitch effects relating to Things—and help you figure out if you're affected by them.

Zeroing in on a specific glitch doesn't usually allow you to change it, but it will enable you to take it into account in deciding how to approach the Thing problem at hand. This is not easy work—to do it, you must head off denial at every pass—but it can make all the difference between success and failure in changing the Thing habits you identified in Part II and may produce positive differences in the rest of your life as well. It's worth doing!

Glitches are not the only phenomena you need to look for in thinking about how you think. In considering your Thing habits, ask yourself not only "What am I doing wrong?" but also "What am I doing right?" In thinking about school, remember not only the classes in which you got C's, D's, or F's, but also those in which you got A's and B's without even trying. In recounting work experiences, think not only about what brought you criticism but also about what brought testimonials. Then ask yourself, "What do all of these achievements have in common? What brain strengths do they reveal?"

Are you exceptionally good at drawing or writing poetry? Do others tell you that you're a good listener? Are you great at golf or basketball? What are your specific strengths within these sports? In golf are you a super putter, are you good at getting out of tough situations, do you have a powerful drive, or what? Are you able to memorize words or dates easily? Are you brilliant at solving math problems? In what specific ways?

Brain strengths are what you'll use to compensate for brain glitches in dealing with Things. If you have a glitch about remembering where particular objects are but a strength at forming poetic metaphors, for example, you can use this strength to invent metaphors to help you remember where Things are. If you have a glitch about staying focused on the task at hand but a strength in responding quickly to external cues, you can set an alarm to go off periodically or ask someone else to issue reminders when you stray from your decluttering course.

The most relevant brain strengths for organizing occur in what might be described as a sixth brain system—"sixth sense"—which we might call the INSIGHT SYSTEM. The insight system, which generates brilliant ideas that seem to come from nowhere, allows you to recognize patterns in your own Thing habits, to devise creative strategies for changing them, and to arrange your belongings in ways that are beautiful and original. Changing your Thing habits is largely a matter of learning to make constructive use of your insight system to compensate for weaknesses in other brain systems as well as the insight system's own excesses.

RESPONSES TO BRAIN STRENGTHS
AND GLITCHES

While it's important to identify both the glitches and the strengths in each of your key brain systems, this is not all you need to do. You also need to understand how you've responded to each glitch and strength. Clutter is caused not only by glitches but also by inappropriate responses to glitches, knee-jerk compensations that do not make use of the higher centers of the brain to reason out a better solution. You may, for example, have been leaving all of your papers out on your desk as a way of trying to compensate for a memory system glitch. If you really thought about this, you'd realize that it's self-defeating, resulting in mountains of paper, and instead would make creative use of some device such as an index, open-topped files, or color coding, to help out your visual memory. If your insight system is in good working order, this should be easy for you.

Sometimes even strengths can cause problems with Things if you don't respond to them appropriately. Many people with excellent memories, for example, respond to their memory strengths by refusing to put anything away, believing they can always find what they need no matter where they put it, because they'll remember where it is. Although they may be right about this much of the time, even the best human memory has its limits, and furthermore, the unsightliness of clutter can cause problems even when losing Things doesn't.

The insight system, which enables you to compensate for many glitches in other systems, is not always a plus for Thing management.

A highly active insight system may make organizing more difficult as you struggle to keep track of all those pieces of paper on which you wrote down brilliant ideas for your next novel. Insights have a way of interrupting the step-by-step courses of action monitored by the attention/executive system, pulling you off track when you're trying to declutter or simply finish a task and put something away. If this happens enough times, however, your insight system may recognize the pattern and enable you to problem-solve about how to break out of it. The insight system creates both problems and solutions with Things.

In *Organizing for the Creative Person,* the first popular book to recognize that organizing problems relate to brain differences, Dorothy Lehmkuhl and Doris Lamping divvy people up into Arbies (right-brain-dominant people) and Elbies (left-brain-dominant people) and attribute disorganization as well as creativity to being an Arbie. Disorganization, in their view, is just the flip side of being creative. Yet we all know extremely creative people who are also well organized. Such people are able to use the strengths in their insight system to compensate for its excesses by devising creative alternative organizing strategies that work for THEM.[10]

What strengths and glitches your particular brain systems contain is not a matter of choice. YOU DID NOT CHOOSE YOUR BRAIN. You do have a choice, however, about how you'll deal with these strengths and glitches. It's up to you whether you'll obliviously allow them to wreak havoc on your life or consciously develop strategies that allow you to make the best possible use of your own brain's chemistry. To make peace with your Things, you must also make peace with your brain.

THE BRAIN IN A NUTSHELL

Each brain is put together differently, which makes different tasks easy, difficult, or impossible for different people, including tasks involving Things. Any given brain performs a great many different tasks. Each task is accomplished by a different brain system. Each brain system is composed of different "hardware," networks of neurons and other physiological equipment. Five brain systems are particularly important for organizing and managing Things: the visual-spatial system, the memory system, the attention/executive system, the motor system, and the affective system. Glitches in any of these systems may cause you problems with Things, while strengths in any of them—as well as a powerful additional system, the insight system—may help you to solve problems. You can identify your Thing glitches and strengths by considering both your findings on your inventory and any general information you have about your performance on different kinds of tasks. The following chapter will help you identify your brain glitches and strengths so as to replace ineffective knee-jerk responses with more effective Thing-management strategies that take your unique brain characteristics into account.

CHAPTER 9

THE FOUR BRAIN-BASED
TROUBLES WITH THINGS

It's time to troubleshoot. The combined effect of glitches in the Five Key Brain Systems is the Four Troubles: four possible brain-based difficulties that may explain why clutter keeps overwhelming you:

I. Trouble tuning in to Things

II. Trouble seeing Things

III. Trouble thinking about Things

IV. Trouble moving Things

Each of these troubles results from a certain set of glitches in one or more brain systems, and each may manifest itself differently in each person who struggles with it, in the form of different combinations of subtroubles. People who have trouble tuning in to Things, for example, may be distractible, have a short attention span, and/or be unable to shift attention from one activity to another. Once you've recognized which of the Four Troubles are causing you problems with clutter and pinpointed specific subtroubles, you can use your own brain strengths to deal with them, as well as the suggestions presented here. As you read about each of the Four Troubles and various subtroubles, circle the ones that you believe apply to you or make a list of them.

TROUBLE TUNING IN TO THINGS

How aware are you of Things? Do you find the inanimate world fascinating or does it bore you to tears? Are you an engineer, who spends whole days and nights pondering the ins and outs of Things, looking for ways to make them go faster or fly higher? If so, you're probably not reading this book. Or are you a philosopher, to whom Things are mere shadows of ideas in your head? Or a people person who regards Things as boring companions? If so, you may choose not to pay much attention to the material objects around you. Many Thing-management problems are simply a matter of attentional preference: Things don't excite your neurons the way people or ideas do, and you CHOOSE to put your attention elsewhere.

Not everyone, however, is able to choose. When you try to concentrate on Things, does your mind fly around all the more? Do you feel bombarded by sights and sounds, all of which seem to compete for your attention? Do you find it hard to stand still and look at a Thing, or do you wander aimlessly from room to room without noticing the Things around you? Do Things sometimes seem to whiz by? Do you rarely *feel* a Thing in your hand when you handle it? Do you buy Things without thinking, leave Things wherever you last used them, find lost Things in strange places, and feel hopeless when you think about decluttering? If so, *trouble tuning in to Things* constitutes one possible reason why your Things keep overwhelming you.

Attention glitches occur primarily in the brain's attention/executive system, the big boss of the brain, but glitches in the affective system—emotional disturbance, in other words—may also cause concentration problems. Attention is not a simple either/or phenomenon but a set of intricately interwoven patterns. You may be able to attend to some stimuli and not others, in some situations and not others. You may be internally or externally distractible or both. Your attention span may be short, medium, or long. You may be able to concentrate deeply on some tasks but find it difficult to shift your attention from one task to another. How your attention level affects what's going on with your Things depends on your specific set of attention patterns.

If you believe you have significant attention problems, you might want to consider getting evaluated for attention deficit disorder (see Appendix for help with referrals). You don't have to have full-blown ADD for wandering thoughts to be part of your problem with Things, however, if the wandering thoughts occur at the wrong times. Attention works differently for each person, and understanding the kinks and curlicues of yours can be liberating whether you have ADD or not.

SUBTROUBLE I. HUMMINGBIRD THOUGHTS (DISTRACTIBILITY)

Jody and Jerry Hummingbird are ten-year-old twin brothers who live with their parents. On Saturday morning, their father informs them that their job for the day is to clean up the back porch, where they keep many of their playthings. If they finish in time, he says, they can all go to the beach. Dad brings out some sorting boxes, and the boys set to work. "You do that side, and I'll do this side," says Jody.

"Sure," says Jerry, wheeling his wagon out onto the patio. Out in the yard he hears a chuckling sound and looks up to see a squirrel running along the back fence. "Hey, Mom," he shouts, "gimme some breadcrumbs. Harry's back!" A sudden high-pitched whining rips through the branches across the way and Jerry pricks up his ears. A buzz-saw, cutting down a tree! As Mrs. Hummingbird appears at the door with the crumbs, her son disappears around the corner of the house.

Meanwhile, Jody is sitting in a wicker armchair staring vacantly at the toys he's supposed to be sorting. Jody's in Switzerland, skiing down a mountainside, winning an Olympic medal. Then he's in Ms. Killjoy's class, getting back a history test with a big red A on it. Then he's in the sporting goods store with his parents, who are buying him a new basketball as a reward. He looks up and sees golden-haired Gloria coming down the aisle. . . .

When Mr. Hummingbird comes out to the porch a little while later, Jerry is nowhere to be seen, and Jody is still sitting motionless, surrounded by toys. Nothing has changed.

Neither Jody nor Jerry is able to pay enough attention to Things to be able to organize them. Both suffer from distractibility, but Jerry's is external and Jody's is internal. External and internal distractibility can cause all sorts of problems with Things. Externally distractible people like Jerry are aware of Things, but usually the wrong Things—those that capture attention and pull it off course. Internally distractible people are aware mostly of imaginary Things, the Things in their heads. While pursuing the Things in their heads, they're able to deal with external objects in automatic mode, but only if what they have to do is not too challenging. They get up in a dream, put their clothes on in a dream, make their beds in a dream, and eat breakfast in a dream. Later they discover that they're wearing socks that don't match and find their toothbrush on the closet shelf. Automatic mode has its limitations.

Suggestions for the distractible:

- Be aware that stimuli compete for your attention and use this to your advantage by using bright colors, flashing lights, loud noises, tactile sensations, and emotional intensity to capture your attention. Whatever it takes. Keep urgent items on your desk in a bright red folder. Put up emotionally charged signs: STOP! PUT ALL PAPERS HERE ON PERIL OF YOUR LIFE!!!

- When decluttering, if your distractibility is external, minimize distracting stimuli in the work area by closing your door, turning off the phone, putting attention-grabbing reading materials out of sight.

- When organizing papers, don't allow yourself to read anything you pick up once you've identified it.

- Try to determine when and under what circumstances you're most and least distractible, and make use of your findings. If you're most attentive in the evenings, for example, schedule decluttering times at the end of your day.

- Choose a small organizing task and challenge yourself to be totally present as you do it. Don't beat yourself up if you can't do this perfectly.

- In setting up an office, place your desk facing away from the door if you're externally distractible, though not necessarily if you're internally distractible, in which case you may actually get more done with noise around you to distract you from your thoughts.

- Don't allow others to lecture or belittle you about your distractibility.

- Don't lecture or belittle yourself when you realize you've been distracted AGAIN. YOU ARE NOT STUPID JUST BECAUSE YOU FIND IT HARD TO TUNE IN!

SUBTROUBLE 2. SNAPSHOT MIND (SHORT ATTENTION SPAN)

People who are distractible often have short attention spans. If you have a short attention span, your brain simply reaches a point where it can't go on focusing on the activity and seeks a new focus. For you, life is a series of snapshots.

The same person may have a short, medium, or long attention span for different activities. Jerry Hummingbird may have a long attention span for Nintendo, a medium attention span for arithmetic, and a short attention span for sorting toys. The same is true for Jerry's mother and father, either of whom may be able to zip through a thriller novel in one sitting but fall asleep after a couple of paragraphs in a textbook. What activities can you do for long periods of time without getting bored? What activities make you want to get up after a few minutes and run around the room? Do any of these involve acquiring, maintaining, or disposing of Things? What is your attention span for decluttering like? Try timing yourself as you work for a few days if you're not sure.

Big decluttering projects are more likely to succeed if you take your attention span for decluttering into account. If you find it impossible to keep decluttering for more than ten minutes at a time, does this mean you're doomed to living forever with whatever clutter you already have? Not at all. Instead of scheduling an hour-long decluttering session each day, which is often what organizing books recommend, try doing ten minutes of work six times a day—before and after every meal, every time the phone rings, or every time a clock chimes—and finish the job. Working with your brain chemistry instead of against it will make the process almost painless.

If, on the other hand, you can go on and on with decluttering, why limit yourself to the daily hour prescribed in the books, unless your time is limited? Not to make use of your brain's natural tendency to keep decluttering would be like taking the sail down on a boat when there's still plenty of wind, and paddling to shore instead. The brain power is there, so why not make use of it while it lasts?

In either case, the key is self-knowledge. Remember that though it may be more convenient to have a long attention span than a short one, time is time, however you chop it up. It's all about learning to make best use of whatever your brain does naturally, setting limits when you must and going with the flow whenever you can.

SUBTROUBLE 3. BRAIN SUCTION (OVERFOCUSING)

While some activities may lose your attention rapidly, others seem to suck on your brain. You have a feeling that if you suddenly stopped doing what you're doing, there would be a loud, smacking sound, like a plunger being pulled from a wall. Brain suction—also known as overfocusing or inability to shift attention—is a matter of degree: you may experience no suction at all while working on your taxes, a moderate amount while solving a crossword puzzle—you could stop, but with effort—and feel totally incapable of extricating yourself from a gripping video even if the house burns down around you. If you cannot keep yourself from persistently engaging in a high-suction activity despite extreme negative consequences, then you may have a compulsion and need to get help.

Sometimes brain suction happens not because an activity is pleasurable but because of compulsive perfectionism. Suppose you decide to spend Saturday morning decluttering the basement. In one corner are some bankers' boxes in which you have stored old records and receipts from past years' taxes. You haven't gone through them in a long time. You open the first box and see that some papers are over ten years old. Sitting down on an old chair, you begin to sort through the papers, then realize that if you continue, you may spend the whole morning on a single box and not get to the rest of the base-ment at all. You know you should do this part later and start going through the shelves, but you can't stop. The more you try to pull yourself out of your chair, the more you feel that you're glued to the seat, knowing that at the end of the morning you're going to feel like a wimp for not accomplishing what you set out to do. This is a com-mon experience. One reason you may put off big decluttering jobs is the fear that you'll get trapped by a part of the task, not accomplish the whole, and feel like a failure.

If you ever become trapped by brain suction, don't try to pull yourself free, which won't work. Brain suction is the result of an esca-lating conflict against yourself, and the more YOU pull, the more IT pulls. Instead, try the following:

- Continue doing what you're doing, but without the intensity. Focus on your breathing and follow it in and out until you feel relaxed.

- Calmly say to yourself, "This is just the suction feeling. It's just a feeling. I can manage it."

- Now imagine a giant magnet with a force that far outsucks the brain suction coming down, pulling you away from the activity, and dragging you over to whatever you need to do next. Or pretend you're caught in the strong current of a stream that pulls you from task to task.

- If this doesn't work and you remain trapped, when you're finally free—either when you become hungry or have to go to the bathroom—do NOT say, "I can't believe I just wasted the whole morning that way." Instead, take some deep breaths and say to yourself, "I did a great job on that one part, and next time I'll use my brain suction strategies and then I'll do better." Visualize yourself flowing smoothly through the rest of the job while breathing slowly and deeply.

Brain suction can sometimes build up with momentum. The more you do something, the more you feel that you can't stop doing it. This can be both a plus and a minus for decluttering. If you're like this, it will NOT work to try to do an hour a day the way the books say you should. An hour for you will turn into a whole day. If you don't have a whole day, you risk being late for work or leaving your children stranded somewhere when you can't stop decluttering. If you DO have a whole day, however, or better yet, three or four days, you'll get the whole job done—and more. You may even wind up in the *Guinness Book of World Records* for performing the world's longest decluttering feat!

II. TROUBLE SEEING THINGS

"If it was a snake, it would have bitten you." Do you often hear these words? Do you frequently find an object right under your nose after spending half an hour looking for it? When you get home from shopping, do you discover problems with your purchases that you missed in the store? When sorting Things, do you sit staring at something for a long time before you suddenly realize what it is that you're looking at? When you've finished "cleaning up" a room, do neatfreaks annoy you by pointing out places that you missed? Do you feel that you have to have all of your Things in plain sight or you'll forget where they are? Are your shins covered with bruises? Are you great at music or sports but poor at drawing or sewing? Is your handwriting famous with your co-workers for being illegible? Does your writing climb uphill as you write or wander all over the page? If so, *trouble seeing Things* may be one of your problems.

"Seeing things," as used here, is not about your eyes taking in images. It's about how your brain makes sense out of what you see, both outside and inside your head. This kind of seeing is an INTERACTIVE process, in which your brain relates what your eyes take in to pictures and sounds on the inside in order to make sense out of your world. Seeing, in other words, is about understanding. For those with certain glitches in the visual-spatial and memory systems visual understanding happens more slowly, with greater difficulty, and less fully than for others.

SUBTROUBLE 4. SEEING WITHOUT SEEING
(VISUAL PROCESSING PROBLEMS)

"I'm done!" announces Melinda Snakebitten, slamming the file drawer shut despite the loose papers sticking out around the edges.

"Are you sure?" asks Judy Stackwright. "Look around you." Melinda looks down and sees papers strewn across the floor that she hadn't noticed before.

"Whoops, well," says Melinda, shamefacedly gathering up the papers, "guess I missed a few."

Melinda has visual processing problems. Her brain is supposed to go "aha!" every time her eyes encounter papers lying on the floor or sticking out of folders, but it doesn't. People like Melinda often get labeled as careless or heedless when in reality they're not: they just have trouble making sense out of what they see. When someone draws their attention to what they fail to notice, they may feel ashamed, and they have nightmares about being hooted at when everyone else sees that they forgot to put their pants on before going out onstage.

Learning specialists talk about visual, auditory, and kinesthetic learners, whose brains are wired to experience the world through different channels: visual people learn best through seeing, auditory through hearing, and kinesthetic through physically doing. People who are mostly auditory or kinesthetic in their orientation may not process visually very well. They are the musical geniuses who wear socks that don't match or the talented athletes with reading problems.

But visual processing is not just realizing that an object is physically there. It is also a matter of HOW you become aware of it. You may do this quickly or slowly, in full detail, or as a mere outline. How fast you process visually is critical in managing Things. If this happens slowly—as is the case in dyslexic brains, according to John Ratey—you will shop, use, organize, and do everything with Things slowly. It takes a long time to reorganize your books, for example, when you have to stand staring at each individual volume for five minutes before your brain finally tells you what you're looking at.

If your brain doesn't take in a lot of visual details, this is also limiting. Some people experience the visual world as cartoons: outline drawings with nothing filled in, while others see only the details and miss the big picture. Most of us do something in between. When it comes to Things, detail people are at an advantage over outline people, who may fail to notice that the pants they're buying have no hems or that one tax form says W-2 and another says W-4. Suggestions for those with visual processing problems:

- In considering what needs to be put away, scan the floor of the room and every surface systematically, from left to right and from front to back, as if you're reading a page. Use

Sandra Felton's "Mount Vernon Method" (as described to her by the cleaning staff at Mt. Vernon) of going linearly around each wall when decluttering.

- Invite others into your space regularly. When you know someone's coming, you'll be more likely to notice problems you overlooked before.

- Hang up mirrors on one wall of a room: this will double the chance of your seeing something out of place.

- Take pictures of your space, preferably with a Polaroid camera. Looking through a camera viewer forces you to see, and you may observe Things in photos that you don't otherwise notice.

- Where details are subtle, make them less so. Instead of writing little reminder notes for yourself, print a note in big block letters on a full-sized sheet of paper with magic marker. Use bright colors, etc.

- Ask a trusted friend to inspect the premises and point out problems—or hire an organizer. MAKING USE OF SOMEONE ELSE'S EYES DOES NOT MAKE YOU STUPID OR LAZY.

- If you process visual information slowly, set goals that take this into account. Speed in our world is grossly overrated. Most tasks will be done better when done slowly. Let quality, not quantity, of production be your trademark.

- Practice drawing or descriptive writing to train your awareness of visual details.

- Habitually take a second look at papers when you sort them. Ask someone else to presort for you, grouping like with like. Read what's written on papers aloud to yourself or ask someone else to do so.

- Don't overcompensate for your visual processing problems by scrubbing and rescrubbing the floor before your mother-in-law comes to visit, for fear she may notice a place that you missed and draw your attention to it. You won't die if she does. Life is too short to waste worrying about what oversights fastidious people may point out to you.

- Consider arranging for an evaluation by a neuropsychologist to determine the extent of visual processing glitches.

- For a complete program in training visual processing skills, read *Open Your Eyes* by Alexandra Stoddard.

SUBTROUBLE 5. FIGURE AND GROUND CONFUSION (SELECTIVE ATTENTION PROBLEMS)

In almost any Psych 101 textbook, there's a picture that can be looked at two different ways. From one mind-set, it looks like a vase, and from another, like two opposing faces. (Another version shows an old woman—or a young one.) To switch from one view to the other, you don't need to turn the picture around or do anything with your eyes—only with your brain, which constantly makes decisions about what you will and won't consciously see. You can flip from one to the other by doing something purely in your brain.

What you see depends on what you're looking for. Children's activity books often contain pictures in which certain objects are hidden among the details, and the child is asked to circle the ones he or she can see. To find a banana in the picture, Betty Brighteyes must have either a clear image of a banana or a list of banana criteria in her head. Betty's eyes scan the picture while her mind flips through images and criteria and compares them with what she sees until Presto! A match! This is called selective attention, and it plays a key role where sorting, organizing, and getting rid of Things is concerned.

Suppose Betty's older sister, Barbie, is looking at her sweaters, knowing she needs to get rid of some of them. If Barbie's brain is not selectively attentive, all of her sweaters will look exactly the same to her, and what she'll see is merely an amorphous mass of colors. Although she may wear one sweater every day and not have worn others for months, in her mind one sweater is just as good as another: nothing leaps out at her. This makes it difficult for Barbie to decide what to keep and what to give away, which may cause her to throw up her hands and turn on the TV.

If a pile of Things seems totally amorphous to you, try the following:

- Review the lists in the introduction to Chapter 5 to clarify your criteria for keeping Things versus giving them away.

- Use sticky notes to put "grades" on the possessions you're evaluating, A through F, according to how much they mean to you, and get rid of everything that ranks below a certain grade.

- Decide how many of these Things you can keep. Think of someone that you see as epitomizing normality, your doctor, perhaps, or your best friend's husband, or the president of the PTO. How many of these Things would he or she have?

- Suppose you've decided to keep eight of these Things. Imagine your home is a store and you're shopping. Choose eight to "buy" and get rid of the rest.

- Suppose you have to leave on a flight for Australia in two hours and need to make hasty decisions. Things will leap out at you.

- Focus on two Things and compare them. Which one makes you feel the best to look at? Which fits your criteria the best? Then compare a third Thing with the other two. Repeat until you've ranked all the Things in order of preference, keep the top eight Things and let the others go.

- If you still have difficulty, ask a friend to help you go through your Things and discuss them with you as you go. If this leads to endless, time-consuming debates, give the friend permission to choose for you. After he or she finishes, you're allowed to change two choices, but no more. THERE IS NO SHAME IN ALLOWING SOMEONE ELSE TO SUBSTITUTE FOR A PART OF YOUR BRAIN THAT DOESN'T WORK, AND THIS DOES NOT MAKE YOU ANY LESS OF AN ADULT.

SUBTROUBLE 6. OUT OF SIGHT, OUT OF MIND
(VISUAL MEMORY PROBLEMS)

Seeing Things out in the world is one thing; seeing Things in your head is another. Visual Memory is only one type of memory, and for some people it plays a bigger role than for others. It's the type that enables most people to keep track of Things, though kinesthetic memory also plays a role.

Remembering where Things are uses different parts of the brain from those used for recognition. To remember where your tennis racket is means that on your mental map you can see it in the back of your closet behind your boots—in other words, in a particular place surrounded by particular other Things. For some people, this doesn't happen.

Neuroscientists believe that the memory system stores practical, "nonfiction" memories and emotional, "romance-novel" memories in totally different areas of the brain. This is why people who have had a stroke can sometimes remember swear words and other emotional language but nothing else. If the visual part of your memory system is less than optimal, it can be helpful to keep this in mind and use reminders that appeal to the emotional rather than the practical memory areas.

People with visual memory glitches often try to compensate by keeping as many Things as possible in full view. If you look in their closets, drawers, or filing cabinets, they'll be three-quarters empty.

But keeping belongings visible by leaving them out works only if you have a great deal of space and very few Things. Usually this approach results in the vast majority of your possessions being buried under Thing mountains where they're just as invisible as they would be inside containers. Other strategies for dealing with visual memory problems may be more effective, however:

- Whenever possible, use containers that allow maximum visibility: remove doors from cupboards, use milk crates instead of filing cabinets, put action items in desktop cubbies or vertical sorters, hang clothes on hooks or stack them neatly on open shelves, and use clear plastic boxes or Baggies for all kinds of Things.

- When you *do* have to put Things in containers, use color coding, labels, indexes, notebooks, databases, pictures, and signs to tell you where they are. Take Polaroids of the shoes in each shoe box and tape the photo to the box, for example.

- Use labels and pictures that appeal to emotional memory as well as your practical memory. Instead of writing "Letters" on a folder, write "Letters that are driving me nuts." Instead of "Reports," write "Dynamite reports!"

- If you can't visualize where something is, use logic instead— "Where would someone be likely to keep an electric fan?" Go look there.

- Whenever you obtain a new Thing, make a home for it, label the home, and consciously "photograph" it with your mind, the way you might focus on where you parked your car before you walk away from it. Many "memory" problems are really attention problems.

- Have a home for each type of Thing in your house—a tape

home, a thread home, an extension cord home—and be consistent for years and years about keeping Things in the same homes.

- If you choose to leave something out as a visual cue of a task that needs to be done, do so in an orderly way.

- Avoid the temptation to keep designing one new system after another, and don't buy in to other people's claims that you can be rescued by their wonderful new system. What you need is memory aids, not a change of system.

- Don't think of yourself as having a bad memory but simply an overloaded memory. Computers have different-sized memories—why shouldn't people?

III. TROUBLE THINKING ABOUT THINGS

Once your brain has made sense out of what you see, what happens then? Are you able to make plans and decisions about what to do with Things, or does the process break down? When you look at a cluttered room, rather than making a reasonable plan for cleaning it up does your mind simply boggle, causing you to flee from the scene? Do you have trouble deciding how to categorize Things? When you're acquiring, organizing, or trying to get rid of Things, do you ever feel paralyzed? Do you try on one shirt after another when you shop, oblivious to your companion's foot-tapping, and end up either buying none of them or buying them all? Do you sit for half an hour with a piece of paper in midair while you try to decide where to file it? Do you spend weeks debating with yourself about whether to give your old lamp to the Salvation Army or keep it in the basement? Or do you buy or accept Things impulsively, start and stop organizing impulsively, get rid of Things impulsively, never making a decision at all but instead bypassing decision making with knee-jerk reactions to whatever is in view? If so, you have *trouble thinking about Things.*

Although there are lots of ways of thinking about Things, of course, *thinking* here means figuring out what you're going to do with Things. Trouble thinking about things relates to glitches "higher up" in the brain, where more complex thinking takes place, especially in the attention/executive system. When such glitches occur, some people simply become paralyzed by indecision, failing to act at all. Others react impulsively, bypassing the decision-making process altogether and doing whatever the lower, more automatic, brain centers tell them to.

Attention/executive glitches are not the only cause of high-level thinking problems, however. It's difficult to make any kind of intelligent decision if your brain and body are flooded with emotions or paralyzed by anxiety because glitches in your affective system prevent it from regulating excess feelings. When emotions overwhelm you, you may either become paralyzed or react impulsively. But, as neurologist Antonio Damasio points out in *Descartes' Error*, it's also impossible to think rationally if you don't feel at all: feelings are a necessary part of good decision making, and as many problems with Things stem from discounting our feelings as from allowing them to control us.

Whether trouble thinking about things is due to attention/executive or affective glitches or both, the insight system may come to your rescue. The insight system allows you to recognize and alter thinking patterns and come up with ideas about how to circumvent problems that result from attention/executive glitches.

SUBTROUBLE 7. PICASSO PLANNING
(SEQUENCING PROBLEMS)

As you move through a grocery store, going up and down the aisles, groceries present themselves to you in roughly linear fashion: first the breads, then the condiments, then the canned fruits, and so forth, one after another. On the conveyer belt at the checkout counter, the items also advance linearly, this time toward the cashier, who picks up one item at a time to ring it up and bag it. For Things to present themselves to you linearly, either you have to be moving, or they do.

In your own home or workplace, you rarely encounter Things linearly, but rather spatially and simultaneously. In a cluttered room, Things do not line up like schoolchildren for you to put them away one by one: it's up to you to decide which objects to handle first, second, and third. To declutter, you must mentally convert the simultaneous to the sequential, using your memory to envision the future: you must SEQUENCE.

The problem is, some people—as Lehmkuhl and Lamping point out, often unusually creative people such as Pablo Picasso, whose paintings demonstrate nonlinearity in viewing the same object from many angles at once—find sequencing more challenging than simultaneity. This has to do with the left and right hemispheres of the brain.

If your brain has trouble with sequencing, you may feel overwhelmed when you behold a cluttered room. Rather than focusing on one problem after another as your eyes move around the room, your brain tries to process everything at once. In considering where to put your skis, who would want the old ballet costumes, whether or not to build more shelves for your books, how many unused hangers to keep, which corner to move your dresser into, whether your old *Life* magazines might be valuable, and how to reorganize your files all at the same instant, the system crashes, panic ensues, and you may flee from the scene.

If this sounds familiar, there are two approaches you can take to working with Things. The first is to make a conscious effort to sequence:

- When you look at a cluttered room, move your eyes systematically around it, taking in one area at a time. Try to break down what you see into parts, don't just look at the whole.

- Tour the space you'll be decluttering and make a list of the jobs this will involve: clean out desk, get rid of old clothes, reorganize files, and so forth.

- As you work, pick up only one Thing at a time and put it away SOMEWHERE—if only in an "Undecided" box—before you pick up the next Thing.

- Ask someone to work with you and hand you one Thing at a time.

- Mentally say the name of each object as you put it away, the way a surgeon says the name of each tool when requesting it from the assisting nurse during surgery.

- Slow down, slow down, slow down. The slower you go, the better the chance you'll be able to sequence your activities.

The other approach is to forget about sequencing and instead use holistic, metaphoric strategies that may get the job done, though unconventionally. In *Conquering Chronic Disorganization,* Judith Kolberg suggests a number of possible fantasy metaphors on which you can base your organizing efforts: a war room, a human body, scenes from a play, a space ship, an assembly line, mission control, a sporting event, a board game, a dinner party, a road map. Choose a metaphor that fits your unique interests. For some people, turning the job over to a metaphor can energize the process so that organizing happens almost effortlessly.

SUBTROUBLE 8. APPLE/ORANGE CONFUSION
(PROBLEMS SORTING AND CATEGORIZING)

"Where should I put this?" Miranda Grayshade asks Judy Stackwright, who's helping her to organize her papers. "Should it go under 'Marketing' or under 'Development?' I mean it's really both, and I can also imagine putting it under 'Administration.' What I'd really like to do is throw it in the trash, but I might get in trouble if I do that. If I have to file it, I'd rather it go under *B* for 'blue' because it's on blue paper. Isn't that crazy?"

Miranda sighs and glances out the window. "This is why I always put off organizing," she says sadly. "I'm always so afraid I'll put something in the wrong place, and when I do try to sort things I get stuck on the first paper that isn't obvious and give up. So tell me, where should I put this memo?"

"Put it where you're most likely to find it," says Judy. "I can't tell you where that is because I'm not you. If *B* for 'blue' works for you, there's nothing wrong with that."

Miranda has trouble sorting and categorizing. Her brain, like many others, does not allow her to think categorically. Kolberg points out that some people's minds string out thoughts in chains, tangentially: "This letter is about administering tests, which reminds me of exams, which reminds me of X-rays, which reminds me of cancer, so I'll file it under *C* for cancer.'" Other minds build thoughts into hierarchies, grouping Things and groups of Things like pyramids of gymnasts standing on each other's shoulders: "This letter is about administering tests, which goes with teaching classes, which ALL goes under Education, so I'll file it under *E* for 'education.'" As you think about filing papers, notice which way your mind is working. If your mind tends to work tangentially, your best bet may be simply to forget about categories and file your papers alphabetically according to what each paper is, i.e., filing the letter on administering tests under *A* for "administering tests."

Or you may want to use unconventional categories. People with categorizing problems often believe that there's only one right way to set up categories, which has existed since time immemorial, if only they knew what it was. This is not the case. Every brain has its own unique way of making sense of what the eyes take in. While some methods of categorizing are more common than others, nothing is set in stone. Just because categories are unconventional does not make them wrong. If Miranda needs to file the memo under *B* for blue, why not?

Fear of putting something in the "wrong" category can keep some people paralyzed for hours. Behind this fear lies the fear of making a mistake. People whose brains work in unconventional ways often grow up hearing their alternative thinking styles discounted on all sides: "What do you want to put that THERE for?" "Those don't go together! Are you crazy?" "You're going to wear that with THAT?" They learn to mistrust their own unique style of making sense out of the world. This works against them when they try to categorize Things so THEY can find them easily.

If you have problems categorizing and sorting,

- Try to identify the PRINCIPLES by which your mind naturally groups Things: alphabetically, numerically, chronologically, by size, color, age, ingredients, other criteria?

- Keep categories as simple as possible. Whenever possible, keep only one type of Thing in one container. Use color to emphasize category differences.

- If your brain works associatively, consider NOT categorizing papers conventionally but instead filing them numerically or alphabetically.

- Make indexes—lists of categories—especially when dealing with papers. Put indexes in filing cabinets and keep a master list in your desk drawer.

- When sorting, always put an item in the first category that occurs to you. Chances are, that's the first category you'll think of when you try to find it.

- If you prefer to use conventional categories for filing personal business records, you can buy prelabeled folders arranged in a system of conventional categories. If you do this, spend time studying the system as you file, and review it often.

- If none of this works, and you're unable to sort and categorize at all, get help from a friend, secretary, or professional organizer.

SUBTROUBLE 9. SCYLLA AND CHARYBDIS (DECISION-MAKING PROBLEMS)

In Homer's *Odyssey*, Odysseus, on his way home from Troy, was forced into a no-win situation. In order to get home, he and his men had to pass through a narrow strait, on either side of which was an equally horrific danger. On one side was Scylla, a snaky monster with multiple heads that had a nasty habit of snatching men from ships and decapitating them. Charybdis, on the other side, was an immense whirlpool down which countless ships had been engulfed. Many people suffer parallel quandaries in selecting, organizing, and disposing of Things. The pressure can be particularly intense when considering throwing something out: you may fear, on the one hand, that if you get rid of a Thing someone will snatch your head off for this mistake but, on the hand, if you keep it you will only be adding to the whirlpool of other Things in which you feel yourself to be drowning.

Decision making involves not only the attention/executive system but also the affective system. It's both cognitive and emotional and, as Damasio points out, feeling and reasoning are interrelated. When emotions run high, it's hard to make sound decisions, but when feelings are too flat or you're out of touch with them, you lack the impetus to decide anything. Even when your affective system is in good working order, however, you may find decision making difficult just because your brain finds it difficult to go through the intricate sequence of operations involved in making decisions.

Next time you're holding an object in midair, unable to decide about it, try this:

- Trust your gut. Ask yourself what you feel deep down and go by this.

- Pray, meditate, or otherwise open yourself to the "still, small voice" and then listen for an answer.

- Pretend you're someone else, your favorite totally decisive hero. What would Captain Kirk have done?

- Reframe a no-win decision as a win-win decision by imagining positive consequences for either alternative: either I have the memo available when I want to refer to it or I get rid of excess paper. Either way I win!

- Assess your mood. Depression interferes with clear decisions. If you're depressed, stop work and do something to counter the depression. (Seek help if necessary.)

- Leave it up to chance—toss a coin.

- Don't decide—put the object in an "Undecided" box with a date on it, to be disposed of if the contents are unused by that date.

- Set a timer for one minute. If you're undecided at the end of the minute, get rid of the Thing. Many people waste hours on fruitless debates with themselves. The word *decide* comes from the Latin, meaning "to cut off." Cut the quibbling!

- When in doubt, chuck it out.

- Remember that any time you choose one option you don't choose another. That is the nature of life.

The only problem now is, how are you going to decide which of these techniques to use? That's easy. Close your eyes, stretch out your hand, and point. You got it.

SUBTROUBLE 10. STOP, LOOK, AND LISTEN PROBLEMS (IMPULSIVITY)

When you go to cross a street, you habitually stop, look each way, and consider your options, if only for a split second. As a child, you were trained to do this as a matter of survival: nature has a way of selecting out those who cross streets without thinking first. Stepping up to the curb is not the only situation, however, that may require you to stop, look, and listen before moving forward.

While some people become paralyzed by indecision, others don't make decisions at all, they simply act. How they act is determined not by conscious forethought but rather by knee-jerk reaction to whatever happens. With each person, the interweaving of thought and action forms a different pattern, depending on the brain's attention/executive system, visual-spatial system, and motor system, and how effectively they've been trained.

Some people keep their eyes perpetually on the road ahead, never doing anything unpremeditated: Pick up spoon? No reason not to. Put spoon in soup? All clear. Soup too hot? Negative. Take a sip? Roger. Take another? Stop! Save room for the entrée. Righto. People who live this way are often big successes but may be less interesting than those who are constantly diving headfirst into swimming pools with no water in them and have lots of colorful stories to tell. Most of us exist somewhere between these two extremes, behaving impulsively in this situation but not in that one. A lot of power lies in identifying your own unique set of impulse triggers—situations in which you often act without thinking and later regret your behavior—and figuring out how to deal with them.

People may act impulsively with Things in a host of different ways. Without thinking at all, you may buy, accept, steal, rearrange, throw, smash, trash, or give away something and, as soon as you have done so, want to hit yourself on the head. The only effective route to better impulse control, however, is patient, nonpunitive, persistent retraining:

- Make a list of your Thing impulse triggers. What do you feel when you give in to one of them? Some of these impulses may be the result of underlying emotional conflicts. OTHERS ARE SIMPLY THE RESULT OF BRAIN WIRING.

- Instead of beating yourself up after giving in, do an instant replay in your head of what just happened. Mentally slow down the action. Now replay it again, changing your action to a nonimpulsive one. If you can physically walk through the behavior again, do so, altering your action.

- Several times a day, sit down and plan your actions for the next few hours. Ask yourself what impulse triggers may lie in your path and visualize yourself walking by them, nodding and smiling and saying "No, thank you."

- Each time you resist an impulse with Things, reward yourself in some small way, if only with words of praise.

Retraining does not always work. Some brains, especially those of people with ADD, may lack the wiring needed to retrain Thing impulses, although the right medication can help this a lot. This is where damage control comes in—dealing effectively with the consequences of having given in to an impulse. If you impulsively buy too many clothes, you can still take the clothes back. If you impulsively go off task when decluttering, you can go back on.

Those who prove hopelessly untrainable may find Odysseus' siren strategy useful. In Homer's epic, Odysseus and his men had to sail past the island of the sirens, whose music was so seductive that it made men go crazy, jump overboard, and drown. Knowing this in advance, Odysseus filled his men's ears with wax, then tied himself to the ship's mast. Prior to filling the men's ears, Odysseus had told the men not to unbind him until they were well away from the island, no matter what he said or did. As the ship sailed past the island, Odysseus began to make desperate gestures to be released, but his men ignored him and the ship passed out of the danger zone without losing anyone.

If you've learned that you're unable to control a certain Thing impulse in the presence of certain triggers, you can build in safeguards to protect yourself from the songs of the Thing sirens. Rules, setting up your environment so as to minimize temptations, and/or prearranged help from others may protect you from yourself at your weakest moments: Whenever you go to the bookstore, you have to leave the credit card at home. Whenever you start to throw a newspaper on the floor, your spouse has your permission to hand it to you and ask you to put it away.

Above all, don't give up. Impulse control can take a long time to develop, and it will take longer if you beat yourself up each time you give in to a Thing impulse AGAIN. When you feel like doing so, your best strategy is to look yourself and anyone booing you squarely in the eye and calmly repeat the sentence "We all make mistakes" until the boos are discontinued. Repeat as needed.

SUBTROUBLE 11. SHORT FUSES (EMOTIONAL REACTIVITY)

Some people are a lot like Gryzypians. For these people, dealing with Things is an emotionally neutral experience, simply a problem to be solved. These are long-fuse people (LFs), at least where Things are concerned. For others, Things can feel like land mines: these people walk among their belongings on tiptoe, fearing that at any moment they may encounter the Thing or the problem with Things that will trigger explosive anger, intense grief, unbearable anxiety, or endless repetitive thoughts. Such short-fuse people (SFs) are at the mercy of their emotions, wired to go off at the drop of a hat, literally.

Some researchers believe that LF and SF brains do things in a different order. When an LF comes in and sees the hat that her child carelessly dropped onto her favorite chair for the twenty-seventh time, the visual-spatial system sends a message to the attention/executive system, which says, "There's a hat on my chair for the twenty-seventh time. What can I do about this? Maybe I should think about putting a sign on the chair for a while to remind Junior to put his hat on the shelf." Finally, after all this, a message is sent down to the affective system: "Problem addressed—no need to react."

When an SF, on the other hand, comes in and sees the very same sight, the impulse from the visual-spatial system bypasses the attention/executive system and goes straight to the areas in the affective system where experiences are labeled as dangerous and terrible. THERE'S A HAT ON MY CHAIR FOR THE TWENTY-SEVENTH TIME. I'M GOING TO KILL JUNIOR!!!!! From there, messages will be sent to the emergency system, which starts the heart racing, the blood pressure rising, and the lungs pumping air, and turns on the propaganda machine, the twenty-four-hour loudspeaker system that plays the same negative thoughts over and over, sometimes for hours. Then, and only then, the message will finally get up to the attention/executive system, which sends down a message: "False alarm. Not a big deal. Stop the music." Once the propaganda machine has been turned on, however, it cannot be shut down so easily. Instead, it goes on grinding out thoughts: "Junior NEVER hangs up his clothes. Junior is ALWAYS going to be a slob. Junior will never be able to hold a job and will wind up in the gutter. I can't stand this. I'm going to go crazy. I hate being a parent. I should never have had Junior. I knew I would regret it." Such sudden, overwhelming, out-of-the-blue reactions are sometimes referred to as *flooding*.

Flooding was what happened to Professor Tightstring, whose short fuse caused him to vent his fury on his own office. Rage is not the only intense feeling that Things may trigger, however: anxiety, sadness, or even extreme happiness may also subvert your thinking processes so that you begin to think "crazy" thoughts over which you have no control, and sometimes even act them out. These thoughts may repeat themselves for days, even months, while painful past memories may well up out of nowhere to add to your misery.

SFs, whose brains flood easily, may feel vulnerable and thus try to avoid any possible stimulus that may trigger a deluge. They may put off sorting through Things for weeks out of fear that among them will be that Thing which will send them over the edge. Even people who don't experience a lot of full-scale flooding may put off dealing with certain emotionally charged Things in order to conserve energy. The problem is, the Things don't go away, and sooner or later you have to deal with them, flooding or no flooding.

If you have a short fuse,

- Get to know which Things trigger unpleasant feelings for you and, if possible, GET RID OF THEM. You don't deserve to feel bad.

- Get to know what situations with Things may cause you to overreact. Does being unable to find something, breaking something, or making some other Thing mistake often lead to your going ballistic? If so, ask yourself if you've internalized the reactions of someone else in your past. If so, pretend the person is there and tell the person that you and he or she are two different people. Visualize yourself dealing calmly and effectively with your trigger situation.

- Whenever you begin to experience negative feelings in response to a Thing or problems with Things, tell yourself, "I still have a choice. I can flood or not flood. I'm going to keep this in perspective. Things aren't worth flooding over."

- If flooding comes on too suddenly for you to do this, tell yourself, "I'm not crazy—this is just the flooding feeling." DON'T DO ANYTHING. Instead, make use of your Gryzypian to observe and name your feelings.

- If this doesn't stop the flooding, stop trying to control it and go WITH the flooding in safe ways: write down all the craziest thoughts you can, close all the windows and yell, pound a pillow, or cry. DO NOT DESTROY YOUR THINGS. This will only lead to shame afterward (and property damage as well).

- Don't avoid decluttering because of possible flooding. Deal with flooding as it happens and then go on with your work.

Flooding doesn't feel good, but if you allow it to happen and deal with it, over time it may happen less, and you'll be free to deal with the Things—and the people—in your life without interference. In the meantime, rejoice in your ability to feel your feelings: some people can't feel anything at all and are terrible bores. Remember that if you can feel intense feelings of any sort, you have the capacity for joy.

IV. TROUBLE MOVING THINGS

Once you've figured out what you want to do with your Things, do you have trouble doing it? Are you unable to move a Thing from point A to point B? What prevents you? Do you sit in your chair, staring at your unwashed dishes, but find that you can't get up and walk across the room? Do you throw Things down "temporarily" and somehow never get around to putting them away? Or are you a whirling dervish, whose decluttering efforts are constantly undermined by a Thing-scattering high activity level? Are you able to start an organizing or decluttering job but not to keep going? Do you peter out after a short time or get sidetracked into another project? Is there something about finishing a project that is inimical to your personality? Or do you have all the energy you need for managing Things but simply lack the physical coordination to make them do what you want? All of these problems add up to *trouble moving Things*.

Trouble moving Things involves glitches in the attention/executive system, the affective system, and the motor system. The attention/executive system regulates activity level, which has a great deal to do with how effective you are in moving belongings where you want them to go, and enables you to stay focused as you work. The affective system regulates energy, which you need to get out of the chair. The motor system regulates muscle movements, without which no Thing can be transported anywhere.

SUBTROUBLE 12. SLOW, MEDIUM, OR FAST (ACTIVITY-LEVEL PROBLEMS)

Freddy Whizbang races down the avenue at top speed in his red convertible. Turning a corner on two wheels, he pulls up suddenly in front of an apartment building, tires squealing. Freddy jumps out of the car, rushes up to the door of his student apartment, flings it open, and shouts, "I'm home!" His roommate, Randy Stonebottom, quietly studying at his desk, inwardly groans. Freddy charges over to the refrigerator and stands in front of it tapping his foot and slapping his knees as he pauses for an instant to consider what he'll have for a snack.

Thinking about it is too much trouble. Freddy is a man of action. He grabs a Coke from the front of the refrigerator and zooms over to the TV, picks up the remote, switches through thirty channels, one after the other, throws down the remote, spills his Coke, walks across the room, shuffles through some magazines and leaves them scattered on the table, opens a book, leaves it splatted out on the desk, goes back to the kitchen and grabs a bag of chips, pours the chips into a bowl, scattering crumbs on the counter, walks to the stereo, sorts through a pile of CDs, pulls one out and puts it into the CD player, dropping the rest to the floor, then turns up the stereo full blast and begins to dance. When Randy comes out to make dinner, he complains about Freddy "trashing the place" and Freddy obligingly stops dancing and starts cleaning up at top speed, breaking a bowl and knocking over a lamp in the process.

Randy stands watching Freddy for a moment, sighs, and goes into the kitchen. Rejecting the idea of cooking himself a hamburger as too much trouble, Randy instead puts a couple of pot pies in the oven and sits down in front of the TV. Soon he's dozing. After dinner, Randy goes back in his room and sits in a chair with a book. Occasionally he looks up and glances idly around the room.

At the foot of Randy's bed is a pile of suitcases that he was going to take down to the storage cage after he moved in. That was in September, but soon he'll be using them for the Thanksgiving holidays, he considers, so he might as well leave them where they are. The wastebasket next to Randy's desk is overflowing with papers. When it gets bad enough, he'll empty the trash, but it's still not quite bad enough to be worth walking to the kitchen, getting a garbage bag, filling the bag, and taking it out to the Dumpster. Randy would rather read.

Some attention/executive systems fail to inhibit people from moving more and faster than others. People who, like Freddy, have a high activity level find it hard to sit still. Sitting in a lecture makes them feel as if they're covered with ants. As children, these people may have been hyperactive Dennis the Menaces. As adults, they usually settle down some, but they may still be more active than most people, which can cause them big problems with Things. It's hard to be careful with Things when you're zipping from one activity to another. You're not likely to take time to put Things away, and you leave a trail of Things behind you wherever you go.

Other attention/executive systems, like Randy's, seem to have the opposite effect, holding their owners imprisoned in a morass of perpetual sluggishness. Without being depressed or suffering from any kind of medical condition, people with a low activity level naturally find it easy to be couch potatoes. They never stand when they can sit and never sit when they can lie down. Their life's ambition is to conserve their energy. These folks don't get many Things out, but the Things they do get out stay out. Over time, they create Thing Mountains.

Both Freddy and Randy have problems with messiness because they're unaware of how their activity level affects them. In order to prevent an unusually high or low activity level from affecting your behavior with Things, you simply need to become more consciously—and more constantly—aware of it. This is called "self-monitoring."

There are various ways to self-monitor:

- Set an alarm to go off at regular intervals. Each time it goes off, ask yourself how your pace is affecting you. If you have a high activity level, do you need to slow down and put some Things away? If you have a low one, do you need to keep moving and declutter?

- Ask a close, nonjudgmental friend to help monitor your activity level. Instruct the friend to limit reminders to two words such as "Slow down" or "Keep moving" and let it go at that.

- Get someone to videotape you. Play the tape back, pause it periodically, and rate your activity level from 1 to 5.

- Put up extra mirrors to increase your awareness of how fast you're going.

- Choose an activity such as a game and practice performing it at high speed and in slow motion.

SUBTROUBLE 13. PERMANENT TEMPORARINESS (PROCRASTINATION)

Johnny Temporary has just moved into a new apartment, a temporary sublease, of course. The first night he comes home from work Johnny hangs his coat temporarily over a chair, throws his mail temporarily on the dining room table, and sets his briefcase down temporarily by the door. Then he goes into the kitchen, pours himself a drink, and sits down in his favorite armchair to read the paper. When he gets up to make dinner, he sets the empty glass temporarily on the table next to it and leaves the newspaper sections temporarily spread all over the floor. After dinner he leaves his dishes temporarily in the sink, then takes some papers out of his briefcase to work on and leaves them temporarily spread across the desk. Then he undresses, leaving his clothes temporarily in a pile, and climbs into bed.

The next morning Johnny gets up and leaves everything from the night before temporarily where it was when he went to sleep. That night when he comes in he hangs another coat temporarily over the one on the chair, throws another pile of mail temporarily on the table, and sets a couple of bags of Things from the hardware store temporarily by the door. By the end of the week, Johnny is surrounded by Thing mountains in a dozen different places. In a few weeks, Johnny is complaining to his friends about being overwhelmed by mean, nasty Things, which insist on piling up in his new apartment "no matter what I do."

Johnny is a procrastinator. He continually procrastinates in minute ways of which he's barely aware and then feels victimized by the collective consequences of his inactions. It's hard for him to believe that he actually caused the mess in his apartment because he created it so gradually. Due to attention/executive system glitches, Johnny lives in a perpetual present. The future does not exist for him, and consequently he has trouble believing that what he does or doesn't do NOW may have consequences LATER. Also, due to affective system glitches, he may lack the energy he needs to keep moving until the Thing he just used is back where it belongs.

If Johnny's behavior sounds a little too familiar to you, try the following:

- Rearrange your Things' homes so as many as possible are stored where you actually use them.

- Establish way-station containers for Things waiting to be transported up- or downstairs or out to your car. Instead of leaving objects out, put them in the way station, and empty it at least once a day.

- For one hour, challenge yourself to put away as many Things as possible immediately after you use them. Try to break your record. Play this game at least once a day for two weeks.

- Put up signs that say Do It Now. You don't always have to follow them, and sometimes you shouldn't—a healthy lifestyle maintains a balance between enjoying the present and preparing for the future—but with the signs up, you'll find yourself "doing it now" more often. Train the people you live with to say "Do It Now"—but that's all—when they see you put something down temporarily.

- If you do set something down temporarily, mentally set a time when you'll put it away. When the time comes, DO IT.

- Establish a regular cleanup time to put away all the Things you "temporarily" left somewhere.

- Allow yourself to do small tasks even if they're small. You don't have to wait until the sink is piled high with dishes to do them or until the whole floor needs vacuuming to sweep up a few crumbs.

- Make a rule that anything you leave out temporarily has to be left out attractively arranged. Things don't have to look terrible just because they're uncontained.

SUBTROUBLE 14. THE "GO" VOICE (ACTIVATION PROBLEMS)

In the classic Spanish film *The Exterminating Angel,* a group of people at a party find that when the party's over, they're unable to leave. It's not as though anyone is forcing them to stay—the doors are unlocked—but for some mysterious reason, none of them can muster up the will to walk through the open doors. Instead, they make all sorts of excuses for staying, and begin to settle in. If you have problems with activation, this story will sound familiar. Imprisoned and isolated by Thing mountains, you know what you need to do, and no one's preventing you, but the little voice in your head that's supposed to say "Go" and propel you out of your chair to the piles doesn't.

This can be extremely frustrating, both for you and for those affected by your inaction, who may react to their frustration by labeling you as lazy or interpreting your behavior as passive aggression—

purposeful, malicious nondoing that is an attack on *them*. This is both erroneous and unfair, but it's also understandable. Activation problems may sometimes relate to interpersonal issues, but more often are due to failures of the affective system. Research has revealed multiple biological causes of underactivity, involving neurotransmitters, hormones, immune cell count, and other bodily entities as affected by stress, burnout, and negative conditioning of the "learned helplessness" variety. This is a scary thought. If laziness is wired or conditioned into peoples' brain chemistry, how can you hold anyone accountable for anything? Does it mean if you don't show up for work your boss shouldn't fire you? Ye Gods! This one could turn the whole world upside down.

Although underactivity may be caused by factors beyond your control however, THIS DOES NOT MEAN THERE IS NOTHING YOU CAN DO TO TRANSFORM WILLESSNESS INTO WILL. Conditioning can be reversed by positive or negative reinforcement, and biology can be altered, not only by medicine but by talking treatment and other salutary experiences such as music, exercise, religion, meditation, romance, and humor, to name a few. If you're totally paralyzed with Things, then someone else may have to light a fire under you to get you to move: the spouse who leaves, the boss who fires, the landlord who evicts, the health department that intervenes. But if you have any scrap of will left at all, you can use what you have as "starter" to generate more will, the way a small bit of sourdough culture is used to grow a whole lot of sourdough.

Strategies for transforming willessness into will in dealing with Things:

- Consider the state of your body. Have you been getting enough sleep, exercise, nutrition, and appropriate medical care? If not, forget about Things and go fill the gaps. The "go" voice is much more likely to speak to people who are healthy than to those who are not.

- Shift your focus from outside—the papers that need to be sorted—to inside—your thoughts about what you're thinking. Invite your Gryzypian to observe your thoughts and feelings. Are you horriblizing? Are you "shoulding" on yourself? Review "Detoxifying Things" in Chapter 2 on how to deal with negative thoughts.

- Reframe. Think of times when the "go" voice is silent as recharging times, not as evidence that you're a Terrible Person.

- Imagine yourself in the hands of some other force stronger than yourself. Feel yourself being shot out of a cannon, caught up in the current of a river, or placed on a conveyer belt and propelled toward the Thing mountains where your hands will be unable to keep from sorting. If this does not lead to immediate action, don't worry—let the play of your imagination be an end in itself—have fun.

- Put yourself in a relaxed state and visualize the outcome you want to achieve: imagine your tidy desk, your spiffy new closet system, your neatly ordered files. Think about how this success might be the beginning of other successes. Visualize whatever you'll do to celebrate your success—the walk in the park, the ice cream cone.

- Accept the fact that you cannot MAKE the "go" voice speak. It may come from inside you, but it's not something you can control. All you can do is increase the chance that it will decide to speak.

No matter how much research is conducted on activation, the "go" voice will probably always remain a mysterious phenomenon. We can know what conditions are likely to make it clam up, but we can never hope to understand exactly what makes it speak to us at the moment that it does.

Ramona Dwindle is working in her office with Judy Stackwright. She has scheduled her organizer for the entire morning and plans to spend the afternoon working on her own. For the first half hour, Ramona works quickly and steadily, making decisions right and left about which papers to keep, which to recycle, which to act upon, which to file. Ramona is excited about her progress and her mind races ahead, calculating how long it will take at her present rate. She figures that if she keeps going she can have her whole office decluttered by the end of the day.

As she moves into the second half hour, Ramona feels something in her brain begin to change. Her decisions are not so swift and decisive as they were. By the second hour, Ramona's mind begins to seriously wander, even though she persistently yanks it back on track. As time goes on, she feels more and more as though her brain is filled with glue. At the end of another hour, Ramona sits motionless with a piece of paper in her hand. The thought of deciding what to do with the paper suddenly fills her with nausea. "I have to stop," she says, putting down the paper, "I just can't keep doing this."

Brains, like bodies, get tired. Some brains get tired faster than others, and different brains get tired by different tasks. "The brain can only retain its intense focus for a certain period of time," Richard Restak, author of *Brainscapes,* writes, "a period that differs from one person to another." The task of making decisions taxes the attention/executive system as well as the affective system. When you make a decision, you make a kind of quantum leap from indecision to decision. One moment you haven't decided: the next moment— BANG—you have. Decisions are like scientific discoveries on a small scale. This takes a lot of mental energy.

You may feel physically fine while decluttering and yet suddenly run into a wall. Some essential chemical in the brain seems to get used up, and the system shuts down until it has had a chance to replenish itself. Problems due to simple mental fatigue may be compounded by factors such as hypoglycemia, lack of sleep, low testosterone, and the brain's natural tendency to cycle between greater right brain and left brain dominance during different parts of the day.

If your decluttering efforts often fail, this may be because you assume that your brain will be able to keep working at full speed for the whole session. This rarely happens, and you may become discouraged when you don't meet your own expectations. Having a brain that gets fatigued easily makes an all-day decluttering marathon a bad idea. What helps is to study how long your particular brain takes to get tired while decluttering, realizing that rapid mental fatigue is not the same thing as stupidity. To do this, start decluttering, noting the time that you begin. As you work, stop every ten minutes and ask yourself how you're feeling. Make notes: 10:00—started decluttering kitchen cupboards. 10:10—still going strong. 10:20—still okay. 10:30—beginning to get bored. 10:40—feeling sleepy. 10:50—let me out of here! 11:00—I HAVE TO STOP. Sitting down to read. 11:10—better, but still tired. 11:20—enjoying reading, but need to get back to it. 11:30—ready to go.

Now that you know that you can work for an hour before you burn out totally, and need half an hour to rest, you can plan to work in sessions of one hour with at least half an hour between them. Planning this way will save you the valuable energy you previously spent calling yourself lazy for not being able to keep going and trying to analyze what's wrong with you. NOTHING IS WRONG WITH YOU. We all have our mental limits, even you, and success is largely a matter of learning to take them into account.

SUBTROUBLE 16. SIDE-TRIP SEDUCERS
(PROBLEMS STAYING ON TASK)

Maria Branchoff is spending Saturday reorganizing her files. She decides to purge the existing files first. In the first folder she comes to, Maria finds a catalogue sent to her by an antiques dealer. Maria opens it and is soon enthralled by the pictures of antique clocks. One clock in particular appeals to her. Maybe she'll just go downstairs and measure the space in the hallway to see if it would fit. But where is the tape measure? Maria digs through her desk, and in doing so finds an old love letter from her ex-boyfriend, Wilbur Rat. That does it. The memories come crowding in and suddenly Maria is back on Wilbur's back porch looking up at the moon. Where is Wilbur now? she wonders. Doris, that's it. Doris would know. She'll call Doris as soon as she can find the phone book. She turns the house upside down and finally finds it in a basket of dirty clothes.

Peuwww! How could she have let them pile up this way? Better do something about it NOW, Maria tells herself, Wilbur or no Wilbur. Hauling the basket down the basement stairs, she begins stuffing clothes into the washer. While she's in the basement she notices the grime that has built up between the washer and drier and reaches for a sponge. The whole basement really needs cleaning, she thinks. . . . At the end of the day, Maria feels depressed, wondering what happened to her plan to reorganize her files. "Too many interruptions," she tells herself, forgetting that the vast majority of interruptions came from her own brain.

You may be better at staying on task than Maria, but you need to ask yourself how often and under what circumstances you fall prey to side-trip seducers—internal and external stimuli that pull you off task—and what impact this has on your dealings with Things. Most off-task behavior is simply one form of impulsivity. The big boss fails to intervene and hence no voice in your head goes "Stop! Is this really what you want to do? You're supposed to be doing so-and-so, remember?"

This can play havoc with your Things. When you move from one activity to another without thinking, you may leave belongings out along the way. In the course of her wanderings, Maria left the file drawer open, the catalogue opened facedown on her bed, the desk drawer contents scattered all over the floor, the phone book on top of the birdcage, and the dirty clothes in the washer with no soap and the washer door open. In addition to causing you to leave a trail of Things behind you and thus create clutter, side trips also seduce you away from decluttering projects.

Strategies for dealing with side-trip seducers:

- Self-monitor for side trips when you declutter. Set an alarm to go off every fifteen minutes and ask yourself the question, "Am I on task or off task?" Ask someone to remind you, put up signs, or train yourself to ask this question every time the phone rings, the children want something, or Nature calls.

- To identify side-trip patterns, keep an ongoing map of your activities, showing where you branch off from the main task and branch off from the branch-offs. You may discover that printed materials or the Internet or Things that need cleaning or Things that bring up memories pull you away from the job at hand while other potential seducers don't. You may find that you have more trouble staying on task as more time goes by, or at certain times of day.

- When you realize that you've fallen prey to the seducers, don't beat yourself up about it. Even if this is the case, it doesn't mean that Thing Mountains are inevitable. You can become as side-tracked as you like if you make a rule that each time you switch activities, you have to put everything away. Or schedule regular cleanup times every few hours.

- In planning decluttering projects, don't set yourself up for failure by expecting to work on a project for three hours straight: set minigoals and reward yourself when you achieve them. Instead of cleaning out a dresser, clean out a drawer. Part of why you may get sidetracked is love of variety.

- Use strategies—as described on pages 137–138—to resist the snares of side-trip seducers as you progress through your day. If you want to clean out your desk and not get sidetracked, shut yourself in your office, turn off the phone, make a rule that you're not allowed to read anything that you find, and ask someone to knock on the door every ten minutes and ask you if you're still at it or, if you have a friend you can trust, ask your friend to sit next to you and GENTLY guide you back on course every time you venture off the road to an organized desk.

Side-trip seducers vary in the magnetic intensity that they exert. Some are more powerful than others, and the more powerful the seducer, the stronger the measures you need to take to counteract its influence. Doing so takes a lot of energy, however. If your brain is susceptible to off-tasking, give yourself a vacation from struggling with your impulses now and then and deliberately allow yourself to follow your nose. Start in a particular room, say, the living room, and put Things away until you come to something that belongs elsewhere, for example, in the office. Then put Things away in the office until something merits a trip to the basement, and so forth. It can be fun to declutter this way, and if you do it for an extended period of time, it may lead to your finishing every room in your house on the same day!

SUBTROUBLE 17. THE SENSE OF AN ENDING (TASK-COMPLETION PROBLEMS)

Jackie Makit loves crafts. Jackie knits, sews, crochets, weaves, macrames, paints, shellacs, glazes, carves, and solders. Jackie makes baskets from soda straws and hats from baskets and lamps from hats. Far into the night, Jackie sits gluing bits of broken eggshells onto burlap, covering Styrofoam with nylon net, and stringing necklaces out of dyed macaroni shells. One would think that such exemplary industriousness would result in a house filled with clever knickknacks in every nook and cranny. Wrong.

The nooks and crannies in Jackie's house are occupied not by knickknacks but by sleeves of sweaters still on the knitting needles, unused piles of gilded pinecones, paint-by-numbers pictures of horses with half the colors filled in, torn pattern pieces pinned to fading materials, unpainted papier mâché pumpkins, and dozens of other half-finished projects. Jackie is a person with task-completion problems. This affects all areas of her life, including what she does with Things.

There could be a lot of reasons why someone starting with step A might not make it to step Z, both psychodynamic and neurological. Jackie's task-completion problem may actually have less to do with endings than with beginnings. If her brain is wired a certain way, she may crave the feeling of novelty and the adrenaline kick (adrenaline is an addictive substance!) it elicits. As the novelty wears off and the adrenaline begins to dwindle, the exciting new project becomes less exciting. If you're a person who's perpetually dropping some tasks in order to start newer, more exciting ones, knowing that you have a biological predisposition to do this is half the battle. Whenever you feel the urge to go West, say to yourself, "It's just the novelty feeling," finish the job at hand, and THEN reward yourself by starting something new. Set a rule that says each project has to be finished before you can start the next one.

Love of novelty is only one possible explanation for task-completion problems, however. Jackie may also have a brain like Ramona Dwindle's, which easily falls prey to mental fatigue. This may affect how Jackie experiences time as she move through a task. Einstein talked about how traveling near the speed of the light causes distortions in time to occur. But going fast is not the only phenomenon that turns time into the stretchy, squeezy pancake clock that appears in Salvador Dali's famous painting: doing a job you aren't crazy about also has this effect.

Suppose Jackie, for example, is cleaning out a closet, a project that takes a total of about four hours. According to what might be called the theory of drudgery relativity, each of the four hours of work does not take the same length of time. The first hour, when she's filled with energy and enthusiasm for the closet cleaning, takes ten minutes, the second and third hours take an hour each, and the fourth hour takes about five or six hours and feels like a bad movie running in slow motion as she forces her leaden arms to pick up the last, infinitely heavy hatbox and drags her leaden legs across the infinitely wide floor so she can finish the job by putting the hatbox on the closet shelf. In planning for decluttering projects, you need to take the drudgery relativity factor (DRF) into account and plan short enough sessions to forestall it. The DRF is only a problem for task completion if it takes you by surprise.

You might also try to induce Flow. Flow is the one big exception to the DRF. If, by some stroke of luck, Flow kicks in and turns drudgery into a joyful dance, then each of the four hours will take zero hours, minutes, and seconds. Flow places you outside of time altogether. It's impossible to force Flow to happen, but you can facilitate it by paying conscious attention to your breathing and accepting every moment of experience as it goes by, no matter what it contains. Don't screw your face all up with tense thoughts trying to MAKE Flow happen—just sort of hope that it MIGHT happen and let it go. If it doesn't happen, you can live. Then, if you're fortunate, Flow will kick in, and you'll be finished with the job before you've begun.

SUBTROUBLE 18. HANDS AND EYES (COORDINATION PROBLEMS)

Energy and freedom from distraction are not all you need to move an object from point A to point B. Your brain also has to be able to tell your hands what to do, and your hands have to cooperate. Glitches in the motor system as well as various orthopedic problems may prevent this, which can be EXTREMELY frustrating. The motor system controls not only muscle movement but also motor planning, the process by which actions are mentally organized and sequenced. While for most people this occurs automatically once an activity has been performed a few times, for some, automaticity requires more repetitions.

Even minor motor-system glitches can cause you to make more messes with Things in the first place by dropping, spilling, knocking over, and bumping into Things. They can also make it difficult to clean up the messes, since you may do all of the above in the process.

If every time you put a paper in the files, you drop three others on the floor, reorganization is not going to happen quickly.

You may find it easier to use some muscles than others, and consequently avoid dealing with Things that require the use of certain muscle groups. Kolberg observes that some people only seem to deal with Things at a certain spatial level—waist-high or above, for example. Is this the case for you? If so, how does it relate to physical comfort and coordination? Do you avoid squatting, sitting on the floor, reaching up, or climbing onto chairs and ladders? Are small muscle movements or large muscle movements easier for you? How does this affect your organizing style?

The challenge, when you have motor problems with Things, is to keep your frustration from escalating into rage, especially if impatient people have abused you for your clumsiness. Old tapes easily become part of your thoughts. "Don't you know how to make a bed? I've already shown you about six times how to do it. What's the matter with you?" becomes "I don't know what's the matter with me—I just can't seem to make a bed right." "Come on, hurry up, get those clothes picked up NOW!" becomes "I don't know why it always takes me so long to hang up my clothes." The good news, however, is that such tapes can be reprogrammed once you become aware of their sources. Review the section on detoxifying Things in Chapter 2.

If you have problems making the Things around you look like the Things in your head,

- Look straight at your organizing efforts without either evading or horriblizing about what you see. Acknowledge the disparity between what you aimed for and what is. Now you can begin to do something about it. Remind yourself that the real will never perfectly match the ideal—all you can do is improve.

- Slow down, slow down, slow down. The slower you go, the better your brain will be able to anticipate, and therefore control, your actions.

- Think of an organizing task as a dance, staying conscious of each movement you make throughout the task. Look at this as PRACTICE rather than as a performance.

- Ask a friend or hire an organizer to help put your ideas into effect for you. He or she provides the hands, while you provide the brains.

- Think of the kindest, most patient teacher you ever had. When you make a mistake, think of what he or she would say to you.

- Make a list of the people who've been critical of your lack of coordination. Write them all letters, explaining that your problems were due to neurological differences for which you're not to blame. Tell them you didn't deserve their unkindness. Express your anger any way you like, then burn the letters without sending them.

- If you have serious coordination problems, consider getting help from an occupational therapist.

THE FOUR TROUBLES IN A NUTSHELL

Now that you've read about the Four Troubles with Things and the specific subtroubles associated with them, it's time to consolidate what you've learned. Circle your own particular troubles and subtroubles on the following list:

I. Trouble Tuning In to Things

   Subtrouble 1. Hummingbird Thoughts (Distractibility)

   Subtrouble 2. Snapshot Mind (Short Attention Span)

   Subtrouble 3. Brain Suction (Overfocusing)

The items you've circled are *your specific troubles and subtroubles,* caused by combinations of glitches in different brain systems. Now that you know what your troubles and subtroubles are, all you have to do is figure out what to do about them. Review the suggestions in each section that relates to you. Next make a list of your own brain strengths. How can these strengths help you to deal with your troubles and subtroubles? If you aren't sure, don't worry. Part IV will help you with this.

ONE LAST WORD ABOUT THE BRAIN

The brain is an incredibly complex organ, composed of billions of neurons and interconnected in countless ways with the rest of the body. By necessity, everything in this book about the brain and its glitches and strengths is oversimplified. You didn't want to read a one-thousand-page neurology textbook, did you? Our purpose here has simply been to reprogram your Gryzypian to beep in some new concepts that relate to how the brain works. The more you work with these ideas, the more this will happen: BEEP—hyperactivity—BEEP—coordination problem—BEEP—emotional reactivity—BEEP—procrastination—BEEP—overfocusing. This is what your thoughts will begin to sound like. Whenever you hear such words in your head, the suggestions given here, along with those generated by your own insight system, will help you know what to do. As time goes on, you'll find that the Four Troubles—trouble tuning in to Things, trouble seeing Things, trouble thinking about Things, and trouble moving Things—are no longer Troubles with a capital *T* but have diminished into non-troubles, and you never again have to feel stupid, lazy, or crazy because of brain-based problems with Things.

CHAPTER 10

YOUR THINGS AND
THEIR THINGS

Eliot Status, Olivia Ostrich, Nancy Neatfreak, Elsie Clutcher, and Griselda Backglance are all in a therapy group together. They're doing inner-child work with their psychodynamic therapist, Gloria Driftwood. In their sessions, they begin to remember childhood experiences. Eliot remembers his big brother, Bruno, snatching away the new red fire engine he got for his birthday. Olivia remembers her father shouting at her alcoholic mother to clean up their squalid apartment. Nancy remembers her friends at camp making fun of her for not knowing how to make her bed. Elsie remembers her grandmother taking her shopping for clothes while her parents were in Europe for three months. Griselda remembers her mother sobbing after little Griselda knocked the whatnot down and broke the china angels her aunt had left them.

No brain exists in a vacuum. A brain is located inside a skull that's attached to a body that interacts with other bodies that also have brains in them. What those other bodies do and say can drastically alter the development of any given brain and mind. Thus, if you want to pinpoint the sources of your Thing-related habits, you can't just consider your brain. You also have to take a look at the people, past and present, who helped to shape your neurochemistry, your beliefs, and your behavior, and how you continually interact with others around Things.

There is more than one mechanism by which we influence each others' Thing habits. The most powerful form of influence is what we do with Things ourselves. Modeling is a powerful form of persuasion. Little Janie Neatfreak's mother hangs her clothes over a chair at night; Little Janie hangs her clothes over a chair at night. Roger Suburb buys a new power mower; Eliot Status buys a new power mower. Millie Squalor throws her clothes on the floor; Joe Squalor throws his clothes on the floor. The woman on TV buys a bottle of Stinkbomb perfume; Ruthie Reactor buys a bottle of Stinkbomb perfume.

The instinct to imitate is wired into the brain to enable one generation to transmit what it knows to the next. If it weren't for imitation, we'd all have to figure out how to walk, speak, and tie our shoes by ourselves, starting from scratch. This would result in a lot of people tripping over their shoestrings. But somehow, we don't like to admit to ourselves that we're imitating someone when it comes to Things.

Another mechanism by which we influence each others' Thing habits, consciously or unconsciously, is conditioning. Conditioning means that every time A happens, B happens, until when someone says "A" we automatically think "B." Every time little Huey Havit throws a tantrum in the grocery store (A), his parents buy him a candy bar (B). Every time Gloria Gorgeous wears a new dress (A), she gets asked out on a date (B). Every time Rebecca Treadmill cleans up her living room (A), Roberto Treadmill messes it up (B).

Thinking of A and B together leads to the development of expectations, which may or may not be met. If we expect B to be pleasant we'll tend, over time, to do A more and more. Huey expects candy bars and throws more and more tantrums in the store. Gloria expects dates and buys more and more new dresses. If we expect B to be unpleasant, we'll do A less and less. Rebecca expects frustration and cleans up less and less.

Sometimes circumstances change and we fail to notice that A doesn't lead to the same B anymore. Archibald Tyrant's wife waited on him hand and foot until she ran off with the milkman. Every time

Archibald put a Thing down (A), his wife put it away (B). But now, Archibald is living alone. Every time he puts a Thing down now (A), it stays where he puts it (B), and Thing mountains are the result.

Where Things are concerned, some A's produce much more immediate B's than others. Spilling a big jar of marbles makes an immediate mess, while leaving one paper out on your desk and then another and another may take a long time to produce clutter. When unpleasant B's happen only slowly as the cumulative result of a lot of little A's, your brain may not get it, so you go on doing more little A's.

A third mechanism by which we affect each others' Thing habits is words. Words can, in fact, serve as substitutes for both modeling and conditioning, though they tend to have less power than actions. "We're putting in a new closet system," Roger Suburb tells Eliot Status, and Eliot goes to the phone to order one for himself without ever seeing Roger's. "When you've put all your Lincoln Logs away, then we'll go to the hobby shop," little Mickey's mother tells him, and he goes to work.

Since actions have more influence on us than words, whenever the two are in contradiction, the actions win out. This can be confusing. Olivia Ostrich's parents constantly harped at her to clean up her room, but *did* nothing to encourage her to do so, while they themselves lived in squalor and spent most of their time in front of the TV. Olivia quickly learned that her parents' harping was meaningless and began to spend all of her time in front of the TV too. Now her parents are gone, but Olivia continues to follow the example they set despite their nagging words in her head, spoiling all the fun during her Thing escapes.

Except when action contradicts words, words gain in influence when they're repeated. If they're repeated enough, they don't even have to make sense to influence us. In fact, repeated words work better if they don't, as every advertiser knows.

How deep an influence someone's words and actions may have on your behavior with Things depends on how emotionally connected you are to the person. If you're emotionally connected to someone who is not emotionally connected to you, the person may give you Things to try to make up for love that is lacking. This doesn't work, and it may cause all sorts of problems in how you deal with Things, from compulsive buying to rebellious cluttering to hanging on to Things forever and ever. If this is what's going on, you need to come to terms with the other person's failure to love you and see it as HIS OR HER failure—not yours. Then you need to stop playing games with Things and begin looking for people who can give you the love you crave and deserve.

Most of us, wanting to be independent, grossly underestimate how much influence others have had and still have on our dealings with Things. Paradoxically, the only way to become truly independent is to analyze the ways in which others' modeling, conditioning, and words have affected your Thing habits and figure out how to counter any negative influences. What you may discover in doing so is that the people who shaped your Thing habits by means of these mechanisms were not mad scientists doing experiments on you but people who had been modeled, conditioned, and worded into dealing with Things in certain ways themselves by the families, neighborhoods, and cultures in which they lived.

MOM AND DAD AND THINGS

In talking about who influenced us, the people we're most likely to allude to are moms, dads, and anyone else who played parent to us. Being a parent isn't easy, and part of every parent's job is to teach his or her child how to deal with material possessions. While most parents try consciously to condition their child to deal effectively with Things, the child learns a great deal more from modeling, i.e., what the parents themselves do with Things.

Since children generally begin life as concrete thinkers, discovering abstract principles only during adolescence, Things loom very large for them. Childhood is a time when your whole future seems to hang on whether or not you receive a new bicycle for your birthday. Childhood is also a time when brains and muscles are not yet fully developed, making interactions with Things more problematic than they will be later in life. Children spill milk, scribble in books, break toys, lose mittens, and leave tools out on the sidewalk. Not all parents react to such behaviors in the same way, and some handle them better than others. One key to understanding your current Thing dilemmas, then, lies in your memories of caregivers and Things.

Questions to ask yourself about Mom, Dad, and Things:

1. How did each of your parents go about acquiring Things? What were their behaviors regarding shopping, gift giving, and dealing with mail?

2. How did your parents organize—or not organize—their Things? What was the home you grew up in like? Was it chaotic or orderly? How did you feel when you walked in the door of your home? Did either of your parents have problems with losing Things and how did he or she react when this happened?

3. If your home was chaotic, why was this the case? Was the chaos the result of substance abuse, mental illness, or marital discord?

4. Did your parents blame each other or the children for chaos? Did either parent ever abuse the other over Things? If your home was superorderly, what price did your family pay to achieve this? Did you ever resent it?

5. How did your parents dispose—or not dispose—of Things they no longer needed? Did they give Things to charity, sell them, have yard sales, or throw them in the trash? Did either of your parents hoard large numbers of certain Things and refuse to get rid of them? How did the rest of your family react to this?

6. What routines and rituals did your parents have—if any— for shopping, cleaning, organizing, or otherwise dealing with Things? What role were you expected to play in these rituals?

7. How did your parents go about training—or not training— you to keep your Things organized? Were they ever unfair or abusive to you over Things? Did they pick up after you or require you to pick up after yourself? Were they consistent in enforcing rules about Things? How did they help you— or not help you—learn to deal with dangerous Things?

8. Did your parents ever give you Things to reward positive behaviors? Were the rewards appropriate for the behaviors? Did you ever feel that they gave you Things to substitute for love or attention?

9. Did your parents encourage you to save for Things you wanted or simply buy them for you? If you wanted a particular type of Thing because all your friends had one, how did your parents respond to this? Did you feel deprived of "normal" Things?

10. Did you feel that your siblings or cousins got more or better Things than you did? Did you and they ever engage in Thing wars? Did they ever abuse your Things or abuse you over them? Did you ever abuse them? If a sibling was destructive to your Things, how did your parents react?

11. Did your parents ever promise you a Thing and then disappoint you? Did you ever expect a Thing for a birthday or holiday and get disappointed? Did you ever desperately want a Thing you couldn't have?

12. Did your family ever lose a lot of Things due to sudden financial losses? How did this affect you?

13. Did your parents encourage you to share your Things with others? Were you made to feel guilty if you chose to keep all of a Thing for yourself?

14. How much effort did your parents put into dealing with Things? Did you ever feel that they cared more about their Things than about you? Did you ever feel sacrificed to a parent's desire to impress others with their Things?

15. If something traumatic happened during your childhood, were Things involved in the incident? In what way? How would you deal with this event if it occurred now?

Once you've answered these questions, compare your answers with your inventory of Thing-related habits and feelings. How do your current Thing habits fit with what your parents did? What impact did they have on your Thing feelings? Do you do just exactly what they did without questioning its appropriateness to your current situation? Or do you do the exact opposite even if your situation merits otherwise? If you're following either of these paths with Things, you still have work to do in making peace with your Things. You are not your mom. You are not your dad. Nor are you still dependent on Mom or Dad. Your situation is different from theirs at the time you were growing up, and if your Thing habits do not address your current situation, your job is not finished.

If your parents are still living, one good way to begin to change this is to talk with them—in a nonblaming way, of course—about what material Things mean to them. If they're no longer alive, you can ask older relatives about them, read letters, journals, or books they may have written, or simply use what memories you and/or your siblings may have to consider how they dealt with Things.

Questions to ask Mom and Dad:

1. What Things are especially precious to you? What memories are attached to them?

2. Did you grow up in a poor family or a poor society?

3. Were you deprived of Things because of wars or other catastrophes?

4. What were *your* parents' beliefs and attitudes about Things?

5. How did your religious, cultural, and political beliefs, if any, affect your feelings about Things?

Meanwhile, you'll need to process any negative feelings brought up by looking back at the past. All of the usual techniques for processing feelings are appropriate: writing letters and burning them; making tapes and destroying them; writing affirmations; performing healing rituals. Some healing rituals involving Things:

1. "Exorcism" ritual: Open all the windows and doors in a room you want to declutter. Stand in the middle of a room and address the ghosts of the past. Say aloud, "This is MY room. I will organize this room in ways that work for ME. YOU don't need to be here. GET OUT!" Imagine the ghosts flying out of the windows and doors, yelping with pain. Slam the windows and doors shut. Now you're free to deal with Things in your own way.

2. Resignation ritual: make two lists—parents' Thing habits you would like to imitate and parents' Thing habits you want to stop imitating. Keep the first list and burn the second list, saying the words: "I am resigning from the job of doing these things just because you did them." Add whatever you'd like.

3. Purification ritual: Make a pile of nonvaluable Things associated with someone who abused you. Give the nonvaluable Things to a charity that helps survivors of abuse, sell them and donate the money, or give yourself the catharsis of tearing up, stomping on, burning, or otherwise destroying them.

As you begin to put Mom, Dad, or caregivers into perspective where Things are concerned, you may experience a new sense of freedom both to do and not do what they did with Things. For the first time in your life, you may feel free to develop your own set of habits with Things, designed to fit whatever life you've made for yourself and the people with whom you now live.

THINGS AND YOUR FAMILY

Caregivers do their jobs within the context of a larger family system, which is more than the sum of its parts. Within a family system, whether functional or dysfunctional, Things may serve a variety of functions:

- Things as definers: If you want to be sure everyone in your family knows who you are, surround yourself with the right Things. If you want to be sure others know who THEY are—or who you want them to be—give them the right Things. You are what you own.

- Things as connectors: If you want to get closer to someone in your family, share a Thing with the person. Or two or three.

- Things as dividers: If you want to separate from someone in your family, start a Thing war or surround yourself with Things he or she can't stand. It's all part of growing up.

- Things as distractors: If you don't want to talk to someone about what you feel, talk about Things instead. Buy now, pay later.

- Things as bribes: When you want to make someone in your family do something, offer him or her a Thing. The more you do this, the more control you may gain over the person. Control yes, love no.

- Things as replacements: If you don't love someone in your family but feel that you should, give the person Things instead. If you lose someone, buy a Thing to cheer yourself up. Trouble is, Things can never really replace people.

Consider your grandparents and your aunts and uncles and cousins as well as your own immediate family and ask yourself who used which Things for what. Does one Thing function stand out over the others?

Different families have different rules about Things which usually get passed down through the generations. Most of us grow up believing that our family's rules are the natural way of doing things, even if our parents are compulsive shoppers who overindulge us with Things they can't afford, skinflints who keep us deprived of Things, hoarders who bury us under Thing mountains, or lockhorns who engage in constant Thing wars. Some types of Thing rules we inherit are the following:

- Rules about shopping: when it's okay to buy what, where to buy it, and how much to buy.

- Rules about sharing: whom to give what to, when, and what to do when you're given to.

- Rules about legacies: whom to leave what to and what to do when you inherit.

- Rules about arranging: what belongs where.

- Rules about maintenance: what needs to be done to what and when.

- Rules about disposal: what to dispose of and how.

What's important to remember about all these rules is that although they may have been in your family forever, you will not get arrested if you decide not to follow some of them. Most of your family's Thing rules probably made sense at one time, in the circumstances with which the family was dealing, but some of them may not make such good sense now. Before you can decide which rules you still want to follow and which you don't, you need to know that you ARE following certain Thing rules, and figure out what they are. Make a list of your family's Thing rules and compare them with your current inventory of Thing habits. Question everything.

THINGS AND YOUR FRIENDS

Past influences are important in shaping how we deal with Things, but they're not everything: the present counts too. A lot of what we do is simply a response to the behavior of people surrounding us in the here and now, in our schools, homes, neighborhoods, and workplaces. This is partly because we are an imitative species, and our current friends and associates continually provide us with new models for imitation. It's also partly because in our minds, our friends have a way of becoming our parents and others from our past.

In Sociology 101, instructors teach students about a famous experiment known as the Asch experiment, in which groups of "subjects" were given lines of different lengths to compare. Only one person was really a subject, however. The others were in cahoots with the experimenter, who had instructed them to pretend to see two lines as being the same length when they obviously were not. Most of the real subjects placed in such groups ended up agreeing with the majority, discounting the evidence of their own senses, though a few exceptionally strong-minded individuals resisted.

What this experiment illustrates is that not only our ideas but even our *perceptions* may be influenced by those around us. This is important where Things are concerned, especially in determining which items we'll choose to buy and keep. When we spend enough time around other people, we begin to see things the way they do, and because we see the way they do, we act the way they do. "I don't know why people are wearing such baggy pants," you say, "I think they look terrible." Then your friends start wearing baggy pants and before long you're wearing baggy pants yourself. By that time, they look fine to you—much better than close-fitting pants—and you go through your wardrobe and get rid of all those boring old fitted pants.

The people around us influence not only what possessions we have but also how we organize them. If your friends are all messy, chances are you'll be messy yourself. If they're all neatniks, you'll feel pressure to become a neatnik too. UNLESS you're one of the strong-minded people who in the Asch experiment would not have gone along with the crowd. Some such people feel that they have to do the opposite of what everyone else does: the more messy others become, the more compulsively they organize every paper clip, and vice versa. Others simply march to the beat of their own drum.

Because your friends may remind you of Mom or Dad, you may fall into behaving as if they ARE Mom or Dad. If a co-worker complains about your messy desk, you may feel all the same emotions you felt when Mom nagged at you to clean up your room. This can lead to Thing wars. But if you talk back to the co-worker or even go to your boss and complain, the co-worker can't spank you or put you in time-out. It's easy to forget this. When you're at odds with someone over Things, ask yourself if he or she reminds you of anyone in your past. Then try to compare the two people as objectively as you can. How are they alike and how are they different? Your co-worker is short and your mom was tall. Your co-worker speaks softly and your mother spoke with a loud, angry voice. Your co-worker has no power over you. Mom had all kinds of power.

Questions to ask yourself about Things and your friends (the term is used loosely here to include everyone with whom you currently associate):

1. Are the Things you own generally similar to or different from your friends' possessions? If different, how much so?

Do you choose Things that blend in with those of others or which stand out as distinctive? If your Things are distinctive, does this make you feel special or simply lonely?

2. Are your Things more or less organized than those of your friends? If they're less so, how do your friends react to this? Do you have any friends who criticize or abuse you over your clutter or your Thing habits? Who, if anyone, does this person remind you of from your past? How does your current response to such people relate to your responses to the originals?

3. Are any of your "friends" destructive to your belongings? Does anyone intrude on your space with his or her Things? Are you currently involved in any Thing wars with anyone? What does the conflict represent to you?

4. Do you ever buy objects you don't really need or want just because everybody else has one? Do you feel inferior because you don't have what everybody else has? If so, what past memories does this bring up for you?

5. How do most of your friends get rid of their excess Things? How do their habits compare with yours? Do you feel shamed by those who are more conscientious than you are about recycling? Do you feel disgusted by others' carelessness? What memories does it trigger?

If you frequently feel inadequate about your Things, you may need to get in touch with feelings from the time in your life when owning the right clothes or the right toys was SO IMPORTANT. You're not that age anymore. Whoever you are, by now you have at least some accomplishments to feel good about, and you no longer need Things to define yourself. The key is to stop thinking in terms of "better" and "worse" and begin thinking in terms of "different."

People have many different ways of dealing with Things, differences that make life richer for all of us.

MEN, WOMEN, AND THINGS

Brad and Cheri Gridlock are complaining to their couples' counselor, Edwina Blissful, about each other and Things. They're in the process of moving into a new house, and this has led to countless Thing battles between them.

"I don't know why Cheri has to hang on to so much stuff from her family," Brad complains. "All of these ridiculous little cups and things, she's spent hours packing them to just sit on the shelves at the new place—"

"They're demitasse cups and they're NOT ridiculous," Cheri interrupts. "They came from my aunt Ethel, whom I dearly love.

"Brad could care less about anything that came from HIS family," Cheri tells Edwina. "I was looking in the garbage and there was the afghan that his very own mother had crocheted. He'd thrown it away!"

"It was full of holes," said Brad. "*I* don't need all this old stuff to be secure. *I* see it for what it is—junk. I like things I can use. You wouldn't see me throwing away a good screwdriver or an electric drill. I'd like to put up a workbench."

"Is he good at carpentry?" Edwina asks Cheri.

"He is," says Cheri, "but he leaves his silly tools all over the house. If he would just—"

"Stop," says Edwina. "I want to say something. Have you two ever talked at all about how men and women are different where Things are concerned?"

Brad and Cheri shake their heads.

"I can't help but feel," says Edwina, "that a lot of the problems you're having come from your expecting the sexes to be more alike than they are."

A lot has been written in recent years about how intimate relationships are affected by male-female differences.[11] Women are said to be oriented to bonding and communicating, men to competition and achievement. Some people ascribe these differences to biology, others to culture, and still others to a combination of the two. Whatever their source, these differences do seem to affect how men and women experience material Things. In their interviews described in *The Meaning of Things,* Csikszentmihalyi and Rochberg-Halton asked questions about what particular possessions people most valued. They found that women favored objects that connected them to others, often Things not to be used but merely contemplated, such as photographs, embroidery, and china figurines. Men, on the other hand, valued "action items"—Things they could use like TVs, stereos, and tools—and "status items" such as trophies.

Any organizer can tell you that when Things pile up, men and women seem to respond differently to this state of affairs. A man often views a pile of Things as The Enemy. He believes that if he applies enough brute force—mental or physical—he can conquer the pile once and for all and establish a system that will work forever. A woman, on the other hand, may see her piles as The Abuser. She believes herself to be the helpless victim of her Things, from which she can only be rescued by somebody else. Until men *and* women learn to assess their own Thing habits, understand what's behind them, and take action in making changes, any Thing peace they achieve will be temporary.

Meanwhile, psychological tests have shown most men and women to have different cognitive strengths, which may translate into different strengths in managing Things. Doreen Kimura, in *Sex and Cognition,* describes some of these findings from studies done by various psychologists:

- Men score better on the average at hitting targets with Things. This may help them avoid making messes in the first place—

if they throw a wad of paper at the wastebasket, it's more likely to go in!

- Women score better on fine motor tasks, such as putting pegs on a peg board. Hence many women's superior craft skills.

- Men score better on "mental rotation"—recognizing an object when it's viewed from different perspectives. An advantage for planning arrangements of Things.

- Women score better on recalling both the identities and the locations of objects. This makes it easier to create homes for Things and remember where they are.

- Men score better on creating and using maps. Another planning advantage.

- Women score better on tests of "perceptual speed," the ability to make rapid comparisons among letters, numbers, or pictures. A big plus for sorting, especially papers.

Whoever may be naturally better at organizing and managing Things, it's clear that in most societies, as Sari Solden points out in writing about women with ADD, the burden of actually DOING so falls mainly on women. Though men have traditionally played a major role in making and building Things, women have been expected to make sense out of that humungous pile of Things called a home. This is easier for some women than for others. Those for whom it is not easy are made to feel as though they're not women. A "real" woman is supposed to be able to choose the right shade of carpeting, remember to get more dog food, know which kitchen utensils do what, keep the silver polished, separate the hand wash from the machine wash, get the broken toilet fixed, buy the presents, run the yard sale, and never stop smiling.

If you and your partner are inclined to get into Thing battles or maybe even Thing wars, you would do well to consider how your difficulties may relate to male-female biological and/or cultural differences. This may be true even if you're a gay or lesbian couple, as one partner may have a more "female" and the other a more "male" brain. It's also true that in some straight couples, traditional roles—and brain strengths—may be reversed. Questions to ask yourselves about gender differences:

1. How are your attitudes, behaviors, and feelings different about Things? Are your differences traditional or nontraditional in relation to gender stereotypes?

2. Which of you is most attached to Things associated with people? How does this relate to the need to connect? Which of you is most attached to Things associated with achievement? How does this relate to the need to do and win?

3. What are your strengths as a couple relating to Things? Is either of you exceptionally good at acquiring, building, organizing, fixing, or decorating Things and are you divvying up labor so as to make best use of your strengths? Are there any Thing activities at which both of you are weak? If so, are you making use of help from outsiders to deal with these deficits?

4. Are you ever jealous of your partner's Things? What do they represent to you?

5. How are your families' attitudes about Things different? What differences in your own attitudes can you attribute to family history and what differences to gender differences?

Once you've begun to understand your Thing-related differences, then you can begin to problem-solve for win-win solutions that take differences into account. In Brad and Cheri's case, this might mean Cheri would agree to get rid of SOME of the heirlooms she likes the least to make room for Brad to buy SOME of the tools he wants most. Or, better still, Brad could use his carpentry skills to build shelves and create more space for both kinds of Things.

Whether your differences about Things are gender related or not, taking the time to try to understand them might make the difference between your relationship lasting and not lasting. As you and your partner begin to work on transforming blame and shame into simply defining your differences about Things, you'll find that this becomes more and more a habit, until Things are no longer an issue between you. Vive la différence!

THINGS AND YOUR CULTURE

Culture is a multi-layered concept. When we talk about our culture, are we talking about ethnic culture, religious culture, corporate culture, national culture, eastern or western culture, global culture, or what? We need to be specific. For our purposes, all levels of culture that may predispose any given individual to certain Thing habits are relevant.

Merriam-Webster's Collegiate Dictionary defines the word *culture* as "the customary beliefs, social forms, and MATERIAL traits of a racial, religious, or social group." This implies that one key aspect of culture is Things. Any group of people that shares a common history is likely to have developed customary or traditional ways of dealing with certain objects. Most cultural groups, first of all, have certain privileged Things, those that are regarded as sacred or symbolic of the group's values: a flag, a statue, a book, a crown, a building, a robe, a bell. But privileged Things are only one aspect of the relation between cultures and the material: different cultures may also have different attitudes about Things in general, although it's difficult to say which cultures have which attitudes. Some discernible attitudes are summarized here:

1. Thing restrictive: Certain Things are verboten, and having too many Things in general is regarded as sinful. Clothes without buttons, floors without carpets, hair shirts.

2. Thing conservative: Less is more. Simplicity and understatement are the aesthetic ideals. A beautifully tailored suit, a single exquisite vase on the table, a perfect rose. Excess Things are not considered sinful but merely vulgar.

3. Thing abundant: More is more. Things are to be enjoyed. Bountiful, brightly colored, swirling, sensuous, glittering Things mixed together every which way, spilling out of horns of plenty, painted across chapel ceilings or woven into rich carpets. Multiple gold bracelets, baskets of grapes, silks and satins.

4. Thing natural: Only Things God made are beautiful: everything manmade is inferior. Natural equals safe and pure. Herbal teas, organic cotton clothing, hardwood floors.

5. Thing frugal: Waste is the ultimate sin. The future is all that matters, and those who are grasshoppers rather than ants deserve to starve when winter comes. Piggy banks, bank books, corn cribs, canning equipment.

6. Thing organizing: A place for every Thing, and every Thing in its place. Order is good and chaos is evil. The more order, the better. Filing cabinets, tackle boxes, closet systems, databases.

7. Thing idolatrous: Things displace spiritual beings as the center of the universe. You are what you own. Ownership is what matters, not enjoying the Things that you have. Do whatever you have to do to get more Things, even if it means sacrificing families, breaking promises, stealing, or committing murders. All Things so acquired, often loud and flashy.

8. Thing generous: Whatever Things you have, share them with one and all. Everybody is just one big, happy family. Thanksgiving baskets, holiday gifts, group photos.

Although any given culture may seem to fit one or more of these patterns, within that culture, as within any family, a whole range of different attitudes toward Things may exist. Each member of a culture or family is an individual whose Thing habits may or may not conform to those of the majority.

Questions to ask yourself about Things and your culture (or cultures):

1. What Things in your culture are privileged? Are they sacred or merely symbolic? What do they represent? Which are associated with holidays and life transitions?

2. Does your culture regard Things in general as good or bad? Are only some Things seen as one or the other? What are they?

3. What are your culture's attitudes about acquiring, keeping, organizing, sharing, or disposing of Things? What rituals relate to these attitudes?

4. What events in your culture's history have shaped its attitudes about Things? How are these attitudes still being played out with Things?

5. What do your culture's proverbs, slogans, songs, or folktales say about Things?

6. How consistent are your own Thing habits with your culture's attitudes? Do you use Things to rebel against your culture? Do you sometimes deal with Things in ways that would have made good sense at another time in history but no longer make sense in the present, purely because of

tradition? What do you feel will happen if you defy your culture's traditions about Things?

YOU are more than your culture, and understanding your culture's attitudes toward Things is not going to tell you everything you need to know. It will, however, provide you with one more piece in the puzzle and thus move you a step closer to understanding and solving problems with Things once and for all.

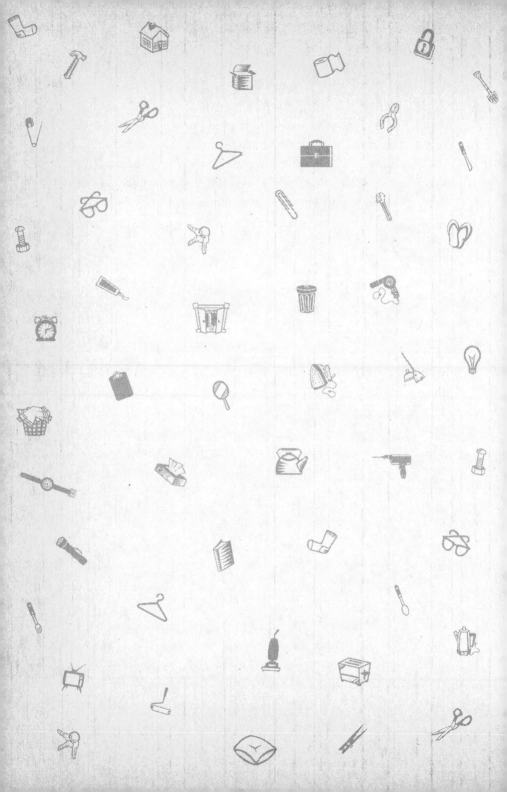

PART IV

WHAT TO DO ABOUT THINGS

By now you know what your Thing habits are: you know where your Things come from, what you do with them while you have them, and how you get rid—or don't get rid—of them. You also know very specifically WHY you do what you do with Things in terms of your situation, your brain strengths and glitches, and the other people in your life, past and present. All this new insight is worth absolutely nothing, however, if you don't begin to translate it into action. Now is the time to act, the time to begin making the changes that can bring peace with your Things for the rest of your life.

What kinds of changes do you need to make? Two kinds: Thing habit changes and environmental changes.

Most people for whom Things are an issue mistakenly focus only on decluttering and reorganizing their environment while doing nothing to improve their Thing habits. Consequently, their efforts are rarely successful. Once you've removed all your Thing mountains, they'll quickly reaccumulate unless you also modify the habits that produced them. A set of new, insight-generated Thing habits allows you to maintain whatever level of organization you find comfortable.

If you simply focus on changing Thing habits, however, and do nothing about the Thing mountains you already have, you'll go on living perpetually with the status quo. This will not leave most people feeling that the issue of Things has been resolved. Somehow, you must manage to change both your environment and your Thing habits at the same time.

To do this, you need to establish specific Thing goals and Thing plans that address BOTH the external and the internal dimensions of the problem. Each day, you'll take some actions to change your Thing habits and some actions to restructure your environment. You also need to take steps to address the sabotage factors that otherwise will prevent you from achieving your Thing goals. *Important: "Sabotage" here does NOT refer to a deep, unconscious desire to fail, as in "self-sabotage," but to any factor, internal or external, that may undermine your success.* YOU WILL SUCCEED AT YOUR GOALS TO THE EXTENT THAT YOU ADDRESS YOUR SABOTAGE FACTORS. If you've failed to accomplish your Thing goals in the past, it was most likely because you ignored your sabotage factors. Now, however, if you set clear Thing goals, identify sabotage factors, and make a reasonable action plan, you'll be placing yourself much more solidly on the path to being at peace with your Things.

CHAPTER 11

TAKING A LOOK AT THINGS

Thus far in this book, we've focused mainly on the INSIDE sources of external clutter and have said relatively little about how to create order on the OUTSIDE. Now that you understand the INSIDE sources of your difficulties, however, it's time to rethink the OUTSIDE dimension. If you're going to make peace with your Things, you do, after all, have to transform INSIDE changes into OUTSIDE ones. This is a good time to get out all your favorite externally focused books and review all the systems they describe and all the creative tips they suggest. It's also time to take a Thing tour.

TAKING A THING TOUR

It's Gryzypian time again, but this time applied to the Things in your environment, not to yourself. As you tour your space from front to back and top to bottom, notebook in hand, listen to the voice of your detached, objective Gryzypian. No horriblizing, no self-chastising, just a string of ACTIONS you need to take based on what you see: BEEP—declutter closet—BEEP—file papers—BEEP—haul away old furniture—BEEP—buy new bookshelves. To help your Gryzypian, make a list of the ACTIONS you need to take in each room. Take or draw some "before" pictures if you like.

Along with this, there are six other things you need to do on your tour:

1. Make a list of Things that are ALREADY organized. What did you do to create these areas of order within the chaos? How did you arrive at the decision to keep THESE areas clutter free? Can you apply any of your past methods to your current situation?

2. Make a list of your "Things of choice," Things of which you have an enormous quantity compared to everything else. Many people's clutter is composed mostly of a superfluity of just one or two types of items. Some favorites are papers, newspapers, books, magazines, memorabilia, clothes, toys, plastic bags, and food containers. If this is the case, the problem of getting rid of excess is going to be relatively simple.

3. Rate the rooms, or parts of rooms, for clutter on a scale of 0 to 10. A score of 0 means any objects in the room are perfectly organized. A score of 10 is a room completely filled with randomly jumbled possessions. What's important is not the individual scores but how they compare with one another, which tells you what's going to need the most work.

4. List your five biggest irritants (BIs). BIs are not necessarily the places that look the worst but rather the areas that bother you the most. Are you having nightmares about cockroaches in your kitchen cupboards? Is it becoming more and more impossible to function in an office knee-deep in papers? Can you no longer get your car comfortably into your garage? Rank the BIs in order of how irritating you find them. Don't list more than five things, as the purpose of this step is to prioritize. Once you've taken care of the five BIs, you can list another five.

5. Make a list of the activities in which you typically engage in each room. How handy are the Things you need for these activities? What Things do you need to make more readily available? What containers do you need for them?

6. Estimate how the volume of any given set of Things relates to the volume of containers available to hold it. Do you have enough file cabinets, jewelry holders, dresser drawers, bookshelf space? If container volume is insufficient, how are you going to deal with this—by getting rid of some Things or by getting more containers? What will you need to buy? Don't rush out and buy a lot of new furniture and equipment at this stage—wait until you've done some decluttering first and use what you have in the meantime.

Touring your space is beneficial not only in helping you to plan for decluttering but also in detoxifying. Notice any negative self-talk that manages to sneak by your Gryzypian. Identify distortions, and replace negative tapes with more realistic ones.

VISUALIZING THINGS

Open the door of your messiest room. Stand in the doorway and survey the scene. What do you see that bothers you and what do you see that feels good? Don't let yourself horriblize. Instead, take a deep breath and blow out any shame feelings you may have. Now close your eyes and imagine that your fairy godmother has put everything to rights. How does the room look in your mind's eye? Is it beautiful or merely functional? How has the furniture been rearranged? Are there any new pieces of furniture or organizing equipment? What eyesores have been removed? What Things that were visible are now hidden away? What Things previously out of sight are now where you can use them? Now picture yourself and your family and friends in the room, doing whatever you most love to do, with everything going smoothly, all the Things you need available at your fingertips. Which Things are in what area? How do you feel when you imagine this?

Visualization is easier for some of us than for others. Some of us simply don't think very visually, so how can we possibly visualize? If you're one of the nonvisually inclined, there are two possible routes to go. One is to work consciously to expand your visual capabilities—assuming you've ever been fully sighted—and the other is to use nonvisual methods of "visualizing," as described in some of the suggestions below. Anything you can do to become more aware of what you see OUTSIDE yourself will make it easier for you to see visions on the INSIDE. Try the following:

- Buy some home decorating magazines and look at the pictures. Note how Things are organized in the rooms. What Things are in what containers? Some magazines or issues of magazines may focus specifically on storage: these are particularly valuable, as are books and magazines on interior design.

- Ask well-organized friends to take you on a tour of their space. Photograph, draw, or write descriptively about what you see. (Keep in mind that what works for them might not work for you. This is an idea-gathering mission.)

- Draw, write about, or make three-dimensional models of real rooms, then of your imaginary rooms. Describe the rooms to a friend (real or imaginary) while looking at or visualizing them.

- If you can't mentally "see" a room, can you hear words describing how you want it to be? What are the key words? Put them all on one piece of paper in big letters. Look at each word and photograph it with your eyes. Now close your eyes and try to translate it into a mental picture.

- Imagine yourself in the room, moving from one area to another. Feel yourself sitting down in a chair, opening a file drawer, taking a garment off a hanger. Imagine the experience of flowing smoothly from one action to another. Where are the Things you need located? Describe this in words or open your eyes and make a map.

- Imagine the payoff. See yourself walking around the newly organized room enjoying a sense of accomplishment. See your friends in the room admiring what they see, and hear their compliments in your mind. Imagine whizzing through a task at your desk that normally takes hours, a model of efficiency now that you know where everything is. Visualize an external reward such as buying yourself a new art object to put in the room.

When it comes to making lifestyle changes, some techniques work without it being all that obvious WHY they work. Visualization is one of these. If you think this is a lot of hooey, try it anyway. You might be surprised.

THINGS AND BEAUTY

Sandra Felton maintains that visualizing efforts may be more effective if they involve not only utility but beauty. But what makes a Thing—or a room filled with Things—beautiful? The person seeing, hearing, tasting, touching, or smelling it. If a Thing gives you a good feeling to perceive, then to you it's beautiful. Philosophers and poets who write about beauty are really just writing about what sets THEIR neurocircuits humming, not necessarily what affects anyone else that way. Because large numbers of people have brains that are wired for neurons to light up at the sight of similar objects, certain Things have generally come to be seen as beautiful in themselves. Yet each brain is also unique, and not everyone thrills at the sight of the Grand Canyon, for example.

Some people don't seem to care about beauty at all. These people would be content to live in a basement storeroom with steel utility shelves and no windows. Others would shrivel up and die in such an environment. THEY MUST HAVE BEAUTY. Yet oddly enough, such aesthetes often live surrounded by Thing mountains. Jackie Makit, with her mountains of uncompleted craft projects, is such a person. For desiring beauty and being able to create it are, alas, not the same thing.

For the more aesthetically inclined, however, a vision of beauty can sometimes have great motivational power when it comes to reorganizing. People who may be totally uninspired by the thought of clearing their desk of papers and their floor of books may go into action when they get the idea to create an "Impressionist" room with sky blue walls, white ruffled curtains, and framed reproductions of Monet and Degas. Somewhere along their path to realizing this image, they'll rearrange all of their Things so as to pave the way for their idea of beauty. Energized by a vision, the aesthete declutters almost without thinking and goes on to create the room of his or her dreams.

This can work only if the vision is genuine. A genuine vision of beauty comes to us all at once in living color, unfolding in all directions. You could not stop the vision if you wanted to, as your whole being becomes focused around your efforts to realize it. Helpers are recruited, money is spent, ladders are brought down from the attic until at last, THERE IT IS.

Just as you cannot stop the vision from being born, neither can you force it to happen. It comes if and when it chooses. You can, however, do things that may make a vision more likely to choose to emerge. You can look at pictures of rooms in magazines, visit other people's rooms, and make yourself generally room conscious. You can ask yourself where you have felt the best in your life and how you might create a room that makes you feel this way. Ask yourself what appeals to YOU. A shady pine forest? A sophisticated art gallery? An Italian restaurant with red-checked tablecloths? A candlelit church, temple, or mosque? A view of city lights at night?

This is the preparation stage of the creative process. Once you've done some deliberate, conscious studying of rooms and their contents, back off and forget about the whole thing. If you're lucky, lightning will strike, and you will be blessed with a central theme, an IDEA for a room around which to focus your efforts. You will have been given a gift that makes organizing easy, a mere means to an end. This is how real progress happens: one flash at a time, one insight at a time, one vision at a time. Simply repeat the experience with each room in your space, and soon, very soon, you will discover that for you, Things are no longer an issue.

CHAPTER 12

GETTING STARTED WITH
THINGS

THINGS GOALS: THING-HABIT GOALS
AND ENVIRONMENTAL GOALS

You've looked at yourself. You've looked at your Things. Now it's time to decide what YOU will do with THEM. It's time, in other words, to set some Thing-habit goals and some environmental goals.

To determine your Thing-habit goals, review the "You and Your Things Inventory" sections in Part II. List the ten most problematic Thing habits you identified relating to where your Things come from, what you do with them while you have them, and how you get rid of—or don't get rid of—them. For example:

1. I compulsively buy too many clothes.

2. I leave mail piled on the dining room table for several days before opening it.

3. I rarely put Things away after I use them.

4. I have no regular decluttering time.

5. I often start decluttering projects that I don't finish.

6. I spread papers all over my desk instead of filing them.

7. When Things break, I put them in the basement and forget about them.

8. I spend a lot of time on the Internet in order to avoid dealing with my Things.

9. I never get rid of clothes.

10. I let dead Things pile up on the back porch for months before disposing of them.

Now list your ten most important Thing-habit goals, one goal per problematic Thing habit. For example:

1. Shop for clothes only four times per year and spend no more than $200 per time.

2. Sort all mail as soon as I receive it.

3. Put all VITs away after I use them.

4. Declutter routinely every morning.

5. Finish every decluttering job I start.

6. Put unfiled papers in a "to-file" tray.

7. When something breaks, get it fixed within one month or give it to charity.

8. Sign on to the Internet only if all of my Things are in their homes.

9. Take a load of clothes to Salvation Army every six months.

10. Put dead Things in recycle bin or trash as soon as they die.

To set your environmental goals, make use of your notes from your Thing tour and your ideas from visualizing. Environmental goals should be general, listed room by room or area by area, as if completed, always answering the question, How will my environment be different when I've finished? Make a list of your ten most important environmental goals, for example:

1. Way stations set downstairs and up

2. All pictures mounted on walls

3. Living room clutter-free

4. Bedroom closet reorganized

5. Linen closet reorganized

6. Kitchen cupboards and counters reorganized

7. Kitchen curtains hung

8. All papers sorted and filed

9. Basement decluttered

10. Garage cleared and cleaned

Now look at your two lists. If you accomplish all of these goals, you still may not be perfectly at peace with your Things, but you'll be a lot closer to peace than you are now. When you reach this point, you can repeat the process if you wish. Don't worry if the goals you've set seem hopelessly unattainable. Accomplishing your goals, especially your Thing-habit goals, will take time, and you won't have to work on them all at once.

THING-SABOTAGE FACTORS

Along with lists of your Thing-habit goals and environmental goals, also make a list of those factors that may interfere with your achieving them, your Thing-sabotage factors. To identify these, review the Why's in Part III as well as the section from Part II on Thing feelings. Now list your ten most important Thing-sabotage factors. For example:

1. Health: depression

2. Change: recent divorce

3. Visual processing problems

4. Trouble making decisions

5. Activation problems

6. Mental fatigue

7. History: didn't have as many clothes as friends had growing up

8. History: old mental tapes of ex-spouse nagging

9. Deprivation feelings

10. Shame

Now look back at your problematic Thing habits. How do your Thing-sabotage factors explain your current Thing habits? What do you need to do about them? Power to make peace with your Things comes from making connections between these two lists. NOTE: YOU WILL NOT BE ABLE TO ELIMINATE MOST OF YOUR THING-SABOTAGE FACTORS. What you *can* do, however, is begin taking them into account in making your Thing Plans.

Now review the suggestions listed in the section relating to your Thing-sabotage factors and make a list of your countersabotage actions: list one to three specific actions you can take to help counter each Thing-sabotage factor. THIS IS A VERY IMPORTANT LIST. For example:

1. Depression

   - work out three times a week

   - chart moods for three days

2. Divorce

   - find out about divorce support group

   - move all ex's Things out to garage

3. Visual processing problems

   - buy colored folders, magic markers, and colored labels

   - read *Open Your Eyes*

Identifying your Thing-sabotage factors and the specific actions you need to take to address them can make a HUGE difference in how successful you'll be at achieving your Thing goals. DO NOT SKIP THIS STEP.

THING PLANS

Thing goals are about WHAT you want to do. Thing plans are about HOW you're going to do it, especially about *when you're going to do what*. In Chapter 11, we talked about sequencing activities by deciding what to do first, second, and third. Planning is a process of sequencing. In order to decide when to do what, you'll need to decide what's most important to you. Planning also involves prioritizing.

You may think that what you need to do now is make a gigantic monster plan delineating every single action you need to take to accomplish every one of your Thing goals. This approach has several major drawbacks. First, you may be setting yourself up for a lot of frustration when your water heater springs a leak the third day into your plan and everything has to be shoved back to a later date so you can deal with the emergency.

Also, chances are you learned how to plan from your parents and teachers, whose purpose it was to train you to follow THEIR plan. Consequently, any plan, even your own, may elicit feelings, especially rebellious "I WON'T" feelings that may undermine your success at achieving your goals. Having a big, scary monster plan is going to invite a lot more of these feelings than a series of smaller, less ambitious plans. So, please: stop drawing circles and arrows and throw away your Plan to End All Plans, which, if you manage to follow it at all, will only make you feel as though you're in a military boot camp. Instead, choose two or three goals at a time, make a plan for accomplishing them, and follow it until you've done so. Then go on to the next two or three goals.

Planning is not supposed to be a onetime marathon but an ongoing process that you do every day. Ongoing planning is essential. Your number-one priority must be to train yourself to spend an hour or so each month making plans and a few minutes each day clarifying them. NOTHING ELSE WILL HAPPEN IF YOU DON'T DO THIS.

For Thing planning—and all other planning as well—you need some type of planner. The planner does not need to be a leather-bound Franklin planner or Day-Timer: these may give you a nice corporate-executive feeling, but a homemade planner in a loose-leaf notebook will do just fine. Palm Pilots and computer programs are also okay. What's essential is that your planner have adequate space both for scheduling appointments and for listing to-do's for each day.

List only those Thing to-do's you think you can accomplish in the next month, based on your list of Thing-habit goals, environmental goals, and countersabotage actions. Prioritize your Thing to-do's as follows:

First Priority: PLANNING TIME

Second Priority: Countersabotage actions

Third Priority: Thing-habit actions

Last Priority: Environmental actions

Now schedule all these Thing actions using your planner:

1. PLANNING TIME: Write "Plan" on the to-do list for each day for the next month and schedule an hour of PLANNING TIME both today and one month from today.

2. Countersabotage actions: Decide when you'll take each action and put it on the to-do list for the day you plan to do it. If it's an ongoing activity such as "work out three times a week," write it in every Monday, Wednesday, and Friday for the next month, for example.

3. Thing-habit actions: Look at your list of Thing-habit goals. These goals are not simply to accomplish a task once, as are your environmental goals, but to achieve certainty that you'll continue to take—or not take—a particular action over and over. If your goal is to establish the habit of sorting your mail every day as soon as you receive it, you can't simply write "Sort mail" one day in your planner and then check it off as finished. For most people it takes at least a month of doing something every day to feel certain they'll keep doing it. Circle the three Thing-habit goals on your list that you care most about accomplishing. Pick one of these goals. If it requires daily action, write it on the to-do list for EACH day. (Yes, I know it's tedious but it's worth it!) If it's a weekly or monthly action, write it on the to-do list for the appropriate days. Some Thing-habit goals may require onetime start-up actions such as purchasing equipment or setting up a system before you can begin to change the Thing habit. Write these start-up actions on the to-do list for the first day of your Thing Plan.

4. Environmental actions: Look at your list of environmental goals. These goals, unlike your Thing-habit goals, only need to be accomplished once. Once they're done, they're done. Notice how you feel as you look at each one. Some may seem relatively benign, while just thinking about others may make your pulse speed up. Breaking goals down into steps can help to counter this anxiety. Some goals will take many more steps to accomplish than others. Decide when you'll do each step and add it to your to-do list on the appropriate day.

This is all the planning you need to do for now. At your next monthly planning session, you'll repeat this process. Meanwhile, you'll need to clarify and prioritize the actions you've listed for each day on that day, both for Things and for other areas of your life. Label actions A (important and urgent), B (important but not urgent), or C (neither). You may or may not want to schedule to-do's at specific times of day, depending on your level of comfort for structure.

Some days, when you have to rush your cat to the vet, call the plumber, and finish an overdue report, you'll find it impossible to do all the actions you've listed. This is life. When interruptions prevent you from doing what you planned, do NOT waste precious time and energy blaming yourself and others. Instead, reenter the undone tasks in the next open slots in your planner. If interruptions occur constantly, you're overcommitted and may not be able to work toward your Thing goals until some free time opens up. This does not make you a terrible person—just an overcommitted person who will have to travel slowly instead of quickly toward peace with your Things. Reread the section on time and Things in Chapter 7.

Keep all your plans simple, and do not overplan. Making use of spontaneous motivators to declutter—someone coming over, a wave of anger, a change of seasons, getting ready to paint—is at least as important as following a plan. WARNING: PLANNING CAN BE AN

ADDICTIVE ACTIVITY! More than half an hour per day spent on planning is too much. And be forgiving toward yourself if you occasionally go out for an ice cream cone instead of doing what The Plan tells you to do. You're a human being, not a robot, and it's only human to rebel against your plan now and then. Remember that planning is always a means to an end, not an end in itself. Some people may even perform better without a plan, allowing their intuition about what to do next to carry them along.

PLANNING FOR THING DISPOSAL

Along with planning your own Thing actions, you also need to make plans for Thing disposal. Review Chapter 5, consider the list of alternative methods for getting rid of Things, gather information about these options—your community's waste management office may be of help—and—*arrrrrgh!*—make some decisions. Keep a running list of your Thing-disposal decisions.

What excess belongings might you give to someone else? Which might you give to individuals, and which to charities? Research the charities in your area to learn which agencies accept which kinds of Things, where they're located, when they're open, and whether they do pickups. Talk to individual family members or friends to get an idea of who might want what.

Do you have Things you might sell? If so, decide how you'll do this. Do you need to place an ad in your local newspaper? How about using an Internet marketplace? Are any neighborhood yard sales coming up or could you hold one yourself? Would some of your Things be appropriate for a consignment shop or antiques dealer? If so, call and get information about what kinds of Things they accept, percentages, membership fees, and hours of operation. Would any of your friends be interested in trading some of your Things for theirs?

If you don't know already, find out what Things can be recycled in your community. Can you recycle them as they are, or do you need to prepare them? Will someone else pick them up, or do you need to take them to a recycling station? When is the station open?

You will not, of course, be able to decide how you're going to dispose of every last article before you start decluttering: as you work you'll get many new ideas about what you might do with any given Thing. However, the more decisions you make about general groups of Things and the more information you gather ahead of time, the more easily Things will flow from where they are to where they need to go as you begin to consider them, one Thing at a time.

PUTTING A FREEZE ON THINGS

Courtney Chasetail is determined to change her ways with Things. At the outset, Courtney's household is in chaos. Some rooms are so cluttered she can't even get into them. She hasn't had anyone over for years, she is so ashamed. But Courtney has taken a Thing tour and knows exactly what actions she needs to take to make peace with her Things. Courtney plans to declutter her whole house before worrying about changing her Thing habits. When the house is perfect, she thinks, she'll begin "maintenance" in order to keep it that way. Maintenance should be easy compared to the monumental job of decluttering, Courtney tells herself.

Courtney has time to work on decluttering for about two hours a day. She begins her first session in her bedroom, picking clothes up off the floor and reorganizing her dresser drawers. Then, to reward herself, she goes on a shopping spree. She buys two new dresses, a sweater and pants, a lot of underwear, a new purse, and some shoes. When Courtney gets home she takes out all the new clothes and tries them on, leaving them strewn over chairs and hanging out of dresser drawers.

Next she goes downstairs to the family room, takes out her latest bead-stringing project, and works on it for half an hour. When the phone rings, she sets her tray of beads and strings on top of the piano so she can take up where she left off later. Meanwhile, the mail arrives, and she adds it to the pile on the dining room table. Tired from her two-hour decluttering bout, Courtney spends the evening in front of the TV.

Courtney sticks with her decluttering schedule for six months, starting at the top of the house and working her way down. But when she's finished decluttering the basement, she's dismayed to realize that the rest of the house is no better than it was when she started. Courtney can't understand this. She complains to her best friend that no matter what she does, her house remains a mess. She feels hopeless and doomed.

If you're a person with an extremely cluttered dwelling who's determined to change your lifestyle, you might think that you must first declutter your house, then build some new Thing habits that will enable you to keep your home clutter free. Wrong. As long as you approach the problem this way, you're probably destined to stay trapped in clutter forever.

In resolving the issue of Things, your first priority must be to STOP MORE NEW THINGS FROM PILING UP. You can only do this by putting countersabotage and Thing-habit actions before environmental actions. If, for the sake of morale, you want to begin taking small environmental steps toward one or two environmental goals each day, you can do so, but only after you've first taken your countersabotage and Thing-habit actions for that day.

Until you've accomplished all of your environmental goals, you may need to make some special rules, especially when it comes to bringing Things into your space. Ask yourself what particular Things overpopulate your space and put a freeze on acquiring any more of them until you've finished decluttering. Tell other people not to give you anything that can't be consumed—food, flowers, money, and tickets to events are okay. Cancel magazine subscriptions. Contact the Mail Preference Service at www.the-dma.org/consumers/off mailinglist.html or by writing to them at P.O. Box 9008, Farmingdale, New York 11735-9008, and ask that your name not be sold to any mailing list companies. To stem the flow of E-mail, go to www.email

preferenceservice.com and register. To discourage yourself from ever buying anything again, read Don Aslett's *Clutter's Last Stand,* which designates practically everything as junk, from cover to cover twice. If you absolutely *must* buy something new, immediately get rid of something else of the same type. Post a simple equation on your wall: Things Out > Things In = ↓ Clutter.

SETTING UP A MAIL-SORTING SYSTEM

During your predecluttering phase you also need to set up a mail-sorting system to stem the in-flow even if the backlog has to wait. Try this: the moment you next encounter your mail, go through it and throw everything you can into your recycle bin. Now make three piles: mail to give or send to someone else, mail to act on, and mail to file. Get rid of all the mail that goes to someone else. If you need to forward it, do so NOW. Set up boxes or cubbies for mail belonging to others in your house and let *their* mail be *their* problem.

This leaves you with two *piles*: action and file. Set up a horizontal "to-file" tray or, if you have a lot of papers to file, a "to-file" box. Put the action items in an "IN" tray or set up an action system to break down the papers further. To maximize visibility, place a vertical sorter on top of your desk and put colored accordion-style folders in it with labels for different kinds of actions such as "to phone," "to write," "to copy," etc. In addition, write "Urgent" on a red folder and "Financial" on a green one. You also need a "to-hold" folder or tray for papers you can only act on once you've heard from someone else.

Put the urgent and financial items in the appropriate folders, then file the other action papers according to the NEXT action you need to take. Open all bills, write the due date and amount of the bill in large numbers on the outside of the envelope, and stuff the bill back into the envelope. Put bills in order of due date in your financial folder. This will ensure that the bills due the soonest get paid first. KEEPING TRACK OF UNPAID BILLS IS A TOP PRIORITY!

This is only one type of action system, based on one recommended by Judith Kolberg. If it doesn't work for you, experiment until you discover what does, referring to organizing books, but don't make yourself crazy over it. Remember: only new habits can rescue you, not a magic system. The key to success with any action system lies in cultivating especially one very important habit: BE SURE TO LOOK IN YOUR ACTION FOLDERS EVERY DAY. To ensure that you'll do this, put reminders in your planner, ask someone to remind you, or put up signs in strategic places.

Also, remember that you still have to DO something with the papers in the folders. Sticking them in there and forgetting them will soon lead to overflowing folders. Again, use your planner, writing in reminders about locations of particular papers if you need to. Reward yourself each day in some small way when you've finished sorting your mail until it becomes automatic.

SETTING UP A THING-SORTING SYSTEM

Before you begin any household decluttering project, you need to set up a thing-sorting system. First, gather together all your sorting supplies. If you don't have the supplies you need, go buy them. Basic Thing-sorting supplies include the following:

1. Eight fairly large cardboard boxes—bankers' boxes with handles can be purchased at office supply stores and put together or you can use boxes you already have—note: really big boxes are harder to carry when full

2. Assorted smaller boxes—plastic or cardboard—to fit in drawers or on shelves

3. Paper, including graph paper for maps

4. Pens and pencils

5. Felt-tip markers

6. Scotch tape

7. Scissors

8. Large trash bags

9. See-through Baggies of different sizes

10. Label maker, if you have one

11. Sticky notes

12. Any organizing equipment you already have

13. Cleaning supplies and equipment, depending on space being decluttered

14. Anything else you think might be helpful with this particular project

Use the felt-tip markers to label four big boxes: "keep," for Things to stay in the room you're decluttering; "elsewhere," for objects that belong in other rooms; "recycle," for Things to recycle; and "share," for everything you're planning to give, sell, or trade, regardless of recipient (you can break this category down further later—keep it simple for now). Clear a space in the middle of the room and arrange your boxes neatly. Use a fifth box to hold all your smaller Thing-sorting supplies. Set the other three boxes nearby to use as others fill up. Line a wastebasket with a trashbag and set it nearby.

Now, stand back and look at the nice pocket of order you've created in the middle of your space. If you can maintain this pocket of order as you work, it will help to keep you centered. Having all your supplies neatly arranged and ready to go will give you a boost that can make it easier, and a lot more fun, to start each new job as you come to it.

Be it ever so humble, each Thing that you own deserves to have a home. This includes twist ties, thumbtacks, screws, rubber bands, odd keys, and the S-shaped gadget you use to unclog the garbage disposal. As you visualize your future environment, you need to begin to decide upon or at least clarify your Thing homes.

If you're like most people, you probably have already created homes for many of your belongings, while others may perpetually float around, homeless. Think back to when you first moved into your current dwelling. What homes did you create for your Things then? Which Things are you still keeping in their original homes? Which have become homeless? How did this happen?

Making Thing homes is easy when you move into a new space. Every time you put an object away as you unpack, the place where you put it becomes its home. All you have to do is keep putting the Thing back there until it's properly trained to stay in its home except when it's being used.

The trouble is, you may not. Instead, the next time you take the Thing out you may put it away somewhere else, and then somewhere else, until soon the poor, confused Thing is wandering around homeless. Making a decision about where a Thing's home is to be is only the first step: to really establish a home, you have to be consistent about keeping it there. In order to be consistent, you have to REMEMBER where it goes, though you may use written memory—labels and/or indexes—as well as neurological memory to do this. What makes a home a home for a Thing is memory.

Creating homes for Things is harder when you're already moved in, and the shelf you want to use for your ice skates already has luggage on it. This is a lot like colonists making their homes on land that already belongs to the natives. It creates problems. Each time you make a home for an object where something else already lives, you have to make a new home for the old Thing, and your mind gets tied up in knots trying to make it come out right.

One possible response to this dilemma is to empty the contents of all containers out into boxes in the middle of the room. This means that now you have to make new homes for everything all over again, which can take a lot of time. To spare yourself the trouble of starting all over, leave your Things where they are and draw some maps as you tour your space. Graph paper works best, but blank or lined paper will do.

Begin first by mapping out the homes, if any, that you've already established for Things. Now ask yourself what works and what doesn't work. If a home is working for you, leave the objects in it and remove only the other Things from their current containers. Now draw a second map with the objects left in their homes and fill in the others where you'd like them to be. Don't get too nitpicky about this. You won't be able to anticipate where every last nut and bolt is going to go until you actually try some Things in different homes and see what fits where. Draw your map in pencil and revise it as you go. When you've finished, you'll have a nice reminder of where to put Things back when you've used them. Fasten the map to the wall in a prominent place until you've committed it to memory.

Maps are helpful, but they're not absolutely necessary for creating homes for your Things. Another option is to create a few new homes for specific types of objects every day as you declutter and concentrate on keeping them there, using labels as needed. In time, a more and more logical system of homes will evolve.

Making homes for Things is a decision-making process. While there are no wrong homes, some make more sense than others for any given Thing. Certain principles can help you make good decisions about homes:

- *The principle of convenience*: In general, the best home for something places it nearest where it's used. This minimizes disruptions to Flow when you need to use the item. Julie

Morgenstern suggests making a list of all your activities and creating "zones" where the Things you need for each activity are kept, as in a kindergarten classroom.

- *The like-goes-with-like principle*: Keep an object with related objects—baseball bats with baseball bats, cookie cutters with cookie cutters, buttons with buttons.

- *The principle of simultaneous use*: Things used together belong together—baseball bats with baseball gloves, cookie cutters with cookie sheets, buttons with needles and thread.

- *The principle of simplicity*: Wherever possible, use only one home for each category of Thing. If your system of homes is too complicated, it will be harder for you to remember where the homes are and the system will break down.

- *The principle of containment*: The more Things you keep in containers, the less potential for visible clutter there is. The right home for most Things is an appropriately sized container.

As a rule, Things that can be grouped with other like Things are easy to keep in their homes. When dealing with oddball Things, those one-of-a-kind objects that don't seem to fit anywhere, it helps to make a firm decision and announce out loud to all and sundry, "From now on, this soccer ball belongs HERE!" Put a label on the spot until you get used to it. Something in you may rebel against putting the ball next to the artificial Christmas tree, craving a category in which to place it with other like Things. You can deal with such feelings by creating a new category in your mind: oddball Things.

For homes to continue being homes, it's not essential that every single object be in its home at all times. At any given moment, all sorts of Things may be out. But when you put them away, always put them in the same home. In this way, Things are like people. Most of us leave our homes to go other places all the time, sometimes remaining away from them even for years. Yet when we go home, we always go to the same place.

Some Things, however, DO need to stay in their homes except when you're using them: your VITs (Very Important Things—see Chapter 4). Because you use them so frequently, you can waste hours looking for VITs if you don't keep them consistently in their homes. Make a list now of your VITs and assign homes to them. If your house has several stories, you may want to create a home for a given VIT on each floor.

If you put your Things away in the same homes every time, eventually you'll have a map in your mind that includes homes for every object you own. Once you have such a map in your mind, you'll feel more at peace, whatever the state of your Things.

THING HELPERS

Facing chaos can be lonely and even frightening. Having to let go of Things to which you're attached can make it even more so. Many of us feel able to face the chaos and let go of Things only if we have someone else with us for moral support. If you feel this way, asking a friend, relative, employee, or professional organizer to help you achieve your goals may make the difference between success and failure.

This is not to say that you absolutely must have someone at your side to make peace with your Things. Many creative people love solitude and are hypersensitive to intrusion. These people need to honor their feelings as much as those who are more socially inclined, and may well choose to work alone.

While Thing helpers can be supportive, they can also be problematic. Where shame runs high, inviting someone to witness your struggles with Things is not easy. If you feel ashamed, it's important to share these feelings with the helper and let the person know how he or she can help you with them. Someone who says, "Tsk-tsk, how can you possibly live like this?" is NOT a helper.

Even people who aren't deliberately shaming may inhibit your efforts by trying to take charge and do things for you that you're able to do yourself. You may be tempted to go along with this, but in most cases simply turning your mess over to someone else to organize in ways that make sense to HIM or HER is only a temporary solution. In cases where unusually large amounts of clutter have accumulated, you may want to ask a helper to presort in your absence—putting likes with likes and making a pile of possible discards—but YOU need to come back at some point and be the primary decision maker.

In most cases, friends, employees, or professional organizers make better Thing helpers than family members, especially parents and spouses. Family members tend to feel your shame as their shame, which can make it much more difficult for them to help you without being controlling or critical.

Whomever you choose to work with, it is your job to train your helper to help you in ways that are constructive rather than destructive. This does not mean saying things like "Please shut up and let me do it my way," which tend to discourage support rather than improve it. It does mean telling the person what you want: "I don't need you to *do* anything, just be there and be supportive," or "I feel ashamed of my messiness and I need you to challenge me if I start beating up on myself." Be prepared to issue frequent but diplomatic reminders until the person is trained. If this works, keep the helper around; if not, find another helper.

In some cases, a helper may need to do something for you that you really can't do yourself. Visually impaired people may ask someone to supply "eyes" for them, while those with motor handicaps may need someone to move Things from point A to point B. Most of us need someone at times to stand in for one particular piece of our brain that doesn't seem to quite do its job, while leaving the rest of the brain work up to us. If, for example, you have trouble sorting and categorizing, you may want to ask someone to help you with that particular activity.

It's important, in such cases, to be clear with the helper about exactly what that person's job is to be. Do not allow him or her to do anything that you can do for yourself. The helper is to do ONLY that which your brain or body does not do. Many people are afraid to accept help that they truly need for fear of losing their independence. If you allow yourself to use someone else's strengths to make up for your own glitches while continuing to do everything you can yourself, YOU'LL GAIN FREEDOM RATHER THAN LOSE IT. Nobody can do it all, and the most successful people in life are those who know how to make good use of others' talents.

"WHERE SHALL I START?"

You've done a lot of thinking about yourself and Things. You've taken a tour of your space, visualized how you want it to look, set Thing-habit goals and environmental goals, laid out plans, taken counter-sabotage actions, and begun to change your Thing habits. Now you're ready to begin decluttering and reorganizing your home. On Monday morning, you put on your overalls and tie your hair up into a bandanna. You've promised yourself that you'll begin work at 9:00. At 9:45 you're still wandering aimlessly from room to room, unable to decide where to start. It seems terribly important to begin in the right place. Although you couldn't say exactly what will happen if you don't, an ominous feeling hangs over you about what will happen the moment you pick up the wrong first Thing.

If this is you, close your eyes and stretch out your hand. Walk until your hand touches something. Open your eyes and pick the Thing up and put it somewhere that makes more sense than where it is at the moment. Now, did the ceiling come down? The reality is, it makes absolutely no difference where you start as long as you KEEP GOING once you've started. If you KEEP GOING, eventually the whole house will be however you want it to be. THERE IS NO WRONG FIRST THING!

Nevertheless, you might want to keep certain principles in mind in deciding where to stand when you stretch out your hand:

- *The principle of health and safety first*: Anything that is currently threatening someone's health or safety MUST be a first priority. This includes, among other things, fire hazards such as basements stuffed with newspapers, clutter blocking stairways, hallways, and exits, broken glass or sharp pieces of metal, anything someone is likely to trip over, poisonous wastes, and bacteria-breeding filth.

- *The principle of maximum relief*: Out of all the problem areas, which is going to make you feel the best to have under control? Take out your list of five biggest irritants that you created during your Thing tour in Chapter 11, rank the BIs according to how crazy they make you, and start with number one.

- *The principle of visible progress*: When you make progress you can see, you feel motivated to keep decluttering; when you see little progress you feel like giving up. For this reason, to begin by purging your file drawers—a slow, tedious process at best—is probably not a good idea. Far better to haul away the unused exercise equipment and carry your suitcases down to the basement. Removing just one or two big Things from your space will make you feel as if you're really getting somewhere.

- *The principle of encounter frequency*: Chances are you spend more time in your living room than in your attic. Start with the space you spend the most time in and progress to the places you rarely go.

- *The principle of public versus private space*: Some space you share with others in your home and use to entertain outsiders; other space is your alone. If you're easily ashamed or if others are giving you grief about clutter in space you share, begin by freeing up the most public rooms. If, on the other hand, having a sanctuary in which to center yourself is most important to you, begin with your private space and progress.

- *The principle of linearity*: If you have a lot of trouble making decisions and feel befuddled by conflicting principles, you may opt for Felton's Mount Vernon method, which requires that you begin next to the front door, work your way around the walls, and then deal with anything in the middle of the room. Then go on to the next room and do the same.

- *The principle of optimal motivation*: Organizer Michelle Passoff suggests starting in the space you can use for whatever in your life you're making room for by decluttering. If you dream of being an artist, start by decluttering your storeroom and transforming it into a studio. If you have fantasies of working out in the basement, start by cleaning it out and get some exercise equipment.

- *The principle of priming the pump*: If you feel anxious about getting started, you may want to prime the pump by starting with something small and easy to give yourself confidence: a jewelry box, a purse, a briefcase, a tabletop, a junk drawer, a medicine cabinet.

Above all, don't allow yourself to become paralyzed if principles seem to conflict. If you feel conflicted, close your eyes and stretch out your hand toward this page. Swing your hand around in a circle and point to a spot on the page. The principle your finger lands on is the one you should consider first. Now close your eyes, click your heels together and repeat three times: "Starting anywhere will get me there. Starting anywhere will get me there. Starting anywhere will get me there." Then, JUST START!

CHAPTER 13

MOVING THINGS ALONG

ONE THING AT A TIME

As you continue along your decluttering path, don't be surprised if every once in a while you experience a moment of mild to severe Thing panic. You will know when Thing panic hits by what your heart is doing. For long spells, you may not notice much of anything. Then all at once: boom-boom-boom. Thing panic.

When Thing panic hits, the solution is always the same: DO ONE THING AT A TIME. Thing panic comes from mentally skittering far up ahead of yourself. From that vantage point, to remain in any clutter at all for one more instant puts your life in peril: the Wicked Witch of the West will appear and throw you into a bubbling cauldron if you don't get every single Thing in its home NOW. This is a distortion. You have lived in your current state of clutter for weeks, months, or even years, and nothing terrible has happened. Thing panic is just a feeling, and when you zoom in on only ONE THING, you're no longer overwhelmed and can move on.

ONE THING AT A TIME means doing something with your eyes and with your mind. You must, first of all, stop looking at too many Things at the same time. Point yourself in one direction and hold your head still. Do not move your body. You have just eliminated at least two-thirds of the room from your visual field. Now go further.

Make a spyglass using your fist and look through it. Keep closing the "lens" until you can see only ONE THING through it. Shut out not only the Things around you, but also the Things in your head. Tell yourself that right now the ONE THING that you see in front of you is the only real Thing in the world. Say the words, "ONE THING AT A TIME" aloud to yourself. Now decide what to do with the object you've zeroed in on. As the one paper slides into the file or the one broken lamp goes out to the trash, notice how your heartbeat slows down and the Thing panic subsides.

The more you begin to practice this technique, the less frequently Thing panic will strike. In time ONE THING AT A TIME will become a habit. When that happens, decluttering will be virtually painless, and you'll be well on your way to peace with your Things.

THING MINDFULNESS

Next time you're standing in line at the supermarket, notice how different people pick up groceries and place them on the counter. Some people grab the cheese, the marshmallows, or the detergent and throw them down any old way. Others pick up each object and place it on the counter in some sort of discernible pattern—like groceries with like, prices turned toward the cashier, weighables together. The fact that the groceries are going to stay on the counter for only a few moments until someone puts them in a bag does not prevent such people from paying attention to the PROCESS of placing the groceries. In fact, they cannot KEEP from paying attention even if they want to. This is because somehow or other they've developed Thing mindfulness.

To some of us, Thing mindfulness comes more naturally than to others. It is not, however, purely a matter of brain chemistry. Thing mindfulness can be trained, if you're willing to take the trouble, though for some people the training may require more effort than for others. Training Thing mindfulness is merely a matter of consciousness raising, of becoming conscious of something to which you were previously oblivious.

The best way to make peace with your Things is to begin to raise your consciousness of them, to become Thing mindful. When you can no longer pick up a Thing without feeling it in your hand, when you can no longer put a Thing down without noticing WHERE you've put it down and how it affects every Thing—and every person or animal—around it, then you're Thing mindful. Thing mindfulness prevents you from tossing your mail on the dining room table day after day so no one can eat a meal without having to move the piles. Thing mindfulness makes it impossible for you to dump excess Things in your attic, on your neighbor's lawn, or in the Atlantic Ocean, and allows you to share them with others or dispose of them responsibly instead. If enough of us achieve Thing mindfulness, we may even be able to save planet Earth.

How can you achieve Thing mindfulness? By patient, persistent retraining, asking for help along the way in slowing down and being more aware of what you're doing with Things. To begin your Thing-mindfulness training, choose a small decluttering task such as cleaning out a drawer. Instead of dumping the drawer out on the floor, take each object out, ONE THING AT A TIME. Feel each object in your hand as you pick it up. Now carefully PLACE the object—don't toss it—on the floor or in a container. Move slowly and feel your movement every inch of the way, as if you're doing a dance.

Now pick up another Thing. Sort as you place until all of the Things are out of the drawer. Arrange Things neatly as you sort them into piles or containers: Things to put back, Things to put somewhere else, Things to dispose of. Now slowly put all the appropriate Things back in the drawer and carry each other Thing to its destination. Notice how the patterns you created in sorting shift from moment to moment as you put Things away.

Consider your options for Things that need to be disposed of, and make decisions one at a time, then carefully take each Thing where it needs to go—the Salvation Army bag, the trunk of the car, the recycling bin. Even if you put a Thing in the trash, do this with full mindfulness. Now open the drawer and sit quietly looking at your work for a moment. Ask yourself how your decluttering experience felt compared with those you've had in the past. Was it pleasant or unpleasant? Don Aslett writes, "Almost any activity becomes pleasant if the pace is slowed sufficiently."

Thing mindfulness is about process. Tibetan Buddhists spend years creating beautiful, intricate sand designs only to wipe them out in a single instant, to remind themselves of the constancy of change in the universe. What we do with Things is simply one more part of that constant change. Chaos is inevitable: sooner or later someone or something will mess up the drawer that you organized so beautifully, but that's how things are supposed to be. What can save you from despair is enjoying the PROCESS.

Now that you know what Thing mindfulness feels like, try doing one task involving Things mindfully each day. Pay particular attention to how you place Things temporarily. If you're doing dishes, line up the dishes beautifully next to the sink before you wash them, then watch the patterns change as you move one dish at a time into the sink and then into the dish rack. Notice how the water swirls across the plates in the sink and how the bubbles disappear as you rinse the glassware. Feel each plate or glass in your hands when it's dirty, clean, wet, dry. Occasionally, you may want to declare a "Thing-Mindfulness Day" and try to be extra aware of each object you encounter throughout the day.

Thing mindfulness may help you with more than just Things. Cultivating mindfulness in any area of your life has the potential to change your whole life. Once Thing mindfulness becomes a habit, you may find yourself dealing more mindfully with the animate as well as the inanimate world, taking time to listen to others and savoring each moment of change, wherever it takes you and whoever is there.

Sandy Chaser, working single mother of three hyperactive children, is feeling overwhelmed. Her children are at her mother's house, but in only two hours she will have to pick them up. Sandy had promised herself that she would spend these two hours decluttering but this seems futile, given the enormity of the problem. Thing mountains are everywhere, and Sandy is sure that it would take months of nonstop work to make a dent in them—months that she doesn't have and may never have. In despair, she calls Judy Stackwright and asks her what she would suggest. "Forget the chaos," says Judy, "just try to create a pocket of order and keep it organized and see how that makes you feel."

"But there's so much to DO!" Sandy wails.

"One pocket of order," says Judy.

Sandy decides that the pocket of order she will create for herself in the next two hours will be her car. A few days earlier, a colleague had asked Sandy to give her a ride to work, and although she hurriedly tossed all of the squashed Burger King sacks and muddy school papers into the backseat, she felt slovenly and mortified, especially when she saw that the back of her friend's skirt was covered with Playdo crumbs when she got out of the car.

It's a crisp, sunny, October afternoon, and Sandy carries her Thing-sorting supplies and tape player out to the garage. Putting her favorite jazz tape on and opening the garage door to let in the sunlight, she gets busy making her car into a pocket of order. Sandy begins by writing "KEEP," "ELSEWHERE," "RECYCLE," and "SHARE" on four sorting boxes, unfolding a plastic garbage bag for the trash, and arranging the boxes and supplies neatly next to the car. Then she opens the front car door on the driver's side and quickly removes a few leaves and papers from the floor and a used coffee cup from the holder and stuffs them into a trash bag. Groping under the seat, she pulls out a glove she thought she had lost and puts it into the "ELSEWHERE" box.

The passenger side takes a little longer but Sandy sorts mindfully, ONE THING AT A TIME. She throws papers into the "RECYCLE" box, an umbrella into the "KEEP" box, a water pistol and a deck of cards into the "ELSEWHERE" box and two pairs of outgrown sneakers into the "SHARE" box. Then she starts on the backseat, sorting through gym shorts, dog's leash, history books, and many, many papers. After that the trunk, and she's nearly done. All she still has to do is empty the ashtrays and sort the maps and papers from the glove compartment into Baggies.

When she's finished, Sandy carries out the trash and contents of the "RECYCLE" box to the bins and distributes the Things in the "ELSEWHERE" box where they belong inside the house. Then she gets into the car and drives it over to a nearby car wash, vacuums out the seats and rugs, and rolls on through. At home in the driveway, Sandy wipes off mirrors, windows, vinyl, and chrome, places the "KEEP" items back in the car, and puts her supplies away. *Done.*

Sandy goes back out to the driveway and stands for a long time surveying her handiwork with deep satisfaction. Sunbeams gleam off the polished chrome, lifting Sandy's spirits for the first time in weeks. She did this! Glancing at her watch, Sandy discovers that she still has time to celebrate. Hurriedly, she locks up the house, climbs into her sparkling vehicle, puts on her sunglasses, turns on the stereo, and cruises down the boulevard to her favorite sidewalk café.

In the days that follow, whenever Sandy digs through Thing mountains to try to find her daughter's shoe, whenever she wears a wrinkled dress to work extracted from a pile on her closet floor, she thinks about The Car. Visualizing the car during chaotic moments leaves Sandy feeling soothed and energized. Meanwhile, by decluttering the car each time she gets out of it and by demanding that her children do the same, she manages to hang on to her personal pocket of order. Now instead of feeling helpless and victimized, she feels strong and capable, able to create more order in a chaotic universe anytime she chooses.

The next week, Sandy's mother again offers to take the children, and Sandy spends three more hours creating another pocket of order in the upstairs bathroom. Before long, she has many such pockets; in time, she has more pockets of order than pockets of clutter.

Sandy succeeds at creating and maintaining a pocket of order for several reasons:

1. She chooses a task that is doable in the time she has available.

2. She focuses on making the experience of organizing as pleasurable as possible, playing music, taking her time, and enjoying the nice weather.

3. When she's finished, she takes time to survey and appreciate her handiwork.

4. When she's finished, she takes time to reward herself.

5. She changes her Thing habits along with decluttering.

You may have times when it seems impossible to do much at all about your Things, but this does not mean you're doomed to flounder perpetually in chaos. No matter how exhausted, how overwhelmed, how inept, or how grief stricken you may feel, you can always create a small pocket of order in your world and in yourself.

MOVING THINGS ON

In preparing to declutter, as discussed in Chapter 12, you made plans about how you'll get rid of different types of Things. Now is the time to put these plans into effect. In setting up your Thing-sorting system you designated one box, for the sake of simplicity, only as "SHARE" rather than specifying different charities, shops, or individuals.

Once you finish decluttering a room, closet, or other area, however, you'll need to further sort your "SHARE" items in accordance with their specific destinations and GET THEM THERE AS SOON

AS POSSIBLE. If you don't have a car, call a taxi, load the cab up, and give the driver an extra big tip for helping you. If you do have a car, put the "SHARE" Things in your trunk and drive them to their destination. If you can't do this right away, at least put them in your garage or on your back porch. You may allow Things to accumulate while you declutter more than one area so you can take them all at once, but while they collect, try to get them out of your house or, if you have to keep them inside, put them someplace where you can't forget about them.

In the meantime, dispose of all dead Things as quickly as you can. Prepare all recyclables and drive them to the nearest recycling station if your city does not pick them up. Then turn everything that's left over to Oscar the Grouch.

This part may be hard for ecologically conscious folks. It doesn't feel good knowing that these Things will be going into a dump or landfill, but at times you need to give yourself permission to let this happen. While your concern about the environment is more than valid, your home is part of the environment too. To counter uncomfortable feelings, learn everything you can about recycling; join an organization to work for better waste disposal; shop where you can use your own containers; and buy Things that are recyclable or biodegradable whenever you can.

LETTING GO OF THINGS

Elsie Clutcher, recovering clothing addict, is feeling serene. Her closet is loosely packed and beautifully organized, containing only a certain specified quota of each type of garment. Elsie limits her clothes shopping time to one afternoon per month, and each time she buys something new, she puts an old garment of the same type in a bag for the resale shop. Now whenever something upsets her, instead of heading for the mall, Elsie puts on some quiet music and sits down in her favorite armchair to give herself a time out.

This did not happen instantly. Elsie spent many hours with her organizer, filling bag after bag with clothes to sell or give away. When she had finished, she set the bags on the back porch. They stayed there for three months. Finally, she carried them out to her car and put them into her trunk, where they stayed for another month. When she found herself thinking about taking them out again so she could pack the car to go on a ski trip, she immediately climbed into the car and drove the bags to the Salvation Army store. Meanwhile, Elsie attended a support group who cheered her along at every step of the way and gave her a safe place to air her feelings.

Decluttering is a constant process of letting go. For some of us, this is easier than for others. If you're having trouble, try the following:

- Reframe: Imagine your home is a store and "shop" for those items you need, then get rid of the rest. Group Things as "friends, acquaintances, and strangers" and deal with them accordingly, as Judith Kolberg advises.

- Replace: Substitute photos, drawings, written descriptions, or videotapes for real items.

- Memorialize: Take a few, representative samples from a collection, mount them beautifully, and toss the others.

- Limit: Only allow yourself to keep a certain number or volume of Things.

- Wean: Don Aslett suggests an "emotional withdrawal box" for Things to sit in for one to three months before you dispose of them. If you're a true Thing addict, make a list of the types of Things you need to get rid of, rate them from 0 to 10 according to how anxious it makes you to think of doing so, then get rid of the easiest Things first and progress to the most difficult.

- Distance: Team up with a Thing helper whose job it is to put Things in the "RECYCLE," "SHARE," or trash containers under your direction. Kolberg points out that when you touch the objects yourself, you're more likely to want to hang on to them, a phenomenon she calls "kinetic sympathy."

- Interconnect: Remind yourself that nothing is really permanently yours anyway, and give your Things back to the universe from which they came.

Moving through the process of decluttering, you let go not only of burdensome excess Things but also of the thoughts and feelings you associate with them. You cannot let go of one and hang on to the other. The ideal attitude for mindful decluttering is one of complete surrender to the process itself or to a higher power, if you will. In this way all of life may be viewed as a process of "lightening up," of slowly relinquishing the material in favor of the immaterial.

THINGS AND WATER

Consider water. Water is everywhere, cycling and recycling, filling big, black clouds with rain that showers down into puddles and oceans, flowing into bathtubs and toilets and bottles and drinking fountains, swirling down drains and through pipes and into reservoirs to begin all over again. Except in extremely dry areas, there's plenty of water for everyone, so that in most places on earth, water is freely shared. When you give someone a glass of water, you don't feel that you're giving the person something that's YOURS as a gift, but simply allowing your friend to SHARE something that belongs to everyone.

Turn on the faucet and fill a sink with water. Put your hands in the water, then pull the plug. As the water swirls down the drain, try first to hang on to it, to keep it from going down. Doesn't this make you feel ridiculous? Open your hands and let the water flow freely away.

Now imagine that all of the Things in your space have been magically transformed into water. Try to feel the Thing-water flowing through your fingers the way the water flowed down the drain. Envision the Thing-water flowing freely into the places where it needs to go: your closets and drawers, the recycle bin, the box for the library, the bags for the bundle drive and the Salvation Army, the Dumpster or the incinerator. As you work with your Things, don't try to force anything to go anywhere; instead allow your Thing-water to flow naturally.

You can only think about Things this way if you're able to trust in the abundance and generosity of the universe to meet your needs. This may be difficult if the corner of the universe in which you've lived contained neither abundance nor generosity, if you were taught, either by experience or by others, that the world is a place in which there's never enough and that only cutthroat competition and tight-fisted hoarding would ensure that you would always have enough Things to meet your needs.

Paradoxically, it's just such attitudes that have produced the scarcity that many of us fear. The human race has long been tied up in knots over this. In adopting a faith that THERE WILL BE ENOUGH and learning to live by that faith, you begin, at long last, to untie the knots. Remember that your part of the universe is only one tiny corner and that beyond it lies a plenitude of Things as vast as the oceans.

In Mitch Albom's popular memoir, *Tuesdays with Morrie,* Albom's dying teacher, Morrie, retells a story from his deathbed about two ocean waves. One wave is perfectly happy doing whatever waves do until he notices that the waves up ahead of him are all crashing on the shore. When, horrified by this realization, he asks another wave if he doesn't think it's terrible, his friend answers, "No, you don't understand. You're not a wave, you're part of the ocean." As with us, so with our Things.

CHAPTER 14

WHEN THINGS GET STUCK

THING NAUSEA

Blech! It's guaranteed to happen. Sooner or later, as you continue to sort and scrutinize, decide about and dispose of your Things, you will reach a point where you feel that if you have to look at another Thing, you will throw up. You will reach the point of Thing nausea. It happens to everyone. Runners call this hitting the wall. Time starts to slow down, down, down and you feel that you simply can't go on.

The important thing to remember when Thing nausea entangles you in its sticky, green goo is that this is NORMAL. You have not suddenly come down with chronic fatigue syndrome. You are not destined to wind up on a ventilator if you don't stop work immediately to conserve your precious energy. You're probably not even really going to throw up. Thing nausea is just a feeling, not a physiological condition.

The only thing you need to do when Thing nausea strikes is say to yourself the words, "This is just Thing nausea." Then go on decluttering and reorganizing, ONE THING AT A TIME. Do not stop working when you're experiencing Thing nausea. Keep working until you're past the negative feelings and then take a break, setting a specific time to start again and visualizing your next action. If you give in to Thing nausea at all, you may have trouble getting back to work. Thing nausea has caused many a would-be reorganizer to founder, but those who can get past it will make it all the way to the finish line.

Above all, do not act out any wild fantasies you may have—and you *will* have wild fantasies. You will fantasize about taking everything you own to the edge of the Grand Canyon and heaving it over. You will contemplate setting a match to the whole kit and kaboodle, including your Ming vase and your Stradivarius violin. You will seriously consider locking up your house, getting on an airplane, and never coming back. DON'T DO ANY OF THESE THINGS!

Instead, reframe your situation as an opportunity to be a hero. Use your brain's insight system constructively: you're an explorer in the jungle, hacking your way through giant rubber trees with a machete knife; you're a mountain climber, three-quarters of the way to the summit, straining to reach the next ledge; you're a long-distance swimmer with the other shore of the English Channel in sight.

Or simply talk to your Things. Tell them how you feel toward them right now and get it out of you: "I'm sick to death of you!" "I can't stand you!" Swear and curse and stomp your feet. Then neutralize your language, subordinate your irritation, and assert yourself: "I may be tired of you, but I'm not going to stop until I've finished what I set out to do today." "I would like to be doing something else, but I'm going to keep putting you all in your homes."

Wild fantasies are not the only brain tricks that may accompany Thing nausea. Along with fantasies go the rationalizations for quitting that seem like perfectly reasonable thoughts from out of nowhere. You're plugging away and all of a sudden a voice in your head that sounds like your favorite movie star croons, "Why don't you just give yourself the rest of the day off? You've worked hard— you deserve a break—come on, now, let's have some fun, darling." Beware. What tells you that this is the voice of Thing nausea is that its suggestions come to you OUT OF THE BLUE. One moment you're doggedly sorting newspapers with every intention of continuing and the next moment you get this great idea to go bass fishing. If, at the end of a good day's work, you decide to reward yourself by going fishing tomorrow, that is not Thing nausea—that is you, and it is always good to listen to you.

As Thing nausea happens mainly when you're overfocused on the work still left to be done, the best antidote to it is to redirect your attention. Instead of thinking about what's still left to do, look back at what you've already achieved and give yourself credit for it. "I know I can do this—I already reorganized the whole basement, after all, and that was much yuckier." The secret of surviving Thing nausea is not to avoid it but rather to view it as an opportunity to experience the joy of your own strength. If you keep handling ONE THING AT A TIME, no matter what, when the smoke has cleared you will feel proud and strong. And you'll see the light at the end of the garage. You'll see peace with your Things beginning to dawn.

THING SABOTAGE

Jackie Makit, craft enthusiast, has nearly finished organizing her entire house. To do this, Jackie first had to come to terms with her task-completion problems, get rid of many of her unfinished craft projects, organize the rest, and make a one-project-at-a-time rule for herself. This was not easy, and Jackie spent time in therapy grieving her limitations and rethinking her life. Meanwhile, she translated her insights into an action plan for changing negative Thing habits and decluttering her environment. Although Jackie's progress has had its ups and downs, gradually the Thing mountains have begun to disappear, and Jackie has begun to enjoy the new freedom that an organized household has given her. She's even thinking about going back to school to get a degree in art education. All that remains is to clean out the upstairs closets and sort through her photos and she'll have achieved every one of her Thing goals.

In the beginning, Jackie's husband, Willie, was Mr. Supportive. Willie cooked dinner so Jackie could finish sorting her craft projects. Willie spent his weekends helping Jackie rearrange furniture and sorting through his own clothes and books. Willie brought Jackie roses to adorn the beautifully cleared dining room table. Willie told Jackie again and again how proud he was of her for "taking the bull by the horns."

Lately, however, Willie has made such remarks less often. Coming in one evening to a sparkling kitchen with every pot and pan in place, Willie says, "You know you really don't have to overdo this organizing thing. It's getting so I'm afraid to move, for fear of messing something up. The house looks great to me just the way it is. Why don't you take a week off, Honey, and do some crafts?"

Jackie feels the starch go out of her. She also feels confused. Has she been right to do all this work? Maybe she's turned into some kind of neat-nut. But isn't that better than living in squalor? She feels annoyed with Willie, but she bites her tongue because she knows he's just trying to be helpful. Or is he?

Watch out, Jackie. Though Willie may truly want change, he also may not. For whatever reason, most human brains seem wired to maintain the status quo at all costs, to drag us—and those near and dear to us—back to bad old habits just because they ARE old and therefore comfortable. This does not make Willie the enemy. He is not. But, like Jackie herself, he's ambivalent. And just as she must keep handling ONE THING AT A TIME in the face of her own Thing nausea, Jackie must keep handling ONE THING AT A TIME in the face of Willie's Thing sabotage until both have begun to recede, as in time they will.

Thing saboteurs—always those closest to us—employ a variety of sabotage strategies to undermine our efforts to change. Some of these sabotage strategies are the following:

- *The reassurance strategy:* It looks great "just the way it is." "There's nothing wrong with a home looking lived-in. It's a home, after all, not a shop window." Your response: "I appreciate your reassurance, but I still have to finish what I started if I'm going to feel good about myself."

- *The nostalgic sigh strategy:* "Sometimes I really miss the days when this felt like a real home." The saboteur is telling the truth. Change brings grief for everyone concerned, even when it's positive change. Your response: "I know that right now you miss the way things used to be, but I believe that eventually you'll like what I've done."

- *The labeling strategy:* "When did you get to be such a perfectionist?" "You're a different person from the one I married—you didn't use to be so fascistic." Your response: "I know it may seem to you like I'm overdoing this, but I feel that I have to overdo it for a while before I'll be able to trust myself not to go back to the way I was, and I need you to bear with me. In time it should balance out."

- *The implied labeling strategy:* "Don't you think you're overdoing this neat thing?" "Why don't you try leaving something out for a change?" Translation: "You're turning into a neat-nut and I don't like it." Your response: the same as above.

- *The role-reversal strategy:* The saboteur, originally a model of neatness, becomes more and more careless with Things. The saboteur is testing you, fighting to maintain the system's equilibrium. Your response: "Have you noticed that the neater I get, the less you take care of your own Things? I wonder why that is." Do NOT try to force the saboteur to stop making messes. If possible, contain the person's clutter and continue to follow your own action plan for dealing with YOUR Things. See Chapter 7 for suggestions on dealing with Automatic Clutter Makers.

- *The guilt-trip strategy:* "You don't care about me anymore. All you care about is having the neatest house in town. What's happened to you?" Your response: "I love you just as much as I ever did, and I'm willing to do everything I can to help you feel loved. Guilt, however, is not going to keep me from doing what I have to do."

- *The abandonment-threat strategy:* "Maybe we're just not compatible anymore, now that you've changed." "I'm not sure I can stay around if this is how you're going to be." Your response: "When you decide to change, you always risk losing the people you love. If you feel you can't live with a neat person, I'll understand. I hope that's not the case, though, as I still love you as much as ever."

In countering all these strategies, the key is to remember that in most cases, if you remain calm, stand firm, and continue to deal with ONE THING AT A TIME, the sabotage will soon stop. No one can keep hurling himself or herself against a brick wall forever, and in the meantime empathize, empathize, empathize. Though the saboteur may bluster and whine and act downright hateful at times, this is usually temporary: if love was there at all before, sooner or later it will surface again. If you allow your efforts to change to be undermined by the saboteur, on the other hand, your resentment at the control you've given the person over your life may do serious damage to your relationship.

To stay on track, remind yourself that if you're consistent in your own efforts, Thing sabotage will almost certainly be JUST A PHASE. Chances are, once you've outlasted all the tricks and games that the saboteur can devise to test your resolve, he or she will be as delighted as ever with your new, more organized lifestyle and may even begin to profit from your example.

A DIFFERENT KIND OF HELP

Sometimes the help we can get from family and friends with our Things just isn't enough. Family and friends may have problems of their own to resolve before they can be of much help to anyone else. And when they do try to help us with Things, they may be too emotionally involved with us to keep from being critical. There comes a time in most people's lives when they need to get professional help of one sort or another. When it comes to Things, the question is, what kind of professional should you call?

Three kinds of professionals may be helpful in resolving Thing problems: professional organizers/organizing consultants, coaches, and counselors/psychotherapists. For many, the best place to start is with a professional organizer or organizing consultant. (These two roles differ only in that an organizing consultant is unlikely to do "hands-on" organizing FOR the client, while a professional organizer may or may not do this kind of work in addition to helping the client organize.)

An organizer will come to your home or workplace and help you to organize your Things and develop new skills. There are many different kinds of organizers, with all sorts of different specialties. Some are primarily office organizers, while others work mainly in the home. Some specialize in event planning, moving, office design, estate organizing, or helping people with disabilities such as attention deficit disorder. Others specialize in helping people who are chronically disorganized. If Things are a long-term issue for you, these are the organizers that will be able to help you the most.

Not all organizers are geared to helping clients with Thing issues: some aim instead to help fast-track people, mostly in offices, be hyperorganized in order to accomplish as much as they and their staffs possibly can in highly competitive situations. These organizers may have unrealistic expectations when working with chronically disorganized clients, who often require a more flexible and imaginative, though equally professional, approach compared with their other clients.

You can find an organizer in several different ways. The National Association of Professional Organizers has a referral line—(512) 206-0151—(see Appendix for address and Internet URL) and will refer you to organizers in your area. Be sure to ask for an organizer who works with chronically disorganized clients. Or you can look in the phone book under "organizers," watch the want ads, or simply ask around.

You may wonder how you can know if an organizer is qualified. At present, this is not easy, since no formal credentials are yet attached to an organizer's name, as in the case of CPAs, for example, though plans have been made to eventually examine organizers who wish to become a CPO (certified professional organizer). For now, you should ask if the organizer belongs to NAPO, ask about his or her background and experience and, most importantly, trust your own instincts. Working with someone with whom you do not feel comfortable is not going to get you anywhere.

If you feel that your organizing skills are adequate but you have a lot of trouble staying on track in accomplishing goals, you might want to work with a coach rather than an organizer. This can be particularly useful if you have attention deficit disorder. Many individuals with ADD check in regularly with a coach for help not only with organizing and managing Things but in achieving other goals as well.

A coach's job is to provide structure, support, skills, and strategies in accomplishing clearly defined goals. Writers work with coaches when writing a book. Businesspeople work with coaches while starting a business. If your goals are to change your Thing habits and reorganize your environment, a coach is someone with whom you can check in. Coaching is sometimes done in person, but a lot of it is done by phone, E-mail, or fax. Contact is usually frequent—often daily—but brief. It may consist of a ten-minute phone call or a short E-mail to check progress and help with problems, with occasional longer sessions to review progress and work on specific skills.

If you find yourself wanting to spend more time talking about feelings than working or problem solving, this is a sign that you may need to contact a counselor or psychotherapist. You may want to begin with a mental health professional and hold off for the time being on working with an organizer or coach if you have severe, long-term Thing problems or other symptoms that you believe to be abnormal.

In choosing a therapist, you need to look for someone who understands that people have different thinking styles and is not simply going to assume that all of your problems with Things are the result of unresolved conflicts stemming from childhood experiences. Therapists who discount the biological (brain) and societal aspects of clients' problems often do more harm than good. The ideal therapist for people with Thing issues uses a *biopsychosocial model* of treatment, which incorporates a solid understanding of neurological differences, dynamic (other people, past and present) issues, and societal context. THERAPISTS WHO ZERO IN ON ONLY ONE DIMENSION AND IGNORE THE OTHERS ARE NOT GOOD FOR PEOPLE WITH THING ISSUES.

As with organizers and coaches, it's essential that you feel comfortable with your therapist. There may be times when you'll need to feel uncomfortable for a brief period, but if discomfort is the rule rather than the exception, GET OUT OF THERE. Large amounts of money have been wasted on bad "therapy," and that's the last thing you need.

If you can afford it, you may want to work with more than one professional at once—for example, an organizer and a therapist. This can be ideal, especially if you're willing to allow the professionals to communicate with one another. Doing so will ensure that they will not be working at cross-purposes.

INSIGHT, IN MIND

No matter who else you might have to help you, you will always have one friend to guide you through the issue-resolution process from beginning to end: your own insight system and its fruits. Whenever you feel discouraged or stuck, you need only call upon everything you've learned so far about yourself and your Things to move on. What you'll need to do then will depend on what you've learned.

Some insights have to do with how your feelings affect your dealings with Things. By understanding what feelings Things can evoke in you, you can allow yourself simply to name your feelings and KEEP GOING. Griselda Backglance keeps going even though she feels sad. Professor Tightstring keeps going even though he feels angry. Elsie Clutcher keeps going, ONE THING AT A TIME, even though she feels as though she can't let go of her Things.

Other insights have to do with your situation. Albert Juggler has learned that his problem is overcommitment and took two days off to train his new secretary to organize his papers for him. Eric Cramp has learned that he's space poor and is now reading Thoreau and enjoying getting rid of nonessentials. Sandy Chaser has realized how much of her clutter is created by her hyperactive children and asked other parents in her CHADD group to help her set up an ADD-proof household.

Still other insights have to do with your brain. Ramona Dwindle reminds herself, when she feels tired while decluttering, that she's suffering from mental fatigue and needs to take a ten-minute solitaire break every hour before getting back to work. Maria Branchoff, catching herself about to call a travel agent after finding a brochure, remembers about side-trip seduction, sticks the brochure in her "to-phone" folder and goes on purging her files. Melinda Snakebitten, believing she's finished decluttering, remembers that she has visual processing problems, looks again, and realizes that she still has work to do. Miranda Grayshade, frustrated by categories that don't work for her, files her papers alphabetically.

In addition, some insights relate to the influences of others. Griselda Backglance, carting her uncle Albert's fifty albums to the local stamp and coin store, reminds herself for the twentieth time that she is NOT her mother and does not have to keep everything her mother would have kept. Eliot Status, rolling his lawn mower out for the neighborhood yard sale, reminds himself for the twentieth time that he does NOT have to be just like Roger Suburb. Cheri Gridlock, finding the sweater she knitted Brad in the Goodwill bag, reminds herself for the twentieth time that Brad is NOT her alcoholic father.

Finally, the most important insight to keep in mind as you sort through shoestrings and lightbulbs, batteries and tiddledywinks, is the insight that all of life is a mixture of chaos and order and that's the way it's supposed to be. Only balance, not perfection, can bring you peace with Things.

CHAPTER 15

PEACE WITH YOUR THINGS

A SUPER-DUPER THING CELEBRATION

You're done. You just put your last pair of sandals in your bedroom closet and closed the closet door. For a moment, you stand there in the sunlight, feeling dazed. You open the door again and behold your shoes lined up like soldiers, your pants and shirts hanging in neat rows. You wander into the living room and glance around at polished end tables displaying your favorite magazines, then move on to the kitchen to admire gleaming pans hanging over the stove, dishes arranged by size and shape on the shelves. Everything is clean, orderly, and in its clearly defined home. Yet somehow it still doesn't feel as though you're finished. There must still be *something* left to do. With difficulty you restrain an impulse to make a new mess so you can get back to decluttering. This was not how you thought it would be. You feel lost. What should you do next?

What should you do next? That's easy. CELEBRATE! It's time for a super-duper Thing celebration big enough to outcelebrate all the little celebrations you may have previously held to reward yourself for bits of progress along the way. For weeks and weeks you were able to stick with it until you accomplished your last environmental goal. This achievement shows something important about you: you have what it takes to accomplish a long-term goal. If you could finish this job, you can finish other long-term projects: get a degree, write a book, establish a business. This is truly something to celebrate.

Before your celebration begins, however, perform a precelebration ritual in savoring your handiwork to the limit. Walk from room to room, alone or with a supportive friend, and appreciate what you've done. Look inside each closet and drawer and ooh and ah. Bless the room with incense and/or chanting, decorate it with flowers, say a prayer, take pictures, or simply recite a sentence or two in each room: "This is a peaceful and beautiful room. May good things always happen in this room." If you find yourself noticing places you missed, do NOT try to do anything about them. It's time to shift your focus from what's wrong to what's right. The ritual is the serious part—now comes the fun.

If you've always been isolated by your clutter, you may want to begin your celebration by throwing a party. If this feels scary, keep the party small—even a single good friend or special date will do—and invite only people you can rely on to be nice. After your party, be sure to take down the streamers, toss the empty Champagne bottles in the recycle bin, and vaccuum the floor. Your environment should look just as clean and organized as before the festivities. Allow your guests to help you with cleanup if they're willing: you deserve it.

Beyond partying, how you'll choose to celebrate will depend on who you are. Jackie Makit celebrated by allowing herself three weeks to complete unfinished craft projects, decorate her house with her handiwork, and go to a crafts fair. Freddy Whizbang rewarded himself with a trip to a rock festival. Griselda Backglance got her hair done, paid for a manicure, bought a new dress, and attended a singles' dance, where she met a handsome widower she's now dating. Brad and Cheri Gridlock went to a couples' retreat where they learned better communication skills and are now talking about having a child. Professor Tightstring took a badly needed sabbatical and wrote a book.

Don't be surprised if it takes you a while to loosen up and enjoy your celebration. You've been making yourself miserable over Things for a long time, and happiness takes practice, just like everything else. Air any negative feelings that crop up with a friend, therapist, or significant other, and get back to having fun as quickly as you can.

You don't need to dread your Super Duper Thing celebration being over, for the best is yet to come: the adventure of living in your newly organized space and discovering how much more smoothly you now flow through your days and nights. No more hours wasted foraging through Thing mountains to find what you need. No more Thing mountains. Though you may not have realized it, the satisfaction of "I DID THIS" was what you were really craving when you tried so hard to fill yourself with Things. You deserve this satisfaction. You deserve every bit of it. CONGRATULATIONS!

THING TRUST

Hold on. You may have reorganized your space, but that does not mean the issue of Things is resolved. You've taken an important step, but it is *only* a step, and if you assume that the issue is resolved at this point, the Thing mountains will soon be back. To achieve lasting peace with your Things, you need to do more than create homes, declutter to a level you can tolerate, and begin to establish new Thing habits: you must also MAINTAIN your Things habits long enough to establish Thing trust.

Thing trust means trusting yourself about Things. It means feeling absolutely secure, inside yourself, that though Thing mountains may accumulate temporarily now and then, at a certain predictable point in time you will put Things away. There is no quick way for this to happen. THE ONLY WAY TO ESTABLISH THING TRUST IS TO BEHAVE CONSISTENTLY WITH THINGS FOR A LONG TIME.

You can't expect that when your behavior with Things has been out of control for many years you'll immediately begin to trust yourself to follow whatever maintenance routine you've set up. But when you've followed it long enough and consistently enough, at some point it will suddenly dawn on you that Things are no longer an issue.

This realization may seem oddly anticlimactic. No fanfares, no hoopla, just noticing that it's been a long time since you even thought about getting control of your Things. Or you're making up your list of New Year's resolutions and discover that doing something about your Things is no longer at the top of the list. In fact, it's not anywhere on the list. The little black Thing-issue cloud that followed you around for so many years has evaporated while you were looking the other way. Only consistency in building positive Thing habits over time can make this happen.

Note that perfection is not required to establish Thing trust. You can go days or even weeks throwing Things on the floor and still build trust AS LONG AS YOU DO WHAT YOU COMMITTED TO DO. If your Thing routine is to spend a whole day decluttering once a month, you follow that routine automatically each time decluttering day rolls around. How do you keep your commitment to your new Thing habits and thus establish Thing trust? When you have trouble following through, ask yourself five questions:

1. What am I doing?

2. What do I feel?

3. What's my situation?

4. What's difficult for my brain to do here?

5. Who—past or present—is having an influence on me?

What you have to do to get yourself back on track will depend on the answers to these five questions. DO NOT BEAT YOURSELF UP IF YOU GO OFF TRACK. Just pick up the next Thing and put it away as if it's the only Thing in the world.

PEACE WITH YOUR THINGS

You'll know when you've achieved peace with your Things by what no longer happens. You no longer spend much time thinking about your Things, talking about your Things, struggling with your Things. You have reached a point, in fact, in which all of your dealings with Things seem to happen of their own accord, with little or no effort on your part. You still buy Things, use Things, organize Things, reorganize Things, fix Things, sell Things, recycle Things, and do all the other things you always did with Things. But that is all you do. No more sturm und drang.

Any area of your life that has never become an issue or where the issue has been completely resolved is characterized by an absence of analysis. People without eating problems rarely think about why they eat what they do. People who like their jobs are usually too busy to think about why. People in happy marriages spend little time dissecting their relationship. As Things cease to be an issue for you, you will think about, talk about, read books about Things less and less, and eventually hardly at all.

For some people, peace with Things is natural: they seem to come out of the womb organized. These people may look down on those who have to analyze themselves upside down, inside out, and backward to arrive at a point with Things where they themselves have been all their lives. But if you look closely, you'll see such people struggling with other issues that for you are nonissues. Everybody has them.

But can this last indefinitely, this hard-won peace with Things? Maybe, and maybe not. Life is about change. Your situation changes, your emotions change, the people around you change, your memories change, and even your brain may change. Any of these changes may have the capacity to throw your all-but-natural Thing habits into disarray at any time, so you must begin again. Each time you have to resolve again the issue of Things, however, it will be a little easier: next time you'll know where you're going. You'll bring to the issue a deeper understanding of your own place within the material world and the memory of what it feels like to be at peace with your Things and with yourself.

THINGS IN THE BIG WORLD

Ideally, making peace with the Things in your life will be only a beginning. Once you have your own house in order, you may want to apply what you've learned to working with others for more responsible handling of Things in The Big World. The survival of the human species may depend on the success of such efforts.

There is a great deal to be done. At present, overproduction and overconsumption of nonessential Things, especially in the West, is leading to the destruction of the world's resources and habitats. Meanwhile, both between and within cultures, enormous material inequalities exist, resulting in conflicts in many countries. If we are to begin to change the Thing habits that have created these problems, we must first change our attitudes about Things, especially about the ownership of excess Things.

For much of history, those who spent their lives accumulating far more Things than they or their families really needed have been regarded with admiration and envy, while those who lived more simply—either by chance or by choice—have been looked upon by the majority with contempt. We need to find a way to turn this around, to begin to see having dozens of pairs of shoes for one pair of feet not as enviable but as an illness that requires treatment, a condition akin to drug addiction or compulsive overeating.

To save our planet, we need to develop guidelines to help people decide how much of each kind of Thing is enough and how much is too much to be socially and ecologically responsible. We cannot force others to change their Thing habits, but we can encourage them to do so. This must begin with making our own habits exemplary. Of all methods of teaching, example is the most powerful.

And there is hope. Individuals and organizations are beginning to call rampant consumerism into question, and voluntary simplicity is on the rise. Groups have sprung up around the world (see Appendix if you're interested), newsletters and books are being published, and lifestyles are changing. If you want to work for Thing changes beyond your own portals, be on the lookout for opportunities to act. Start a recycling project, write an article, join a Simplicity Circle, serve on a committee. (For suggestions about places to volunteer, see Simple Living Volunteer Opportunities in the Appendix.) Don't get discouraged if you can't do everything at once: DO WHAT YOU CAN. If you're going to take your efforts to this level, however, be careful. Your first responsibility is to keep Things from becoming an issue in your own life again. You've worked hard for peace, and you deserve to maintain it.

THE BEST THINGS IN LIFE

No matter how much effort you put into making peace with your Things, when all is said and done, Things are just Things. Nothing you can possibly do with Things amounts to a hill of beans compared with what you can do with that which lives and breathes. Paying attention to Things is important only insofar as this impacts people—including YOURSELF as well as other living creatures. If hanging up a raincoat or creating a home for your Monopoly game gives you the space or peace of mind to make a discovery, fall in love, rethink a problem, or dream a dream, these tasks are worth doing: if not, you might as well use your time some other way.

In the final analysis, the best things in life are not Things but moments. No sane person would think of sacrificing moments with loved ones, moments with nature, moments of spirituality, creativity, growth, success, romance, or discovery for the sake of mere Things—or so it seems. All too often, however, this is what happens:

we pile up Thing upon Thing at the expense of moments that now are forever lost.

This does not mean, however, that the time you've spent rethinking your dealings with Things has been wasted. You've taken an honest look at your own Thing habits and how they need to be changed. You've asked yourself how you feel about Things. You've considered your situation in life as objectively as possible and how it affects your immediate surroundings. You've analyzed how your particular brain strengths and glitches affect what you do with Things. You've thought about how others have influenced what you do with Things. And you've decluttered and reorganized your space while establishing new habits to the tune of constant self-scrutiny. Did you really do all this believing that it was only about Things? Surprise: in changing your Thing habits, you may also have changed your life!

Much of what you've learned about dealing with Things is transferable to other issues. If you can face up to problems with Things, you can face up to problems with people. If you can let go of Things, you can let go of grudges. If you can get moving with Things, you can get moving with your life's work. If you can be mindful of Things, you can be mindful of those who love you. If you can take care of your Things, you can take care of your soul. And you may discover that somewhere along your way to making peace with your Things, you have managed to make peace with yourself. If so, congratulations: there is now no enemy you need to fear and no new challenge you cannot meet.

NOTES

1. Although listed under obsessive-compulsive personality disorder in the *DSM-IV*, in much of the psychiatric literature hoarding is discussed in connection with obsessive-compulsive disorder.
2. See John Bradshaw, *Healing the Shame That Binds You.*
3. Believe it or not, according to historian Susan Strasser in *Satisfaction Guaranteed: The Making of the American Mass Market,* there was a time—before 1900 or so—when most ads in America were more informative than manipulative, and the story of how this changed is worth reading.
4. The psychiatric literature, including the *DSM-IV,* combines impulsive and compulsive buying under the heading of "compulsive buying," which is considered one type of disorder under the heading "Impulse-control Disorders Not Otherwise Specified." For our purposes here, however, it is more helpful to distinguish between impulsive and compulsive buying.
5. See Appendix for information on Spenders Anonymous and Debtors Anonymous.
6. This list was based on lists in *Clutter Free!* and *Not for Packrats Only* by Don Aslett.
7. There are a number of different types of obsessive-compulsive disorder, and hoarding OCD is relatively rare compared with repeated hand-washing or checking, for example.
8. For help, see *401 Ways to Get Your Kids to Work at Home* by Bonnie Runyan McCullough and Susan Walker Monson.
9. I was advised by University of Michigan neuropsychologist Dr. Seth Warchausky that the attention system and the executive system are two separate but related systems, hence their combination here.
10. Although the left-brain versus right-brain approach used by Lehmkuhl and Lamping can still be a pragmatic way of thinking about organizing problems, such reductions have recently been criticized by neuroscientists such as Richard Restak, who, in *Brainscapes,* writes,

Emerging knowledge of the organization and functioning of the two hemispheres led in the 1970s to the oversimplified notion that people can be divided into "right" and "left" brain types, and courses of instruction in painting and writing soon began to encourage students to develop their "right brain." Such teaching ignored the fact that, except under the rare and unnatural conditions of a split-brain operation, we possess two integrated hemispheres that are in constant two-way communication with each other across the corpus callosum. . . . In short, we possess a unified brain.

11. See John Gray, *Men Are from Mars, Women Are from Venus.*

APPENDIX

CINDY GLOVINSKY'S WEB SITE:

www.freshstartorganizing.com

This Web site contains articles, links, resources, and information about Cindy's organizing business, Fresh Start Organizing, as well as information about how to order this book.

RESOURCES FOR HELP WITH ORGANIZING:

National Association of Professional Organizers (NAPO)
P.O. Box 140647
Austin, TX 78714

512-206-0151 information and referral line
512-454-3036 fax

www.napo.net

Gives referrals for professional organizers

National Study Group on Chronic Disorganization
P.O. Box 1990
Elk Grove, CA 95759

916-962-6227

NSGCD@NSGCD.org
www.nsgcd.org

Gives referrals to professional organizers specializing in chronic disorganization

Messies Anonymous
5025 S.W. 114 Avenue
Miami, FL 33165

305-271-8404
1-800-637-7292 (orders)

Gives referrals to Messies Anonymous groups

Clutterers Anonymous
CLA
P.O. Box 91413
Los Angeles, CA 90009-1413
U.S.A.

www.clutterersanonymous.net
e-mail: clawso@hotmail.com

ATTENTION DEFICIT DISORDER:

CHADD (Children and Adults with Attention Deficit Disorder)
8181 Professional Place, Suite 201
Landover, MD 20785

800-233-4050
301-306-7070
301-306-7090 fax

www.chadd.org

Self-help network for parents of children with ADD and adults with ADD

The National Attention Deficit Disorder Association (ADDA)
1788 Second Street, Suite 200
Highland Park, IL 60035

847-432-ADDA
847-432-5874 fax

www.add.org
e-mail: mail@add.org

Self-help and professional organization focusing on adults and young adults with ADD

The American Coaching Association
Nancy A. Ratey, Ed.M. and Susan Sussman, M.Ed., Codirectors
P.O. Box 353
Lafayette Hill, PA 19444

610-825-4505 phone and fax

www.americoach.com

Trains ADD coaches, referrals available

International Coach Federation
1444 "I" Street NW, Suite 700
Washington, DC 20005

888-423-3131
202-712-9039
888-329-2423 fax
202-216-9646 fax

www.coachfederation.org

An organization of personal and business coaches, including ADD coaches; has a coach referral service

OBSESSIVE-COMPULSIVE DISORDER

Obsessive-Compulsive Foundation, Inc.
337 Notch Hill Road
North Branford, CT 06471

203-315-2190
203-315-2196 fax

www.ocfoundation.org
E-mail: infor@ocfoundation.org

Self-help and professional organization, referrals to mental health professionals specializing in OCD available

Obsessive-Compulsive Anonymous World Services
P.O. Box 215
New Hyde Park, NY 11040

Twelve-step groups for OCD sufferers

COMPULSIVE BUYING—TWELVE-STEP PROGRAMS

Spenders Anonymous
P.O. Box 2405
Minneapolis, MN 55402

651-649-4573

www.spenders.org
E-mail: info@spenders.org

Debtors Anonymous
General Service Office
P.O. Box 92088
Needham, MA 02492-0009

781-453-2743
781-453-2745 fax

www.debtorsanonymous.org

These groups may also be listed in your local directory for referrals in your area

SIMPLE LIVING/VOLUNTEER OPPORTUNITIES

The Simple Living Network
P.O. Box 233
Trout Lake, WA 98650

800-318-5725

www.simpleliving.net
E-mail: service@simpleliving.net

Support system for people who wish to simplify their lives

New Road Map Foundation
P.O. Box 15981
Seattle, WA 98115

www.newroadmap.org

Organization started by the late Joe Dominguez and Vicki Robin, co-authors of Your Money or Your Life. *Offers "practical tools and innovative approaches for mastering basic lifestyle change"*

Center for a New American Dream
6930 Carroll Avenue, Suite 900
Takoma Park, MD 20912

301-891-ENUF (3683)
301-891-3684 fax

www.newdream.org
E-mail: newdream@newdream.org

Helps individuals and institutions reduce and shift consumption

Co-op America
1612 K Street NW, Suite 600
Washington, DC 20006

800-58-GREEN
202-872-5307
202-331-8166 fax

www.coopamerica.org

Educates and empowers consumers, helps entrepreneurs start environmentally responsible businesses, and encourages corporate responsibility

SOURCES

Albom, Mitch. *Tuesdays with Morrie.* New York: Doubleday, 1997.

Alcoholics Anonymous. New York: Alcoholics Anonymous World Services, Inc., 1976.

Asch, S. E. "Effects of Group Pressure on the Modification and Distortion of Judgments." In H. Guetzkow (ed.), *Groups, Leadership, and Men.* Pittsburgh: Carnegie, 1951.

Aslett, Don. *Clutter Free!* Pocatello, Idaho: Marsh Creek Press, 1995.

———. *Clutter's Last Stand.* Cincinnati: Writer's Digest, 1984.

———. *Not for Packrats Only: How to Clean Up, Clean Out, and Live Clutter-Free Forever.* New York: Penguin Books, 1991.

Bird, Mary Ann. "Business: System Overload Excess Information Is Clogging the Pipes of Commerce—and Making People Ill." *Time International* (Internet), December 9, 1996.

Black, Donald W. "Compulsive Buying: A Review." *Journal of Clinical Psychiatry 57* (*Suppl. 8*): pp. 50–55, 1996.

Bowlby, John. *A Secure Base: Parent-Child Attachment and Healthy Human Development.* New York: Basic Books, 1988.

Boyles, Nancy S. and Darlene Contadino. *The Learning Differences Sourcebook.* Los Angeles: Lowell House, 1997.

Bradshaw, John. *Healing the Shame That Binds You.* Deerfield Beach, Fla.: Health Communications, 1988.

Briggs, John and F. David Peat. *Seven Life Lessons of Chaos.* New York: HarperCollins, 1999.

Burns, David. *The Feeling Good Handbook.* New York: Penguin, 1990.

Butschart, Joann. "Let's Get Organized." *The Sacramento Bee,* January 25, 1994.

Covey, Stephen. *First Things First.* New York: Simon & Schuster, 1994.

Csikszentmihalyi, Mihaly. *Flow: The Psychology of Optimal Experience.* New York: HarperPerennial, 1990.

Csikszentmihalyi, Mihaly and Eugene Rochberg-Halton. *The Meaning of Things: Domestic Symbols and the Self.* Cambridge/New York: Cambridge University Press, 1981.

Culp, Stephanie. *How to Conquer Clutter.* Cincinnati: Writer's Digest Books, 1990.

Damasio, Antonio R. *Descartes' Error.* New York: Avon Books, 1994.

Damecour, Claire L. and Maryse Charron. "Hoarding: A Symptom, Not a Syndrome." *Journal of Clinical Psychiatry* 59(5) (1998): pp. 267–272.

Damon, J. E. *Shopaholics: Serious Help for Addicted Spenders.* Los Angeles: Price Stein Sloan, 1988.

Diagnostic and Statistical Manual of Mental Disorders: Fourth Edition. Washington, D.C.: American Psychiatric Association, 1994.

Dominguez, Joe and Vicki Robin. *Your Money or Your Life.* New York: Penguin Putnam, 1992.

Donald, Lee. "Professional Organizing for Women with ADHD." *ADDvance* 2(4), March/April 1998, p. 6.

Felton, Sandra. *I've Got to Get Rid of This Stuff: Strategies for Overcoming Hoarding.* Miami: Five Smooth Stones Communications, 1995.

———. *Meditations for Messies.* Grand Rapids, Mich.: Fleming H. Revell, 1992.

———. *The Messie Manual.* Grand Rapids, Mich.: Fleming H. Revell, 1984.

———. *The Messie Motivator.* Grand Rapids, Mich.: Fleming H. Revell, 1999.

———. *Messie No More.* Grand Rapids, Mich.: Fleming H. Revell, 1989.

———. *The Messies Superguide.* Grand Rapids, Mich.: Fleming H. Revell, 1987.

———. *When You Live with a Messie.* Old Tappan, N.J.: Fleming H. Revell, 1994.

———. *Whiz Bang Guide.* Miami: Five Smooth Stones Communications, 1998.

———. *Why Can't I Get Organized?* Miami: Five Smooth Stones Communications, 1998.

Freud, Anna. *The Ego and the Mechanisms of Defense.* New York: International Universities Press, 1966.

Frost, Randy O., Hyo-Jin Kim, Claire Morris, Cinnamon Bloss, Marta Murray-Close, and Gail Steketee. "Hoarding, Compulsive Buying, and Reasons for Saving." In *Behavior Research and Therapy* 36 (1998): pp. 657–664.

Frost, Randy O. and Gail S. Steketee. "Hoarding: Clinical Aspects and Treatment Strategies." In Jenike, M. A., L. Baer, and W. E. Minichiello (eds.), *Obsessive-Compulsive Disorders: Practical Management,* third edition. St. Louis: Mosby-Year Book, 1998. pp. 533–554.

Gleick, James. *Chaos.* New York: Penguin, 1987.

Gray, John: *Men Are from Mars, Women Are from Venus.* New York: HarperCollins, 1992.

Hallowell, Edward and John Ratey. *Driven to Distraction.* New York: Simon & Schuster, 1994.

———. *Answers to Distraction.* New York: Bantam, 1994.

Hedrick, Lucy. *Five Days to an Organized Life.* New York: Dell, 1990.

Hempshill, Barbara. *Taming the Paper Tiger.* Washington, D.C.: Kiplinger Books, 1997.

Holmes, Jeremy. *John Bowlby and Attachment Theory.* London: Routledge, 1993.

Homer. *The Odyssey.* New York: Harper & Row, 1965.

Howard, Pierce J. *The Owner's Manual for the Brain.* Austin: Leornian Press, 1994.

Hyman, B. M. and C. Pedrick. "Hoarding OCD." In *The OCD Workbook: Your Guide to*

Breaking Free from Obsessive-Compulsive Disorder. Oakland: New Harbinger Publications, 1999, pp. 145–151.

Joseph, Rhawn. *Neuropsychiatry, Neuropsychology, and Clinical Neuroscience.* Baltimore: Williams & Wilkins, 1996.

Kelly, Kate and Peggy Ramundo. *You Mean I'm Not Lazy, Stupid or Crazy?!* New York: Simon & Schuster, 1993.

Koehnline, Caroline. "Confronting Your Clutter." In T. Hartmann and J. Bowman, eds., *Think Fast! The ADD Experience.* Grass Valley, Calif.: Underwood Books, 1996.

Kolberg, Judith. *Conquering Chronic Disorganization.* Decatur, Geo.: Squall Press, 1998.

———. *Surviving Chronic Disorganization.* FileHeads Professional Organizers, 1989.

———. "Surviving Chronic Disorganization." *ADDvance,* 1(5) May/June, 1998, p. 4.

———. *What Every Professional Organizer Needs to Know About Chronic Disorganization.* FileHeads Professional Organizers, 1998.

———. Editor's comments, *The Chronicle,* April/May 1998, p. 4.

———. Editor's comments, *The Chronicle,* July 1998, p. 1

———. Editor's comments, *The Chronicle,* August 1998, p. 2.

———. Editor's comments, *The Chronicle,* January 1999, p. 2.

———. Editor's comments, *The Chronicle,* February 1999, p. 1.

———. Editor's comments, *The Chronicle,* July 1999, p. 2.

———. "Trade of the Tips," *The Chronicle,* July 1999, p. 2.

———. "Trade of the Tips," *The Chronicle,* September 1999, p. 1.

Koran, L. M. "Compulsive Buying." In *Obsessive-Compulsive and Related Disorders in Adults: A Comprehensive Clinical Guide.* Cambridge/New York: Cambridge University Press, 1999.

Kuhn, Thomas. *The Structure of Scientific Revolutions.* Chicago: University of Chicago Press, 1970.

Larkin, Geri. *Stumbling Towards Enlightenment.* Berkeley, Calif.: Celestial Arts, 1997.

Lehmkuhl, Dorothy and Dolores Lamping. *Organizing for the Creative Person.* New York: Crown Publishers, 1993.

Lerner, Harriet. *The Dance of Anger.* New York: Harper & Row, 1985.

Levine, Mel. *Educational Care.* Cambridge, Mass.: Educators Publishing Service, Inc., 1994.

Luhrs, Janet. *The Simple Living Guide.* New York: Broadway Books, 1997.

McCullough, Bonnie and Susan Monson. *401 Ways to Get Your Kids to Work at Home.* New York: St. Martin's Press, 1981.

Mendelsohn, Cheryl. *Home Comforts.* New York: Scribner, 1999.

Merriam-Webster's Collegiate Dictionary—Tenth Edition. Springfield, Mass.: Merriam-Webster, Inc., 1998.

Morgenstern, Julie. *Organizing from the Inside Out.* New York: Henry Holt & Company, Inc., 1998.

Nadeau, Kathleen. *A Comprehensive Guide to Attention Deficit Disorder in Adults.* New York: Brunner/Mazel, 1995.

Nadeau, Kathleen, G. *Adventures in Fast Forward.* New York: Brunner/Mazel, 1996.

"News of the Weird." *Atlanta Journal/Constitution,* February 27, 1999.

Passoff, Michelle. *Lighten Up! Free Yourself from Clutter.* New York: HarperCollins, 1998.

Ratey, John. *A User's Guide to the Brain.* New York: Pantheon Books, 2001.

Rechtschaffen, Stephan. *Timeshifting.* New York: Doubleday, 1996.

Restak, Richard. *Brainscapes.* New York: Hyperion, 1995.

Schlenger, Sunny and Roberta Roesch. *How to be Organized in Spite of Yourself.* New York: Penguin, 1999.

Schor, Juliet. *Do Americans Shop Too Much?* Boston: Beacon Press, 2000.

Seligman, Martin. *Learned Optimism.* New York: Simon & Schuster, 1998.

Snead, G. Lynne and Joyce Wycoff. *To Do, Doing, Done!* New York: Simon & Schuster, 1997.

Solden, Sari. *Women with Attention Deficit Disorder.* Grass Valley, Calif.: Underwood Books, 1995.

St. James, Elaine. *Living the Simple Life.* New York: Hyperion, 1996.

————. *Simplify Your Life.* New York: Hyperion, 1994.

Stern, Daniel. *Diary of a Baby.* New York: HarperCollins, 1990.

Stoddard, Alexandra. *Open Your Eyes.* New York: William Morrow, 1998.

Strasser, Susan. *Satisfaction Guaranteed: The Making of the American Mass Market.* New York: Pantheon, 1989.

————. *Waste Not, Want Not: A Social History of Trash.* New York: Henry Holt & Company, 1999.

Taylor, Harold. *Making Time Work for You.* North York, Ontario: Harold Taylor Time Consultants, 1998.

Virgil, *The Aeneid.* New York: Penguin, 1991.

Weiss, Lynn. *The Attention Deficit Disorder in Adults Workbook.* Dallas, Texas: Taylor, 1994.

Wesson, C. *Women Who Shop Too Much: Overcoming the Urge to Splurge.* New York: St. Martin's Press, 1990.

Winnicott, D. W. *Play and Reality.* New York: Basic Books, 1971.

Young, Pam and Peggy Jones. *Get Your Act Together.* New York: HarperCollins, 1993.

FURTHER READING

ORGANIZING

Aslett, Don. *Clutter Free!* Pocatello, Idaho: Marsh Creek Press, 1995.

———. *Clutter's Last Stand.* Cincinnati: Writer's Digest, 1984.

———. *Not for Packrats Only: How to Clean Up, Clean Out, and Live Clutter-Free Forever.* New York: Penguin Books, 1991.

Culp, Stephanie. *How to Conquer Clutter.* Cincinnati: Writer's Digest Books, 1990.

Felton, Sandra. *I've Got to Get Rid of This Stuff: Strategies for Overcoming Hoarding.* Miami: Five Smooth Stones Communications, 1995.

———. *Meditations for Messies.* Grand Rapids, Mich.: Fleming H. Revell, 1992.

———. *The Messie Manual.* Grand Rapids, Mich.: Fleming H. Revell, 1984.

———. *The Messie Motivator.* Grand Rapids, Mich.: Fleming H. Revell, 1999.

———. *Messie No More.* Grand Rapids, Mich.: Fleming H. Revell, 1989.

———. *The Messies Superguide.* Grand Rapids, Mich.: Fleming H. Revell, 1987.

———. *When You Live with a Messie.* Old Tappan, NJ: Fleming H. Revell, 1994.

———. *Whiz Bang Guide.* Miami: Five Smooth Stones Communications, 1998.

———. *Why Can't I Get Organized?* Miami: Five Smooth Stones Communications, 1998.

Hedrick, Lucy. *Five Days to an Organized Life.* New York: Dell, 1990.

Hempshill, Barbara. *Taming the Paper Tiger.* Washington, D.C.: Kiplinger Books, 1997.

Kolberg, Judith. *Conquering Chronic Disorganization.* Decatur, Geo: Squall Press, 1998.

———. *Surviving Chronic Disorganization.* FileHeads Professional Organizers, 1989.

Lehmkuhl, Dorothy and Dolores Lamping. *Organizing for the Creative Person.* New York: Crown Publishers, 1993.

Morgenstern, Julie. *Organizing from the Inside Out.* New York: Henry Holt & Company, Inc., 1998.

Passoff, Michelle. *Lighten Up.* New York: HarperCollins, 1998.

Schlenger, Sunny and Roberta Roesch. *How to be Organized in Spite of Yourself.* New York: Penguin, 1999.

Young, Pam and Peggy Jones. *Get Your Act Together.* New York: HarperCollins, 1993.

TIME MANAGEMENT

Covey, Stephen. *First Things First.* New York: Simon & Schuster, 1994.

Morgenstern, Julie. *Time Management from the Inside Out.* New York: Henry Holt & Company, Inc., 2000.

Rechtschaffen, Stephan. *Timeshifting.* New York: Doubleday, 1996.

Snead, G. Lynne and Joyce Wycoff. *To Do, Doing, Done!* New York: Simon & Schuster, 1997.

Taylor, Harold. *Making Time Work for You.* North York, Ontario: Harold Taylor Time Consultants, 1998.

ATTENTION DEFICIT DISORDER

Hallowell, Edward and John Ratey. *Driven to Distraction.* New York: Simon & Schuster, 1994.

————. *Answers to Distraction.* New York: Bantam, 1994.

Kelly, Kate and Peggy Ramundo. *You Mean I'm Not Lazy, Stupid or Crazy?!* New York: Simon & Schuster, 1993.

Koehnline, Caroline. "Confronting Your Clutter." In T. Hartmann and J. Bowman, eds., *Think Fast! The ADD Experience.* Grass Valley, Calf.: Underwood Books, 1996.

Nadeau, Kathleen. *A Comprehensive Guide to Attention Deficit Disorder in Adults.* New York: Brunner/Mazel, 1995.

Nadeau, Kathleen G. *Adventures in Fast Forward.* New York: Brunner/Mazel, 1996.

Solden, Sari. *Women with Attention Deficit Disorder.* Grass Valley, Calif.: Underwood Books, 1995.

Weiss, Lynn. *The Attention Deficit Disorder in Adults Workbook.* Dallas, Texas: Taylor, 1994.

BACKGROUND

Bradshaw, John. *Healing the Shame That Binds You.* Deerfield Beach, Fl.: Health Communications, 1998.

Burns, David. *The Feeling Good Handbook.* New York: Penguin, 1990.

Csikszentmihalyi, Mihaly. *Flow: The Psychology of Optimal Experience.* New York: HarperPerennial, 1990.

Csikszentmihalyi, Mihaly and Eugene Rochberg-Halton. *The Meaning of Things: Domestic Symbols and the Self.* Cambridge/New York: Cambridge University Press, 1981.

Damasio, Antonio R. *Descartes' Error.* New York: Avon Books, 1994.

Damon, J. E. *Shopaholics: Serious Help for Addicted Spenders.* Los Angeles: Price Stein Sloan, 1988.

Dominguez, Joe and Vicki Robin. *Your Money or Your Life.* New York: Penguin Putnam, 1992.

Gray, John: *Men Are from Mars, Women Are from Venus.* New York: HarperCollins, 1992.

Howard, Pierce J. *The Owner's Manual for the Brain.* Austin: Leornian Press, 1994.

Lerner, Harriet. *The Dance of Anger.* New York: Harper & Row, 1985.

Luhrs, Janet. *The Simple Living Guide.* New York: Broadway Books, 1997.

McCullough, Bonnie and Susan Monson. *401 Ways to Get Your Kids to Work at Home.* New York: St. Martin's Press, 1981.

Mendelsohn, Cheryl. *Home Comforts.* New York: Scribner, 1999.

Ratey, John. *A User's Guide to the Brain.* New York: Pantheon Books, 2001.

Restak, Richard. *Brainscapes.* New York: Hyperion, 1995.

Schor, Juliet. *Do Americans Shop Too Much?* Boston: Beacon Press, 2000.

Seligman, Martin. *Learned Optimism.* New York: Simon & Schuster, 1998.

St. James, Elaine. *Living the Simple Life.* New York: Hyperion, 1996.

————. *Simplify Your Life.* New York: Hyperion, 1994.

Stoddard, Alexandra. *Open Your Eyes.* New York: William Morrow, 1998.

Strasser, Susan. *Satisfaction Guaranteed: The Making of the American Mass Market.* New York: Pantheon, 1989.

————. *Waste Not, Want Not: A Social History of Trash.* New York: Henry Holt & Company, 1999.

Wesson, C. *Women Who Shop Too Much: Overcoming the Urge to Splurge.* New York: St. Martin's Press, 1990.

INDEX